ROOSEVELT UNIVERSITY LIBRARY

W9-DGB-398

THE ARCHAEOLOGY

OF ATHENS

WITHDRAWN

MAY 06 2009

THE
ARCHAEOLOGY
of ATHENS

JOHN M. CAMP

Yale University Press   New Haven and London

To Elizabeth Ann Fisher

Copyright ©2001 by John M. Camp.

All rights reserved.

This book may not be reproduced, in whole or in part, including illustrations, in any form (beyond that copy-ing permitted by Sections 107 and 108 of the U.S. Copyright Law and except by reviewers for the public press), without written permission from the publishers.

Designed by Sonia Shannon and set in Scala and Scala Sans type by The Composing Room of Michigan, Inc., Grand Rapids, Michigan.

Printed in Italy by EuroGrafica SpA, Vicenza.

The Library of Congress has cataloged the hardcover edition as follows:

Camp, John M., 1946–

    The archaeology of Athens / John M. Camp

      p.   cm.

    Includes bibliographical references and index.

    ISBN 978–0–300–08197–8 (cloth: alk. paper)

     1. Excavations (Archaeology)—Greece—Athens.   2. Athens (Greece)—Antiquities.   3. Historic sites—Greece—Athens.   I. Title.

DF275 .C28   2001

938′.5—dc21

                         2001002711

A catalogue record for this book is available from the British Library.

The paper in this book meets the guidelines for permanence and durability of the Committee on Production Guidelines for Book Longevity of the Council on Library Resources.

ISBN 978–0–300–10151–5 (pbk.: alk. paper)

10 9 8 7 6 5 4 3 2

CONTENTS

PREFACE

The city of Athens has played a leading role in the development of European civilization. When we look back through time to the origins of so many of the institutions and activities which thrive or are valued today, we are led to ancient Greece and, most often, to Athens in the Classical period (480–323 B.C.). Time and again we find a connection with antiquity and a sense that little has changed but the technology; this is true in the case of theater, philosophy, art, law, athletics, medicine, architecture, and politics. Every time we watch a marathon, walk through the colonnaded facade of a public building, tell the story of the tortoise and the hare, or vote, we pay tribute to the enduring legacy of ancient Greece.

Of the figures associated with the greatest accomplishments of Classical Greek civilization, many were native Athenians and others were drawn to the city from all over the Mediterranean to contribute to a remarkable period of intellectual and artistic achievement. Statesmen and playwrights, historians and artists, philosophers and orators—Thucydides, Aischylos, Sokrates, Pheidias, Euripides, Demosthenes, Aristotle, and Praxiteles—all flourished here in the fifth and fourth centuries, when Athens was the most powerful city-state of Greece; collectively they were responsible for sowing the seeds of Western civilization.

Here, too, the political institution of democracy first took root under the guidance of Solon, Kleisthenes, and Perikles. Even when the city's political, economic, and military significance waned, Athens remained an influential cultural and educational center for centuries, drawing teachers and students of philosophy, science, logic, and rhetoric until the sixth century A.D. Archaeological exploration of the city and study of its monuments can therefore shed light on all aspects of the early history of modern institutions.

Archaeology is the study of the past using physical evidence: buildings, monuments, gravesites. When we study Athens we are especially fortunate, however, because the abundant archaeological record can be supplemented by an equally rich written tradition. Much of ancient Greek literature is, in fact, Athenian or concerns Athens. The historians Herodotos, Thucydides, and Xenophon provide a narrative account of the fifth and fourth centuries B.C., which can be supplemented by the extant speeches of orators such as Demosthenes, Lysias, and Lykourgos. In the years around A.D. 100 the philosopher Plutarch studied in Athens and later wrote a series of biographies which include considerable information on the monuments and topography of the city. About 150 the traveler Pausanias visited Greece and wrote a detailed guidebook, describing buildings while they were still in use. His tour of Athens is the single most important source we possess for a study of the ancient monuments.

Numerous other authors provide passing references to many of the buildings in the city; this volume draws on no fewer than thirty-five ancient writers to help tell the story of Athens. In addition, the Athenians had a tradition of recording tremendous amounts of information on stone: laws, treaties, public honors, dedications, epitaphs, financial transactions, and inventories of all sorts. Well over twenty thousand inscriptions survive from Athens, a source of information unparalleled anywhere else in the Greek world. All these voices from the past supplement the archaeological record and help us determine who built a given structure, when, and why. This book includes dozens of passages in translation to allow the reader easy access to the variety and richness of the documentary and literary evidence.

Like time, archaeological investigation marches on. It has been twenty-five years since the last general account in English of the archaeology of Athens appeared, and many recent discoveries and a large body of additional research are now available for consideration. Since 1975 claims have been offered for the discovery of the Painted Stoa (from which Stoic philosophy took its name), the Demosion Sema (the public burial ground for war casualties where Perikles delivered his Funeral Oration), and the Lyceum (the gymnasium where Aristotle founded his school). In Attica, we now have reports of the arsenal in Peiraieus, which housed the equipment of the mighty Athenian fleet, the tomb of the Plataians who fought and died with the Athenians on the Plain of Marathon in 490 B.C., and the cave on Salamis where Euripides wrote his tragedies.

The excavations to build the new Athenian Metro throughout the 1990s have brought to light several thousand objects, including hundreds of graves and inscribed or sculpted grave markers. To these new discoveries can be added fresh insights on old monuments, continually being subjected to investigation by an array of scholars devoted to the antiquities of Athens. Among these groups, though not limited to them, one thinks of the team at work restoring the Acropolis monuments, the staff of the first, second, and third Ephoreias of Classical Antiquities, members of the Archaeological Society, the faculty of the University of Athens, the German excavators of the Kerameikos, and the American excavators of the Agora. Given the pace and huge volume of scholarly activity, a new overview should be welcome whenever someone musters the energy to present one.

My own qualifications to do so have more to do with time and interest than ability. It has been my good fortune to have excavated and lectured in Athens for more than thirty years. I have taught the monuments at all levels: to casual visitors from abroad, to local social and business clubs, to undergraduates at College Year in Athens, and to the highly trained graduate students of the American School of Classical Studies at Athens. I have learned from all of these audiences, and much of this volume represents the results of research done preparing those lectures or comes from discussions with colleagues and students.

In my formal academic training I benefited from the expert instruction of Sterling Dow (Harvard), T. Leslie Shear, Jr., Homer A. Thompson (Princeton), and Eugene Vanderpool (American School of Classical Studies). In Athens, dozens of colleagues have enlightened me in numerous ways, and it is a pleasure to record here my debt to, among others, A. L. Boegehold, F. Cooper, D. Giraud, I. Jenkins, M. Korres, J. Kroll, M. Langdon, A. Mantis, M. M. Miles, S. Miller, S. Rotroff, R. Stroud, A. Tanoulas, A. Walker, and S. Walker. Among departed friends W. B. Dinsmoor, Jr., Alison Frantz, Virginia Grace, Lucy Talcott, and John Travlos greatly added to my store of knowledge of things Athenian. Two Greek colleagues, to my mind, deserve special mention for their contributions to Athenian studies: M. Korres for his work on the Acropolis and B. Petrakos for his unparalleled presentation of Oropos, Marathon, and Rhamnous. The final word of appreciation and admiration is reserved for a scholar who has toiled ceaselessly for decades to unravel and share the complexities of Athenian scholarship both ancient and modern, Judith Binder.

No volume of this scope can be free of errors or poor choices of interpretation. Several colleagues have labored to eliminate at least some of its infelicities, and I am indebted to J. Binder, R. Holloway, M. B. Richardson, H. C. Stroud, and R. Stroud for reading the book in manuscript. They are in no way responsible for the errors which remain.

At Yale University Press I would like to thank editor Harry Haskell and manuscript editor Susan Laity for their work in seeing the volume through production.

This book is dedicated to my wife, Elizabeth Ann Fisher, who has contributed to its creation in every way imaginable, both direct and indirect. My hours spent in the library or in the field were possible only through her unselfish devotion and care for both me and our family, often at the expense of her own career.

The text is enlivened by numerous images drawn from a variety of sources. I am indebted to the following for their considerable help in providing photographs and for permission to reproduce them: Craig Mauzy, Kyriaki Moustaka, and Jan Jordan of the Agora Excavations at the Stoa of Attalos; Marie Mauzy, photo archivist of the American School of Classical Studies and curator of the Alison Frantz collection; Hans Rupprecht Goette, photo archivist at the Deutsches Archäologische Institut; and Mrs. I. Ninou and B. Petrakos of the Archaeological Society of Athens. I am indebted also to Peter Connolly for permission to reproduce many of his excellent watercolors of the ancient city.

There are two main approaches to an account of the monuments of Athens, topographical or chronological. Because the city developed over both time and space, either presentation should be acceptable. Most previous works have presented Athens monument by monument (J. Travlos, *Pictorial Dictionary of Athens* [1971]) or in topographical order (I. T. Hill, *The Ancient City of Athens* [1953]; W. Judeich, *Topographie von Athen* [1931]; R. E. Wycherley, *The Stones of Athens* [1976]). For a change, therefore, I offer in Part I a descriptive narrative of the monuments in their historical context, an account which makes up the larger part of this volume. To assist the reader, however, I have supplied cross references to other discussions of the monuments in question. I also include the monuments of Attica in the discussion; they are an inseparable part of the story of the archaeology and history of ancient Athens. Part II, "Site Summaries," is presented topographically to pick up loose ends, present the monuments in their physical context, discuss antiquities or aspects not covered in the narrative account, and provide notes and bibliography. So that each part can be read independently I have retained some degree of overlap or repetition.

Ancient authors, often quoted in translation, are cited throughout the text, as are references to relevant inscriptions, usually cited as *IG* for *Inscriptiones Graecae,* 2d or 3d eds.; they are there to provide both students and nonspecialists access to our principal sources of information on any given monument. In these translations I have retained the ancient references to measurements in feet, which correspond roughly to the modern English measurements (1 foot is roughly 0.3 meters). Acceptable consistency in the transliteration of Greek names into English has proved awkward or elusive, and in each case I have chosen whichever form makes the best sense to me. The dedicatory inscriptions on the buildings at Labraunda give the proper spelling of Maussollos' name, just as the silver coins minted under his authority tell us how Mithradates preferred to have his name written.

The translations in this book are taken (with occasional minor updating) from the Loeb edition (Cambridge: Harvard University Press).

I

THE MONUMENTS OF ATHENS

1

Introduction
The Physical Setting

Ancient Athens consisted of the city itself and the large triangular peninsula known as Attica, which juts southward into the Aegean Sea. In antiquity Attica was settled with numerous villages and towns (*demes*), whose inhabitants were full citizens of the Athenian state. The city of Athens sits on a large coastal plain in northwest Attica, surrounded by mountains. Running through the plain in a northeast-southwest orientation is a long lime-   1
stone ridge. Near its southwest end, this ridge comprises the Acropolis, a steep-sided, free-standing crag which became the citadel and primary sanctuary of the Classical city. The ridge ends at the southwest in two hills west of the Acropolis, the Mouseion (modern Philopappos Hill) and the Hill of the Nymphs, with the Pnyx lying between them. It also continues northeast of the Acropolis, for the most part lying outside the limits of the ancient city; the highest point, a conical peak which reaches 273 meters above sea level, is known as Lykabettos, now a clear reference point rising above the sprawling modern city; beyond, the ridge continues northeast as modern Tourkovouni (ancient Brilessos or Anchesmos).

The Classical city of Athens developed around the Acropolis, which served both as the principal sanctuary and as a fortified place of refuge. Numerous other sanctuaries were es-   2, 3
tablished around the base of the hill (see figs. 239–242). Beyond, a circuit wall 6.5 kilometers in length enclosed the lower city. On gently sloping ground to the northwest lay the Agora, the great open square which served as the civic center and central marketplace (see figs. 243–245). Around its sides were clustered the major public buildings needed to run the city on a day-to-day basis: senate house, archives, magistrates' offices, law courts,

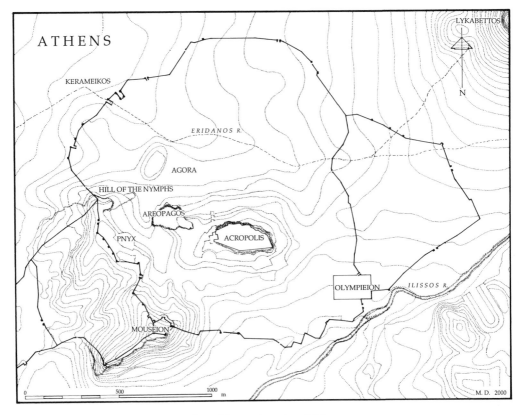

1. Plan of the ancient city of Athens.

2. The Acropolis seen from the Mouseion, with Tourkovouni visible in the left background.

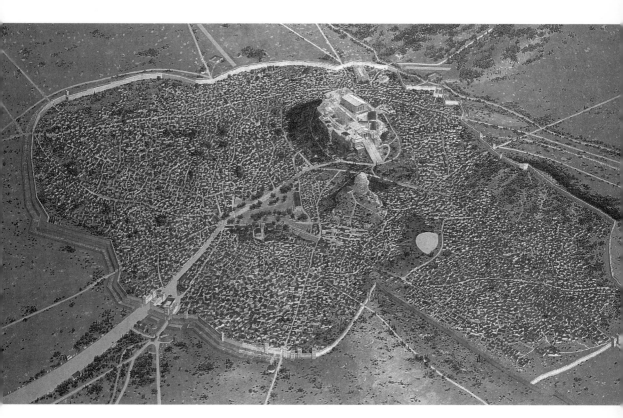

3. Classical Athens seen from the northwest. (Watercolor by Peter Connolly)

bureau of standards, mint, and the like. Just to the east lay the center of town in the Roman
period, represented by the Roman Agora and a great building containing a library donated
by the emperor Hadrian. Some 500 meters to the northwest of the Classical Agora was an
area known as the Kerameikos (potters' quarter; see fig. 246). Here a long section of the city
wall has been found, together with two of the principal gates: the Dipylon (double gate) and
the Sacred Gate. The roads just outside these gates were lined with tombs, and the Kerameikos area served as the most prestigious, though by no means the only, cemetery of the
city.

    Moving counter-clockwise within the city walls, we next encounter the ridge west of
the Acropolis which carried the Pnyx (see figs. 127, 148), the great theatral area cut from the
rock to serve as the meeting place of all the Athenians when they gathered in the assembly
(*ekklesia*). East of the Pnyx a rocky outrunner of the Acropolis rises up. Here was the original meeting place of a council of elders which took its name from the hill: Areopagos (Hill

4

4. The Agora and Athens from the west. The Hephaisteion is at the left, with the Stoa of Attalos in the center, and (left to right) Mount Pentele, Lykabettos, and Mount Hymettos.

of Ares). The area to the southeast of the Acropolis was occupied by the largest temple of Athens, the Olympieion, which was dedicated to Zeus. Individual monuments have been excavated elsewhere, but for the most part the rest of ancient Athens lies buried under the modern town. Outside the city walls were the three great gymnasia of Athens: the Academy, the Lyceum, and Kynosarges. The port of Athens, Peiraieus, lies 7 kilometers away toward the west, a low rocky peninsula with three well-protected, deep natural harbors: Mouny-chia, Zea, and Kantharos (see fig. 260). These sheltered the great Athenian fleet, as well as providing space for the huge volume of sea trade. Just beyond the Peiraieus lies the island of Salamis, an Athenian dependency for much of antiquity.

Opposite 5. Athens and the Peiraieus, seen from the southwest, with the long walls connecting them. In the center is the Kephisos River, which is joined by the Eridanos River from Athens; the Ilissos River is at the right. (Watercolor by Peter Connolly)

Three rivers pass through the plain, the two biggest lying beyond the limits of the ancient city. To the north, the Kephisos River rises in the foothills of Mount Parnes and makes its way, for 27 kilometers, to the sea at Phaleron. To the south, the Ilissos winds along the foot of Mount Hymettos. Between them, the Eridanos rises on the slopes of Lykabettos Hill and flows north of the Acropolis, passing through the Agora. It continues northwestward, exiting the city through the Sacred Gate, and disappears underground several hundred meters farther on, at the edge of the present German excavations of the Kerameikos. From that point it made its way to the sea. It was canalized by the mid-fifth century B.C. for much of its length where it passed through the city. Ancient sources indicate that pollution was a problem even in antiquity:

> In his *Collection of Rivers*, Kallimachos says that it makes him laugh if anyone makes bold to write that the Athenian maidens "draw pure liquid from the Eridanos," from which even cattle would hold aloof. (Strabo 9.1.19)

6. Inscription of the 5th century B.C., limiting the area along the Ilissos River where hides may be tanned.

This concern over pollution of the rivers is attested to for the Ilissos as well; a fifth-century inscription prohibits the washing of hides upstream of the sanctuary of Herakles (*IG* I³ 257).

6

The plain of Athens is bounded by four mountains. To the west, Mount Aigaleos runs down to the sea; a pass through it carried the Sacred Way to the Thriasian plain and the important town of Eleusis, with its sanctuary of Demeter. To the north, Mount Parnes separated Athens from Thebes and Boiotia. To the northeast is Mount Pentele, source of the fine white marble used and exported by the Athenians for centuries. And to the southeast, closing Athens off from the rest of Attica, is Mount Hymettos, crowned with a sanctuary to Zeus as weather god and famous in antiquity for fine honey.

Beyond Pentele and Hymettos lay the rest of Attica, some of it hilly country, part of it a large arable plain. The northeast limit was occupied by the towns of Rhamnous and Marathon, both on the sea, facing the large island of Euboia. The southern tip is Cape Sounion, which was dedicated to the sea god Poseidon.

7

Attica, and therefore Athens, was rich in certain products, poor in others. Grapes and olives have always done well, grain less so. The area is a dry one, and when Athens prospered and the population grew, Attica could not produce enough, and food had to be imported, especially grain. Attica also failed to provide enough timber for Athenian needs; in addition to housing and fuel, immense amounts of timber were needed for the huge fleet from which Athens derived its power. Plato, writing in the early fourth century B.C., describes an earlier time when the ecological system was better:

> But at that epoch the country was unimpaired, and for its mountains it had high
> arable hills, and in place of the moorlands, as they are now called, it contained
> plains full of rich soil; and it had much forest land in its mountains, of which

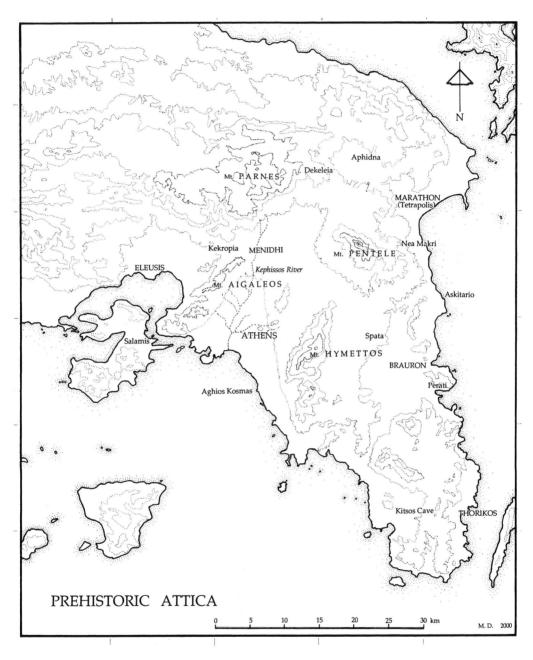

PREHISTORIC ATTICA

7. Map of prehistoric Attica, the territory belonging to ancient Athens, showing the principal Bronze Age sites.

there are visible signs even to this day; for there are some mountains which now have nothing but food for bees, but they had trees no very long time ago, and the rafters from the trees felled there to roof the largest buildings are still sound. And in addition there were many lofty trees of cultivated species; and the country produced boundless pasturage for flocks. Moreover, it was enriched by the yearly rains from Zeus, which were not lost to it, as now, by flowing from the bare land into the sea; but the soil it had was deep and therein it received the water, storing it up in the retentive, loamy soil. (*Critias* III C–D)

Beautiful white marble, large deposits of silver, and excellent clay all contributed to Athenian prominence in the historical period, though they were of little interest to the earliest human inhabitants of the area.

2

The Prehistoric Period

PALEOLITHIC AND NEOLITHIC

For the earliest history of Athens we rely on the results of archaeological exploration, supplemented by the myths and legends familiar to the Athenians of later times. The land of Attica has been inhabited since at least the Upper Paleolithic period (30,000–10,000 B.C.), when humans hunted and gathered their food. Early traces from this time have been found in the Kitsos cave near Laureion and in chance finds elsewhere of early stone tools. Sometime around 6000 B.C. the Neolithic period began with the introduction of cultivated grains and domesticated animals. These new advances appear in Greece relatively quickly, and it is usually assumed therefore that they were developed elsewhere, presumably in the Middle East, and imported into Greece. The changes allowed for a larger and more settled population.

Evidence of human activity in the Neolithic period has been uncovered at various sites in Attica, particularly in caves. At Oinoe near Marathon, excavation of one such cave produced large amounts of pottery of the Middle Neolithic period (5000–4000). At Nea Makri, at the south end of the plain of Marathon, excavations have revealed part of a settlement of several very modest houses of Middle Neolithic date, along with a stretch of the earliest known street in Attica. In Athens itself excavation suggests that the shallow caves and overhangs of the Acropolis rock were used primarily in the latest Neolithic period (3000–2800), a time when the use of caves was widespread throughout Greece. The Klepsydra Spring just below the caves on the northwest slope of the Acropolis hill was also exploited at this time, when twenty-two shallow wells were cut into the soft bedrock.

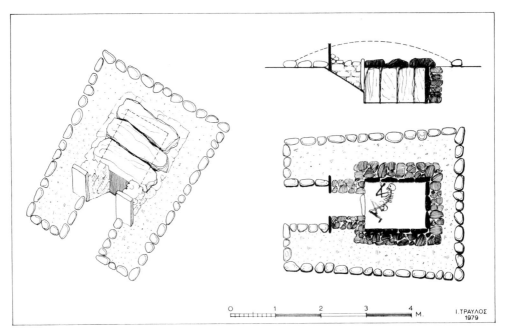

8. Early Bronze Age tombs at Tsepi (Marathon), ca. 2500 B.C.

EARLY BRONZE AGE

With the introduction of metallurgy, the Bronze Age began, and along with it the be-ginnings of a recognizable, distinct history of Athens. The early Bronze Age (3000–2000 B.C.) was an island and coastal civilization, and the clearest evidence for human activity has been found largely in excavations of cemeteries and settlements by the sea (see fig. 7): Aghios Kosmas (near Hellenikon Airport) on the west coast, Thorikos, Raphina (Aski-tario), Brauron, and Marathon on the east. The objects recovered from these sites, includ-ing marble figurines and clay pans with incised decoration, show close affinities with the rich civilization flourishing at this time in the Cycladic Islands of the Aegean. The house walls are built in the characteristic herringbone style of masonry, with cobbled areas in front. Except for a modest attempt at Askitario, the Attic sites lack the substantial fortifica-tions found at Lerna, on the island of Aigina, and at Chalandriani on Syros.

The early cemetery at Tsepi, near Marathon, consists of well-built large family tombs, each with a slab roof and small doorway, marked off as a private plot by rows of large rounded stones. As each member of the family was buried in the stone-lined chamber, the bones of those interred earlier were somewhat unceremoniously piled up in a corner. The area of Athens, in particular the Acropolis, which had been attractive to Neolithic cave

8

dwellers, seems to have been less appealing to the seafarers of the early Bronze Age. These people were probably not Greek speakers, for one of the most enduring and conservative aspects of the countryside—the toponyms—are not, linguistically speaking, Greek. Words ending in *-ssos, -ttos,* and *-nthos* are pre-Greek and must have been adopted from the early indigenous people who occupied the land, remembered in later myth as Pelasgians, Lelegians, or Carians. Just as many Native American names survive today to remind us of the indigenous population of North America before European colonization, so too for Athens. The very names of the mountains (Hymettos, Lykabettos) and rivers (Kephisos, Ilissos) take us back to the earliest memories of Athens and Attica, a time before the arrival of the Greeks.

MIDDLE BRONZE AGE

In around 2000 B.C. new people came into Greece and Attica, apparently by land and from the north: the word for sea (*thalassa*) is also pre-Greek and must have been borrowed from the seafarers of early Bronze Age times. The newcomers brought with them five innovations which allow us to recognize them as a different and distinct culture: a new style of architecture, making use of houses with curved or apsidal ends; new burial customs, with individual rather than communal graves; new pottery: of a gray fabric, sharply angled, and made on a potter's wheel; the horse; and the Greek language. There are no written records from this period (2000–1600), so we are dependent on the archaeological evidence, which suggests that Attica was extensively occupied. Athens, too, was settled, and numerous graves and wells have been found, both on the Acropolis and around the citadel.

With these newcomers came their gods, presumably the Olympian deities that are familiar from the historical period.

9. Middle Bronze Age tumulus (ca. 1700 B.C.), with individual burials, at Vrana (Marathon).

Athens became the city of Athena, daughter of Zeus, warrior goddess and protector of the city. When depicted in later times she is usually shown full-armed with helmet, shield, and spear. Her breastplate was a goatskin (aegis) with snakes along the edges and the head of the gorgon Medusa set in the middle. She was chosen as patron of Athens after a contest with her uncle Poseidon. Athena was thought to have had a hand in building the Acropolis; one tradition explains Lykabettos as a piece intended to further fortify the citadel but dropped by the goddess. She also gave the olive tree to Athens, and both the olive sprig and her favorite bird, the owl, were used in later times to decorate the coinage of the city.

LATE BRONZE AGE

The succeeding period, known as the Late Bronze Age (1600–1100), is the great age of Greek myth and legend, the Heroic Age. To this period the Classical Greeks assigned the Labors of Herakles, the Trojan War, the voyage of the Argo, the story of Oedipus, and the expedition of the Seven against Thebes, to name but a few. Numerous Athenian myths are attributed to this period as well. Attica was thought to have been organized in early times by King Kekrops into twelve cities:

> According to Philochoros, because the country was raided from the sea by Carians and from the land by Boiotians (then called Aones), Kekrops was the first to bring the population together in twelve cities. These were Kekropia, Tetrapolis, Tetrakomoi, Epakria, Dekeleia, Eleusis, Aphidna, Thorikos, Brauron, Kytheros, Sphettos, and Kephisia. (Strabo 397C)

Of the sites on the list which are securely located (Tetrapolis, Eleusis, Aphidna, Thorikos, Brauron), all have significant Late Bronze Age remains, whereas two sites which are not listed, though they were important in later times (Rhamnous, Sounion), have minimal Bronze Age material. Archaeology would therefore seem to indicate that there is a core of truth in these early legends which permits us to regard them with some confidence as part of the history of the city. In addition to Kekrops, Athenian legend preserves the names of two other significant early Athenian kings: Erechtheus and Theseus.

Erechtheus is one of the earliest legendary kings of Athens and was regarded as the founder of the Panathenaic festival. A warrior king, he fought King Eumolpos of neighboring Eleusis, a contest he eventually won, though it took the sacrifice of one of his daughters to ensure success. Euripides' play *Erechtheus* has Athena herself foretelling the construction of a temple in his honor.

10. Athenian red-figure cup by the Codrus Painter,
5th century B.C., showing the labors of Theseus:
the Minotaur is in the center.

Theseus, a generation or so
later than Erechtheus, was the
son of the king of Athens,
Aigeus, though he was brought
up in Troizen, the ancestral
home of his mother. As a young
man he made his way to Athens
to claim his inheritance, having
many adventures en route as he
cleared the road of assorted brig-
ands. These youthful deeds make up a
sort of parallel to the Labors of Herakles
and were a favorite theme for Athenian sculptors and pot painters in later times. When he arrived in
Athens, Theseus was sent to Crete for his most renowned exploit, the slaying of the Minotaur in the labyrinth. When he later assumed the kingship of Athens, Theseus is thought to
have carried out a crucial political reform, the unification of Attica (*synoikismos*), with
Athens as the capital. The procedure is described by Thucydides (2.15):

> For in the time of Kekrops and the earliest kings down to Theseus, Attica had
> been divided into separate towns, each with its town hall and magistrates, and
> so long as they had nothing to fear, they did not come together to consult with
> the king, but separately administered their own affairs and took counsel for
> themselves. Sometimes they even made war upon the king, as, for example,
> the Eleusinians with Eumolpos did upon Erechtheus. But when Theseus be-
> came king and proved himself a powerful as well as a prudent ruler, he not
> only reorganized the country in other respects but abolished the councils and
> magistracies of the minor towns and brought all their inhabitants into union
> with what is now the city, establishing a single council and town hall, and
> compelled them, while continuing to occupy each his own lands as before, to
> use Athens as the sole capital. This became a great city, since all were now pay-
> ing their taxes to it, and it was such when Theseus handed it down to his suc-
> cessors.

The archaeological evidence seems to confirm this tradition in broad outline. In the years around 1400 B.C. the Late Bronze Age settlements are well scattered throughout Attica and were equally wealthy, to judge from the finds. Most significant, perhaps, the elaborately constructed tholos, or "beehive," tombs, which denote a substantial degree of wealth and authority, are also found scattered throughout Attica: at Menidhi, Marathon (see fig. 259), and Thorikos (though none are yet reported from Athens itself). Largely plundered in antiquity, these tombs have nonetheless produced signs of rich grave goods: a gold cup (Marathon), an

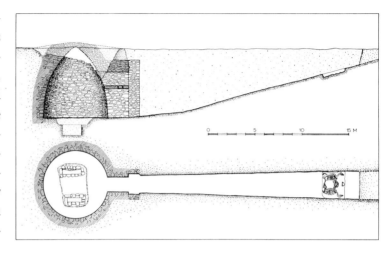

11. Mycenaean tholos tomb at Marathon, 15th century B.C. (Cf. fig. 259)

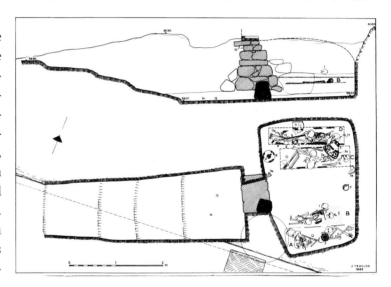

12. Mycenaean chamber tomb from the Agora with multiple burials, 14th century B.C.

ivory lyre (Menidhi), and carved gemstones (Thorikos). By 1250, however, we find the Acropolis of Athens massively fortified—also a probable indicator of wealth and power—whereas none of the other Attic Bronze Age sites, though several are flourishing, is fortified. It appears, in short, as though the scattered and equally wealthy settlements of 1400 had by 1250 become part of a single political unit with Athens and the Acropolis as its dominant center. The synoikismos was an essential step in the develop-

13. Remains of the Mycenaean (cyclopean) fortification wall at the west end of the Acropolis with the Parthenon in background, 13th century B.C.

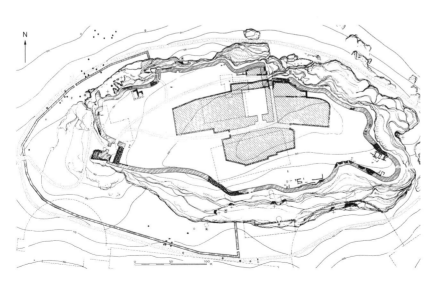

14. The Acropolis in the Mycenaean period, showing the line of the circuit wall and the probable area of the palace (hatched), now lost.

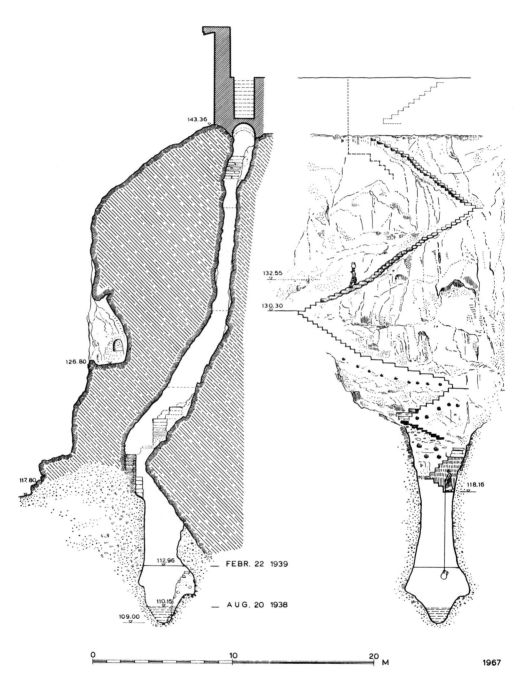

143.36

132.55

130.30

126.80

118.16

117.80

112.96 — FEBR. 22 1939

110.15 — AUG. 20 1938

109.00

0   10   20 M

1967

15. Mycenaean stairway and spring on the north side of the Acropolis.

ment of later Athens; henceforth all free-born inhabitants of the outlying districts of Attica were citizens of Athens, with the same rights as those living in the city. The state of Athens and the limits of Attica were coterminous. So significant was this event that a separate festival, the Synoikia, was established to commemorate it and was celebrated for centuries.

The city itself, according to Thucydides, lay south of the Acropolis in the early period. This is in marked contrast to his own day, when the Agora was the focal point and center of the city, northwest of the Acropolis. Once again, we have reason to place some trust in these later accounts of early Athens, for excavation has revealed far more early material south and southeast of the Acropolis than the cemeteries and limited occupation encountered in the deep layers beneath the Classical Agora to the north. The graves of the Agora area are of more modest construction than their contemporaries in Attica, being rock-cut chamber tombs rather than built tholos tombs. The richest, however, like the tholos tombs contain 12 remnants of considerable wealth, in the form of ivory vessels, gold adornments, and bronze weapons.

As noted, the citadel of the Acropolis was defended by a huge circuit wall, built of immense stones and rising as much as 8 meters in height. So massive was this wall that it was 13, 14 believed by Classical Greeks to have been built by Cyclopes, or giants. The assumption is that this wall protected a palace like the ones referred to in the Homeric epics and known from archaeological work at Mycenae, Tiryns, Pylos, and Thebes. Later occupation and extensive use of the Acropolis as a sanctuary in the Archaic and Classical periods have removed all but the slightest traces of such a palace at Athens. A few short stretches of retaining walls and a single limestone column base are all that survive.

Like the citadels at Mycenae and Tiryns, however, the Acropolis of Athens was provided with a secret water-supply system which allowed defenders within the walls to withstand a long siege. This takes the form of a staircase consisting of eight flights of steps which led from the north edge of the Acropolis deep down into the rock to a hidden spring. The staircase, which collapsed and was filled up at the end of the Bronze Age, was excavated in the 1930s; it descends 25 meters into the fissure. A secondary line of fortification 15 apparently ran around the lower slopes of the Acropolis, probably bringing other sources of water within safe reach of the citadel. Known from several literary sources and inscriptions as either the Pelargikon or Pelasgikon, no part of this early lower wall has ever been found, and it may not have survived, though the area it enclosed was a recognizable entity in the sixth and fifth centuries B.C.

The loss of the palace has also removed possible contemporary written accounts of Athens in the Bronze Age. At other palace sites—Mycenae, Pylos, Thebes, Knossos— archives written in a primitive form of Greek known as Linear B are preserved on clay tablets, carrying records of various administrative transactions. The Homeric epics, how-

ever, do preserve a memory of both the palace and the early worship of Athena on the
Acropolis:

> And she [Athena] made him [Erechtheus] to dwell in Athens, in her own rich
> sanctuary, and there the youths of the Athenians, as the years roll on, seek to win
> his favor with sacrifices of bulls and rams. (*Iliad* 2.546–551)

And:

> So saying, flashing-eyed Athena departed over the barren sea and left lovely
> Scheria. She came to Marathon and broad-wayed Athens, and entered the well-
> built house of Erechtheus. (*Odyssey* 7.78–81)

The great palaces of Mycenae, Tiryns, and Pylos all show signs of violent destruction
and burning, attributed in antiquity to the arrival of the Dorian Greeks from the north. The
collapse of the Late Bronze Age, or Mycenaean, civilization led to several centuries of what
are referred to as the Dark Ages, a time when the level of material culture fell dramatically.
There are no more palaces with ornate frescoes, nor any other monumental buildings, no
massive fortifications, and few examples of the extraordinary objects of gold, silver, ivory,
bronze, ostrich egg, lapis lazuli, and other precious materials which were deposited in
Bronze Age tombs. Also lost was the ability to write: Linear B texts cease and there are no
signs of literacy for almost five hundred years. The tradition for Athens is that the Dorians
passed by Attica, turning aside to enter the Peloponnese. Because later activity has obliter-
ated all traces of a palace on the Acropolis, we do not know how or when it came to an end.

Whatever the case, it is clear that the city shared fully in the Dark Ages which followed
the destruction of the Bronze Age palaces elsewhere. Cemeteries from the end of the
Bronze Age have been found on the nearby island of Salamis and at Perati, on the east coast
of Attica. Six hundred individuals were buried at Perati in 279 graves in a cemetery used for
about a century between 1200 and 1100 B.C. In Athens itself a handful of wells and some
very poor graves are all that survive from the years around 1100 to 1000. To this period can
be dated the first use of the area later known as the Kerameikos, northwest of the Agora, as
a burial ground; in the historical period the Kerameikos developed into the premier cemetery of Athens.

3

Early and Archaic Athens

THE DARK AGES

The grim picture of Athens provided by the archaeological evidence suggests that recovery during the Dark Ages was slow and gradual. As few architectural remains survive, almost all our information comes from wells and graves. Other than a few bronzes and, later, some iron tools and weapons, pottery is the main survival from these difficult centuries (1100–750 B.C.). The pots are decorated in a distinctive style, with painted geometric designs. There is no contemporary written evidence, either literary or documentary, to supplement the archaeological record.

The numbers of wells and graves increase from the tenth to the eighth century, suggesting a steadily rising population. The graves seem to reflect a social structure similar to that found later in the Archaic period (750–500 B.C.), when there was an aristocracy based on ownership of property. The highest propertied class were the *pentakosiomedimnoi,* those whose land produced 500 *medimnoi* (about 730 bushels) of grain a year. A grave found in the Agora dating to the ninth century contained the cremated remains of an Athenian lady buried with a lovely set of gold earrings and other jewelry. Among the grave goods was an unusual box of clay with miniature representations of five granaries on the lid, almost certainly a reference to her high status as a member of the pentakosiomedimnoi.

The second propertied class was the *hippeis* (knights); as the name suggests, these were people wealthy enough to own horses. A ninth-century grave, identifiable as that of a warrior by the iron sword wrapped around the man's burial urn, also contained the iron bridle bits for his horse. Graves of other members of the hippeis can perhaps be identified by

16

16. Burial urn and grave gifts from the tomb of a rich Athenian woman, ca. 850 B.C.; the pyxis with five granaries appears in the left foreground.

pyxides (cosmetics boxes) with small clay horses serving as the handles for their lids. Huge vases, up to 2 meters tall and decorated with geometric ornament and friezes of highly stylized human figures, birds, horses, and deer, were used to mark important graves. Often they depict funerary scenes, with groups of mourners gathered around the bier. Extensive cemeteries from this period (known from the pottery as Geometric) have been excavated in several areas of Athens and at many sites in Attica: Merenda and Anavyssos (finds displayed in the Brauron Museum), Marathon (Marathon Museum), and Eleusis (Eleusis Museum) are among the most extensive.

THE EIGHTH AND SEVENTH CENTURIES

The late eighth century is a time of increased contact with the Orient; locally made bronzes and a few imports of ivory and bronze suggest a growing trade with the Levant at this time. One such import, apparently from Phoenicia, is the alphabet. After five hundred years of illiteracy, we have evidence that the Greeks, and especially the Athenians, were writing again. Some of the earliest examples of writing in mainland Greece come from the sanctuary of Zeus on Mount Hymettos and on a Geometric jug from a grave in the Kerameikos. The earliest examples include alphabets, which people practiced before rapidly moving on to use their new skill to write rude remarks about their acquaintances. To this same time, late in the eighth century, can be dated the beginnings of Greek literature, with the writings of the Boiotian Hesiod and the epic poems of the Ionian bard Homer.

Hesiod wrote not only a theogony but also an account of the hard agricultural life in his native Askra, not far from Thebes. The great epics attributed by the Classical Greeks to

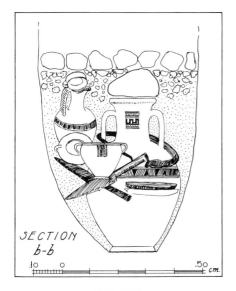

Top left 17. Geometric tomb group from the 9th century B.C., with an iron sword wrapped around the burial urn.

Top right 18. Pyxis (cosmetics case) from the 8th century B.C. with horses forming the handle.

Bottom 19. Amphora with geometric designs and funerary scene, used as a grave marker, 8th century B.C.

Homer, the *Iliad* and *Odyssey,* are thought to have been composed in their final form in the late eighth century, though they reflect the heroic past of the Bronze Age. Athens played no large role in these origins of Greek literature, though the city's artists and craftsmen were among the first to decorate their pottery with Homeric scenes. The epics became a source of artistic inspiration for narrative art for centuries.

The archaeological record for the early seventh century is extraordinarily meager when compared to that of the eighth and suggests that Athens was in a severe decline in the years around and just after 700. The early seventh century is perhaps the only period within a span of several centuries in which the Athenians imported more pottery than they exported. There are fewer graves in both Athens and Attica, and a large drop in the number of wells in Athens. As the city sent out no colonies at this time, we

20. Late Geometric jug with an early example of the Greek alphabet, ca. 730 B.C.

must look elsewhere for an explanation of this decline and apparent drop in population. The likeliest cause may be a severe drought late in the eighth century, accompanied by famine and epidemic disease—a combination of disasters which affected Athens until well on in the seventh century. Most of the wells in the area of the Agora were abandoned in the late eighth century while an especially large number of votives were dedicated at the sanctuary of Zeus Ombrios, a weather god worshiped on Mount Hymettos. The sanctuary of Artemis at Brauron also shows signs of intense activity at this time, and the foundation legend associates her cult with drought and famine.

Pottery made in the seventh century takes off in a completely new direction from the geometric designs of the eighth century. Early on, while Athens is still recovering, the graves in the Kerameikos show a respectable proportion of pieces imported from nearby Corinth. These are decorated with friezes of animals, birds, and mythical creatures such as sphinxes, griffins, and chimaeras, which seem to owe their inspiration to the Orient. In Athens the local Geometric pottery gives way to a period of exuberant experimentation in style, technique, subject matter, and scale. Mythological scenes begin to make a significant appearance in the "proto-Attic" style which flourished throughout the seventh century. From the west cemetery at Eleusis we have a huge amphora (1.42 meters high), decorated with scenes of Perseus killing the gorgon Medusa and Odysseus blinding the cyclops Polyphemos. And a cemetery near the west coast of Attica at Vari has produced some of the largest decorated vases of the seventh century, including one showing Herakles rescuing Prometheus and another of Herakles killing the centaur Nessos. Other archaeological material, such as monumental sculpture or substantial architecture in stone, does not appear in Athens or Attica much before the end of the seventh century. A few scraps of baked terracotta roof tiles with painted decoration found on the Acropolis, along with two poros limestone column bases, may be remnants of an early temple to Athena dating to around 620–600.

We have little information from literary sources for Athens at this period, though

Top 21. Amphora from Eleusis showing Odysseus blinding the cyclops Polyphemos, with a gorgon chasing Perseus below, 7th century B.C.

22. Amphora from Vari showing Herakles killing the centaur Nessos while gorgons pursue Perseus below, ca. 610 B.C.

there is a tradition that the chief magistracy (the archonship), which had been a lifetime office, was changed to a ten-year term starting in 683. This change in leadership was perhaps an attempt to resolve a conflict between aristocratic families for control of the city. Later in the seventh century we learn of a formal body of law which was drawn up by one Drakon in the years around 621. This new code included a series of laws on homicide which remained in force for centuries; copies were carved on a marble stele late in the fifth century B.C. and set up on display in front of the Royal Stoa in the Agora.

Also to the seventh century can be dated an early attempt to set up a tyranny by the Olympic games victor Kylon with the help of his father-in-law, Theagenes, tyrant of neighboring Megara. The coup failed and, though they had taken refuge under the protection of Athena on the Acropolis, many of Kylon's followers were killed by members of the Alkmaionidai, a powerful Athenian aristocratic family. All three of these developments—a change in ruling tenure, a codified body of law, and an attempted tyranny—can be seen as significant changes indicative of an evolving political system, though the details, impulses, and results remain obscure.

One other important element in the creation of Athens was the annexation of Eleusis (see figs. 254–257). Along with the town and territory, the Athenians also gained control of the sanctuary of Eleusinian Demeter. This was her principal cult place in Greece and of panhellenic significance. As the goddess of vegetation and fertility of the land, Demeter was an extremely important deity to the agricultural society of early Greece. The date of the takeover is disputed, but it seems to have been some time in the seventh century. The Homeric *Hymn to Demeter* contains no suggestion that Eleusis is not an independent entity; Athens does not figure in the story at all. By the sixth century, however, the town and its territory were fully integrated into the Athenian state, which administered the sanctuary and the mysteries celebrated in honor of Demeter and her daughter, Kore (Persephone).

To the eighth and seventh centuries belongs the earliest archaeological evidence of worship in many of the sanctuaries in Attica which in later times were adorned with handsome temples and sculptures. In the early period, cult activity is expressed in modest votives, usually clay plaques, bronze figurines, miniature vases, and small items of jewelry in ivory, bone, or semi-precious stones. In addition to Eleusis and Brauron, mentioned above, such manifestations appear in the sanctuary of Athena at Cape Sounion.

THE SIXTH CENTURY

SOLON

By the early sixth century, according to Aristotle, social and political tensions had led Athens to the brink of collapse. Almost all power remained in the hands of a few strong families, and the rest of the population had become restive. The poor had in many cases been forced to sell themselves into slavery in order to survive. An individual named Solon was chosen as a *nomothetes* (lawmaker) and charged with arbitrating the dispute. Plutarch preserves several passages of Solon's poetry which record the difficulties of his task; Solon himself claims that he failed to please anyone.

Solon abolished many debts and arranged for a redistribution—not a transfer—of power among the four classes: the pentakosiomedimnoi, the hippeis, the *zeugitai* (owners of oxen), and the *thetes* (laborers). Political power in the form of archonships, hitherto restricted to pentakosiomedimnoi, was extended to the hippeis; lower offices were available to the zeugitai, and the thetes were permitted to appeal to the courts and to sit on juries. This last measure, seemingly insignificant, was in fact vital to the development of democracy, as we learn from Aristotle (*Ath. Pol.* 9.1–2):

> The people, having the power of the vote, become sovereign in the government. Since the laws are not drafted simply or clearly but like the law about inheritances and heiresses, it inevitably results that many disputes take place and that the jury court is the arbiter in all business, both public and private.

After drawing up his laws, Solon went into voluntary exile so that he could not be pressured into changing them by the Athenians, who had sworn an oath to abide by them for ten years. Although the laws were much disputed in their day, in time Solon came to be regarded as one of the seven sages of early Greece.

The archaeological record has preserved little architecture which can be dated with confidence to the time of Solon: graves, wells, and a few house walls but no remains of any monumental public buildings or temples in Athens. What should be one of the earliest public buildings of Athens, said to have housed copies of the Solonian law code, was the Prytaneion. It apparently stood somewhere on the north slopes of the Acropolis, in an area of the modern city where archaeologists have thus far been unable to dig. The Prytaneion in Athens, as in every Greek city, was in a sense the heart of the city, for it housed a hearth dedicated to Hestia where an eternal flame was kept burning. The practice may go back to primitive times, when households needed one fire which would never be extinguished from which they could rekindle their individual hearths.

By the historical period the Prytaneion served as a sort of town hall, as a repository for laws and archives, and as a public dining hall. Here important men of the city were fed at public expense, sometimes for life, and here benefactors and ambassadors from foreign states were invited to dine. A fragmentary inscription from the fifth century lists those eligible to dine on a regular basis, including the priests of the Eleusinian deities and victors in the Panhellenic games (*IG* I³ 131). Later, generals were included as well, and the meals must have been something, with their mix of priests, ambassadors, athletes, and soldiers. We even hear of an old Athenian mule who worked so long and hard on the Parthenon that he was voted public sustenance from the Prytaneion, though it seems unlikely that he was actually invited to the table.

Early on the fare was simple: leeks, onions, bread, cheese, and olives; late in the fifth century fish and meat were added to the menu. Prytaneia have been found in other cities, and all have certain features in common. Essential is a courtyard and a place for the hearth or altar of Hestia with its eternal flame; also necessary were the dining rooms, usually identifiable from the raised border which carried the couches lining the walls of the room. The Athenian Prytaneion is one of the most venerable of the public buildings of Athens still awaiting discovery.

Though the architectural remains of Solon's time are slight, other findings are noteworthy. This was the period when black-figured vase painting made its first appearance. The style developed gradually out of the proto-Attic ceramics of the seventh century. Characterized by dark figures set against a light background, with the use of incision and polychromy for details and decoration, the black-figured style lasted for well over a century (see figs. 35, 38). It was widely exported and imitated elsewhere, beginning several centuries during which Athenian potters and painters produced the most influential and valued pottery in the Mediterranean.

At nearby Eleusis, the cult of Demeter had been flourishing for at least a century, to judge by the small votive plaques found there. The central cult chamber, which was later incorporated into a huge Telesterion (Hall of Mysteries), was built of bluish limestone blocks set with curvilinear joints. It has been dated by some to the early sixth century. If the date is correct, this is one of the earliest surviving cult buildings known from Athens or Attica.

From Cape Sounion come the earliest examples of monumental marble sculpture from Athens or Attica. Long before there is any evidence for a temple, the sanctuary of Poseidon was filled with *kouroi,* large marble statues of striding nude males. The earliest, which dates to close to 600, is also one of the largest known, standing 3.05 meters high. Other kouroi were added to the sanctuary during the course of the sixth century, and fragments of no fewer than thirteen examples have been recovered in the excavations. The early appearance and large number of such impressive and expensive votives at Sounion suggest that the area may have been home to one of the richer aristocratic families of Athens, the Alkmaionidai, who were said by Herodotos and Aristotle to have had their landholdings on the coast. The kouros type also became popular as a grave marker, and several sixth-century examples have been recovered, many of them from southern Attica.

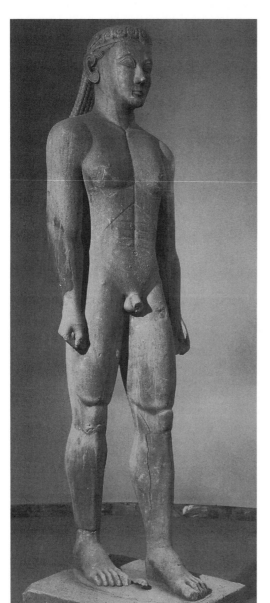

PEISISTRATOS

Despite Solon's reforms, tensions among the aristocratic families continued. Three major factions or clans were involved, each of whom occupied a spe-

23. Marble kouros from Sounion, ca. 600 B.C.

24. A statue of a woman named Phrasikleia and a kouros, found in the cemetery at Merenda (ancient Myrrhinous), in south Attica.

cific geographical part of Attica: the Alkmaionidai, led by Megakles, controlled the coastal areas; the clan of Lykourgos (possibly the Eteoboutadai) held the city and much of the plain; and the Peisistratids, led by Peisistratos, claimed the inland parts of Attica. Shifting alliances among these families kept anyone from seizing full power immediately after the reforms, but a tyranny arose within a generation, starting around 566.

The word *tyrant,* which seems to be Lydian rather than Greek and is first applied to the rich Lydian ruler Kroisos, did not originally carry the strong negative force it held in the Classical period (and retains today). Early on the word meant simply a person who seized and held power unconstitutionally. Often, in fact, a tyrant arose as a champion of the common people against an overbearing aristocracy. Tyranny was a common element in the political development of many Greek states in the Archaic period as they passed from monarchy to aristocracy through tyranny to either democracy or oligarchy. Characteristic of these tyrannies were monumental building programs, usually temples and water-supply systems. For the first time in six hundred years, the two necessary components for such projects were available: accumulated wealth and a strong centralized authority. Many Greek states show this political development, together with a parallel building program: Athens, Corinth, Megara, Samos, and Akragas, to note the best documented.

In Athens, Peisistratos first seized power in around 566 by means of both trickery and alliances with other families. His was a recent, upstart faction compared with some of the others, such as the Alkmaionidai, and it took several attempts and periods of exile before he was able to secure control, in about 545. He reigned until his death in 527, at which time two of his sons, Hippias and Hipparchos, took over until the murder of Hipparchos in

25. Limestone pediment from the Acropolis of a lion attacking a bull, mid-6th century B.C.

26. Limestone pediment from the Acropolis of a triple-bodied creature, mid-6th century B.C.

514 and the expulsion of Hippias in 510.

Peisistratos and his sons were typical tyrants in their approach to public works, and during their reign we find Athens adorned with the first monumental public buildings. On the Acropolis a large temple was built in the Doric order, presumably dedicated to Athena and decorated with lively, brightly painted poros limestone pedimental sculptures depicting lions attacking bulls and scenes from Greek mythology. Numerous pieces of the temple were found scattered around the Acropolis, built into the south fortification wall, and buried in the early fifth century B.C. in great pits southeast of the Parthenon. No certain traces of foundations have been found, and just where the temple may originally have stood remains a matter of conjecture and dispute. The ground plan is also uncertain, though the large number of column fragments make it likely that the tem-

25, 26

ple had colonnades on all four sides. The style of the sculptures and the profiles of the column capitals have led most scholars to date the building to the middle of the sixth century.

Perhaps dating to the second quarter of the sixth century is a rearrangement of the entrance to the Acropolis and the establishment of a cult of Athena Nike (Victory) nearby. The entrance was embellished by a great ramp measuring 11 meters wide and some 90 meters in length, carried on a handsome retaining wall of polygonal masonry, which led up to the Acropolis. To the south of this ramp, an altar of Athena Nike was established on the ruins of the old Mycenaean entrance to the citadel. Part of the altar survives, carrying the dedicatory inscription "Altar of Athena Nike. Patrok(l)es made it," written in early letters (A. Raubitschek, *Dedications from the Athenian Acropolis* [Cambridge, 1953] no. 329). It is tempting to associate these substantial improvements to Athena's great shrine on the Acropolis with another of Peisistratos' contributions: the creation or aggrandizement of the Panathenaic festival.

Ancient sources indicate that the festival was reorganized on a large scale in 566 by Peisistratos, who instituted the great procession during which a hundred bulls were led up to the Acropolis to be sacrificed at the altar of Athena Polias (of the City). The cult statue of Athena received a new robe (*peplos*)—into which was woven a scene of the victory of the Olympian gods over the giants—which was carried at the head of this procession. Accompanying it were priests and priestesses, along with a host of attendants and officials, who appear later on the Parthenon frieze and in the parade described in Aristophanes' plays *The*

27. Polygonal retaining wall for the monumental ramp leading up to the Acropolis, mid-6th century B.C.

28. Limestone pediment from a small building on the Acropolis, showing Herakles fighting the hydra, mid-6th century B.C.

Ekklesiazousai (ll. 730–745) and *The Birds* (ll. 1550–1552): basket bearers, stool bearers, parasol bearers, bearers of hydrias (water jars), musicians (playing the kithara and flute), bearers of trays of honey and cakes, and elders carrying olive branches.

Many more pieces of architecture and architectural sculpture all dating to the middle years of the sixth century have been found on the Acropolis. They can be combined in a variety of ways and suggest that there were between five and seven small Doric buildings up there as well. In plan, these resemble the treasuries built at panhellenic sanctuaries, best known from Delphi and Olympia: a simple room entered through a porch of two columns. The pediments were decorated with lively scenes from Greek mythology, many of them featuring Herakles: Herakles wrestling a Triton, fighting the Lernean hydra, and being introduced to Mount Olympos. Herakles began as a hero and then was promoted to full-fledged god, hence this introduction to his fellow deities.

Like the sculpture on the large temple, these pieces were carved in a soft poros which has preserved the brightly colored paints far better than most ancient architecture or sculpture in marble. It is not clear where these little buildings stood; later quarrying and building on the Acropolis have eradicated all traces of foundations. A possible area would be west of the later Parthenon, facing north. Nor is it known exactly what purpose they served: they seem too numerous to have all been temples, and yet it is hard to see why treasuries would be needed in a local rather than panhellenic sanctuary.

Other areas of Athens grew as well under the tenure of Peisistratos and his sons. North of the Acropolis the Agora, the great square destined to become the civic center and birthplace of democracy, was first laid out. The creation of this public space, replacing what had been a domestic quarter and burial ground in the eighth and seventh centuries, occurred during Peisistratos' reign, and the first public buildings were erected nearby. According to Thucydides (6.54) the younger Peisistratos, grandson of the tyrant, established the Altar of the Twelve Gods in the Agora during the year in which he served as archon, and an inscription dates his archonship to 522/1. The monument served as the central milestone of the city, according to both Herodotos (2.7) and the following inscription:

29. Archaic limestone pediment showing the introduction of Herakles on Mount Olympos: Zeus is enthroned at left, and Herakles approaches him from right, mid-6th century B.C.

30. Plan of the Agora ca. 520 B.C., showing buildings constructed under the Peisistratids.

31. Drawing of the Altar of the Twelve Gods in the Agora, seen from the southwest, 522/1 B.C.

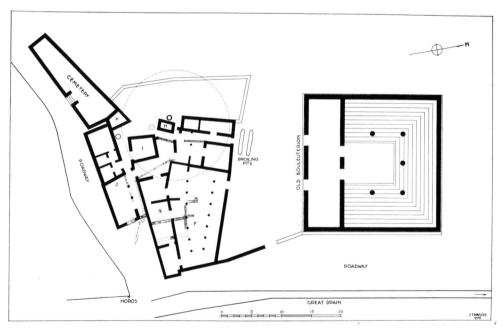

32. Archaic buildings along the west side of the Agora: Building F (ca. 550–525 B.C.) at left and the Old Bouleuterion (ca. 500) at right.

33. Statue of a seated Dionysos from Ikaria, ca. 530–520 B.C.

The city set me up, a truthful monument, to show all mortals the measure of their journeying; the distance to the Altar of the Twelve Gods from the harbor is forty-five stades (ca. 9 kilometers). (*IG* II² 2640)

The area of the altar lies mostly under the modern Athens-Peiraieus railway, built in 1891; part of the sill which carried a low parapet surrounding the altar was discovered just south of the tracks. Nearby was a statue base in situ, which reads, "Leagros, the son of Glaukon, dedicated this to the twelve gods," thereby providing a secure location and identification for the monument.

Across the Agora to the south a small fountain house was constructed, fed by a beautifully crafted pipeline of terra-cotta, which brought water for the hundreds of people now expected to frequent the new public space of Athens. A central lobby which was entered through a colonnaded facade gave access to basins and running waterspouts at either end of the building. Pottery from beneath the floor, the use of Z-clamps to bond the wall blocks, and the Kara limestone set in a polygonal style all indicate that the building should date to the period 530–520. The fact that water was conveyed over a long distance to this specific spot suggests a deliberate attempt to develop the area for public use.

In the southwest corner of the square a large building was constructed as well. The plan, a group of rooms around a central courtyard, with provisions for cooking, seems to indicate a domestic function, though the building is far larger than any known Athenian house of the period. One plausible suggestion is that it served as a palace or headquarters for the tyrants. However it may have been used, the date from pottery found in it is around 550–525, indicating that it too, like the altar and fountain house, was part of the Peisistratid development of the area.

The broad street taken by the Panathenaic procession ran diagonally through the Agora, leading from northwest Athens up to the Acropolis, and it may well be that the laying out of the large open square was primarily motivated by the need to provide a proper

venue for the athletic and theatrical events which made up an important part of the Panathenaic festival.

At some time late in the sixth century, perhaps under the Peisistratids though possibly later, the sanctuary of Dionysos Eleuthereus was established south of the Acropolis, and
a small temple was built for the god. The cult, and therefore the god's epithet, was imported
from Eleutherai, the border area between Attica and Boiotia, the traditional center of his
worship. In later times the plays of the great theatrical festival (the Dionysia) were performed in the sanctuary, though in the sixth century they were produced in an area of the
Agora known as the orchestra. The worship of Dionysos, patron god of wine, theater, and
merriment, had a long tradition in the demes as well. One small deme, Ikaria, had a particular association with his cult (see fig. 258). Here, on the wooded northern slopes of Mount
Pentele, Dionysos was said to have been hospitably received by Ikarios. In return for his
kindness, Dionysos taught Ikarios the art of making wine. A dangerous gift; when Ikarios
shared his discovery with two neighbors, they quickly became dizzy and, thinking they had
been poisoned, killed Ikarios. Ikaria was also the place where Thespis is said to have first
added a narrative actor to the primitive choral performances in honor of Dionysos in 534
B.C., thereby gaining credit as the inventor of both tragedy and comedy (Athenaios, *Deipnosophistai* 2.40a). Excavations late in the nineteenth century uncovered the sanctuary
where these momentous events occurred and were commemorated. In addition to small
temples and a simple theater, a large marble statue, dated ca. 530–520, of a seated figure of
Dionysos holding his wine cup (*kantharos*) was also recovered.

Southeast of the Acropolis the Peisistratids also laid out a monumental temple dedicated to Olympian Zeus. Designed to rival other giant temples built at Samos, Ephesos, and
Miletos at this time, this huge building measured more than 40 by 100 meters but was
never finished. Only its foundations and several dozen limestone column drums were produced. The foundations were carefully laid in a polygonal style, and the drums indicate that
the building would have been of the Doric order, like the great Sicilian temples at Akragas
and Selinous. The project was abandoned when the tyrants were expelled in 510 B.C.

One other monument known to have been built by the Peisistratids does not survive,
though it was famous in antiquity. This was the Enneakrounos, the nine-spouted fountain
house, built somewhere near the bed of the Ilissos River, according to Thucydides, not far
from the Olympieion. It is referred to repeatedly in ancient sources and seems to be reflected in literally dozens of black-figured hydrias (water jars) of the period, painted with
scenes showing young maidens drawing water from a fountain house. Also established in
this southeastern part of town was a monumental altar dedicated to Pythian Apollo by Peisistratos the Younger in 522/1, the same year he dedicated the Altar of the Twelve Gods in
the Agora. The top of this altar was found by the Ilissos River, carrying a handsomely carved

Left 34. Large limestone column drums from the unfinished archaic temple of Olympian Zeus, late 6th century B.C.

Right 35. Black-figured water jar (hydria) showing young women at a fountain house. These scenes became very popular in the late 6th century B.C., a time when the Peisistratids were building fountain houses throughout the city.

molding and part of the dedicatory inscription (*IG* I³ 948) seen and recorded by Thucydides (6.54.7):

> This memorial of his office Peisistratos the son of Hippias set up in the sanctuary of Apollo Pythios.

The territory of Attica received attention from the Peisistratids as well. Plato (*Hipparchos* 228–29) refers to roads in the country marked with posts and carrying moral maxims of the tyrants:

36. Inscribed crowning block from the altar of Pythian Apollo, carrying a dedication by Peisistratos the Younger, 522/1 B.C.

There are two such inscriptions of his: on the left side of each herm there is one in which the god says that he stands in the midst of the city or deme, while on the right side he says, "The memorial of Hipparchos; walk with just intent." There are many other fine inscriptions from his poems on other figures of herms, and this one in particular on the Steireian road, which reads: "the memorial of Hipparchos; deceive not a friend."

One such marker has actually come to light in central Attica near the village of Koropi, halfway between the city and the deme of Kephale (*IG* I³ 1023).

In addition to Ikaria, other demes in Attica show indications of Peisistratid interest in building religious structures. At Eleusis the old sanctuary of Demeter was enclosed in a large circuit wall built with a low socle of limestone blocks set in a polygonal style which carried several meters of sun-dried mudbrick. A common, cheap, and effective building material, mudbrick rarely survives today; the wall at Eleusis is among the earliest and best-preserved examples in the Mediterranean. One of the many phases of the Telesterion should also presumably be attributed to the tyrants.

Finally, Peisistratos was said to have been responsible for the construction of the early temple of Artemis at Brauron, on the east coast of Attica. The sanctuary lay within the territory of Philaidai, the home deme of Peisistratos. Many of the votives go back to early Archaic times, and much of the architecture dates to the fifth century B.C., but limestone

37. Model of the sanctuary at Eleusis, showing the Peisistratid fortification wall and the Telesterion.

fragments of triglyphs and antae suggest that a temple of the Doric order was built originally in the late sixth century B.C.

Thus with the construction program of temples and fountain houses, Peisistratos fits
the mold of an Archaic tyrant. Politically, his reign seems also to have been a success, if we
may judge from the following assessment by Aristotle (*Ath. Pol.* 16.7–8):

> And in all other matters too he gave the multitude no trouble during his rule,
> but always worked for peace and safeguarded tranquillity; so that men were of-
> ten heard to say that the tyranny of Peisistratos was the Golden Age of Kronos;
> for it came about later when his sons had succeeded him that the government
> became much harsher.

Or this, by Thucydides (6.54.5–6), which refers to the building program:

> The Peisistratidai carried the practice of virtue and discretion to a very high de-
> gree, considering that they were tyrants, and although they extracted from the
> Athenians only 5 percent of their incomes, not only had they embellished their
> city, but they also carried on its wars and provided sacrifices for the temples.

In addition, the Peisistratids added considerably to the cultural life of Athens, attract-
ing famous poets such as Anakreon and Simonides to the court and encouraging the
spread of the Homeric epics by having rhapsodes recite them at the Panathenaia. Athens
begins to take form as a city in the sixth century with the laying out of the Agora, the construction of temples and fountain houses, and the organization of the Panathenaia as a primary expression of civic pride. These important new developments were the work of Peisistratos and his sons.

THE RISE OF DEMOCRACY

Toward the end of the sixth century, the Peisistratid tyranny came to an end. In 514, as
the result of a love feud, two men, Harmodios and Aristogeiton, stabbed Hipparchos to death.
They killed him at the Panathenaia, the one day of the year when citizens were allowed to
carry weapons without arousing suspicion. As a result of this attack the reign of the surviving
brother, Hippias, became much harsher, and the members of the principal rival clan, the Alkmaionidai, were driven into exile. Several unsuccessful attempts were made to expel Hippias
and, finally, in 510, he was deposed with Spartan help. A period of civil unrest followed, in

38. Panathenaic amphora, with the tyrannicides as the emblem of
Athena's shield, 5th century B.C., copied from statues of Harmodios
and Aristogeiton set up in the Agora.

which two leaders, Isagoras and Kleisthenes, contended
for power. Getting the worst of it, Kleisthenes called on the
common people for help, gained control, and instituted a
new constitution, which went into effect in 508/7. Other
than his name and the fact that he was a member of the
Alkmaionidai, we know almost nothing of the individual
who brought about such radical change. His new system
of government was the foundation on which Classical
Athenian democracy was erected. Its primary achievement
was to break the power of the old aristocratic families which
had been based on control of different geographical regions
of Attica.

Kleisthenes reorganized the social and political structure of Attica, creating ten new *phylai* (tribes). Each tribe was
made up of three groups called *trittyes* (thirds), and each trittys was
drawn from one of the three geographical regions of Attica. All rights and privileges as a
citizen came from membership in the tribe. A citizen served in the *boule* (senate) in a
tribal contingent. He fought in the army—where his life literally depended on the shield
of the next man in line—in a tribal contingent. There were also special tribal sacrifices.
Each tribe was named after an early hero of Athens, and the members of the tribe dedicated shrines, made sacrifices, and held feast days in his honor in which the other Athenians did not share; each Athenian, however humble, was thereby provided with
a heroic ancestor. Governing, fighting, and feasting with a new group of fellow tribes-
men drawn from all three regions of Attica forged new bonds of loyalty and greatly
diminished the power, influence, and control of the local aristocratic families. The
tribes thus became the new focus for political power as well as for social and religious activity.

The success of the new system was tested almost at once when Athens was attacked

Opposite 39. Map showing the political organization of Attica as a result of the Kleisthenic reforms of
508/7 B.C. Each color stands for one of the ten tribes, each mark for an individual deme. The lines link
the groups of demes which make up each *trittys* (third) of a tribe. The number inside each deme
symbol shows the number of representatives sent annually from that deme to the *boule* (senate).

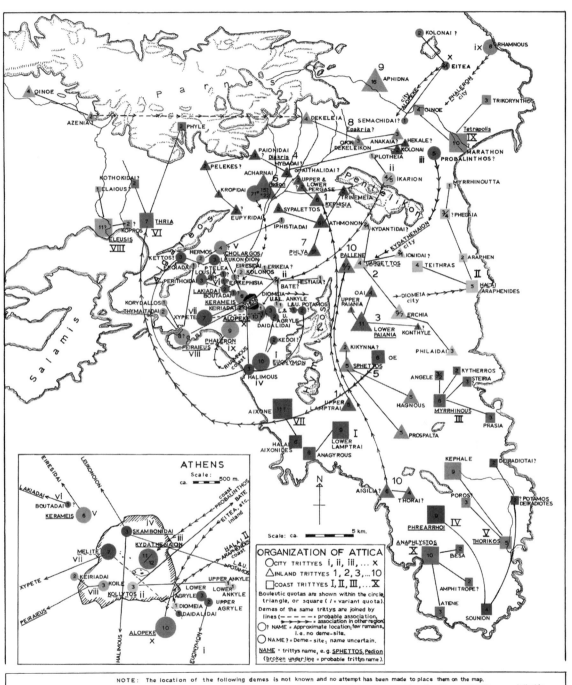

ORGANIZATION OF ATTICA

○ CITY TRITTYES i, ii, iii, ... x
△ INLAND TRITTYES 1, 2, 3, ... 10
□ COAST TRITTYES I, II, III, ... X

Bouleutic quotas are shown within the circle, triangle, or square (/ = variant quota).

Demes of the same trittys are joined by lines (— — — — = probable association, →→→→ = association in other region).

○¹ NAME = Approximate location; few remains, i.e. no deme-site.

○ NAME? = Deme-site; name uncertain.

NAME = trittys name, e.g. SPHETTOS, Pedion (broken underline = probable trittys name).

NOTE: The location of the following demes is not known and no attempt has been made to place them on the map.

Erechtheis	Aigeis	Pandionis	Leontis	Akamantis	Oineis	Kekropis	Hippothontis	Aiantis	Antiochis
△ THEMAKOS 1?	○ OTRYNE ii	○ None	● CHOLLEIDAI iV	○ EITEA V	● HIPPOTOMADAI Vi?	● PITHOS 7	△ ACHERDOUS 8?	○ None	● KRIOA X
△ PHEGOUS 1?			△ AITHALIDAI		△ TYRMEIDAI 6?		● AURIDAI VIII?		● EROIADAI X
■ PAMBOTADAI I?			or HYBADAI 4			● EPIEIKIDAI Vii	■ HAMAXANTEIA VIII?		
▨ SYBRIDAI I?			△ OION KERAMEIKON 4			or 7			

J. S. Traill, Demos and Trittys, 1986

by the Boiotians and the Chalcidians of Euboia together on a single day in 507/6 and defeated both armies, according to Herodotos (5.78):

> Thus grew the power of Athens, and it is proved not by one but by many instances that equality is a good thing; seeing that while they were under tyrants the Athenians were no better in war than any of their neighbors, yet once they were quit of their tyrants they were far and away the first of all.

To celebrate the victory a bronze horse and chariot group was set up on the Acropolis. Parts of its inscribed base have been identified (IG I² 394), though the sculpture itself does not survive. Also dedicated were the chains with which the Athenians bound their many prisoners.

Other monuments on the Acropolis are probably to be dated to the period of the new 40, 41   democracy as well, including a large temple to Athena. Its foundations survive in place near

40. Foundations of the old temple of Athena on the Acropolis, ca. 510 B.C.

41. The marble statue of Athena from the pediment of the old temple of Athena.

the center of the Acropolis, just south of the later Erechtheion, and numerous pieces of its superstructure have been recovered. It was a Doric peripteral building of limestone, with six columns across the ends and twelve down the sides. It was adorned with marble sculptures, and in one pediment was depicted a battle of gods against giants, with Athena prominently featured. The Athena temple shares stylistic affinities with the temple of Apollo at Delphi, built by the Alkmaionidai during their period of exile, and should be close in date, perhaps around 510–500. There is no record of who paid for the new temple.

The Acropolis was also adorned at this time with a forest of free-standing dedications, mostly statues and *perirrhanteria*. A perirrhanterion was a broad, shallow marble basin, resting on a columnar support and looking like a modern birdbath. In antiquity, they held water used by visitors at a sacred area to carry out a token ablution. Perirrhanteria were apparently regarded as especially appropriate gifts to Athena: no fewer than fifty examples bearing dedications inscribed on the rim have been found on the Acropolis.

Of the statues, numerous examples in marble survive. The most common type by far was the *kore,* a standing draped female figure, exquisitely carved, often shown holding out an offering with one hand. The clothing is rendered with care, and enough paint survives 42, 43
to indicate the elaborately woven patterns which decorated the borders of the real garments of the day. In all, several dozen examples from the Acropolis survive, many found carefully buried near the north wall of the citadel. Other statue types, though far less common than the korai, survive as well: a hound, horses with riders, and seated scribes.

A number of statues which do not survive are represented by the inscribed bases on

42 and 43. Kores from the
Acropolis, 6th century B.C.

which they once stood. Cuttings in the tops of these bases
indicate that many of the missing statues were of bronze; the
metal could be melted down
and reused, whereas a marble
statue was less easy to recycle.
In all, counting statues and
bases, we can say that several
dozen statues adorned the
Acropolis by around 510–490.
Almost all the statues were dedicated to Athena, and sometimes the dedicator gives his
profession: architect, potter,
ship's captain. Except for the
bronze chariot, most of the votives are gifts by individuals rather than the Athenian state.
Soon after the establishment of the democracy, then, we find the Acropolis provided with a
handsome new temple and numerous expensive free-standing votives.

In the lower city new buildings were required to house the different branches of the
new political system, and the Agora was transformed into the civic center. A *bouleuterion*
(senate house) was built along the west side of the square to house the new council (boule)
of five hundred citizens who each served for a year. Only the lowest foundations survive;
these indicate that the building was roughly square in plan, about 30 meters a side, with interior columns to support the roof. In addition, a small stoa, or colonnaded building, was
constructed at the northwest corner of the square. Though there are problems with its date
and later history, we know that it served as headquarters for the *basileus* (king archon), the
second-in-command of the Athenian government and the official in charge of religious
matters and the laws. The building faced east onto the square and had eight Doric columns
across the front, with four inside. Immediately outside the building was a huge, unworked
stone measuring 0.95 meters by 2.95 meters which has been identified as the oath stone of
the Athenians, described by Aristotle as follows (*Ath. Pol.* 7.1):

44. Northwest corner of the Agora. At left is the Royal Stoa, originally built ca. 500 B.C.(?).

Inscribing the laws [of Solon] on the pillars, they set them up in the Royal Stoa.
The nine archons, taking an oath at the stone, declared that they would set up a
golden statue if they transgressed any of the laws; this is the origin of the oath
they still take.

The identification of the building is secure, thanks to a description of this part of Athens
written by Pausanias in about A.D. 150 and to two inscribed bases, dedicated by king archons to commemorate their year in office, which were found in place right on the steps of
the building (Agora Inventory 7168 and 7185).

The formal limits of the Agora square were also more carefully defined in the years
around 500 B.C. Marble boundary stones were set up wherever a street entered the square,
carrying the text "I am the boundary of the Agora." Two such stones have actually been
found in situ along the west side. The square needed to be defined for two reasons. First, it
was public land and the stones were necessary to ensure that private individuals did not
build on it. Second, the Agora was a quasi-religious area and certain people were not allowed into it: anyone convicted of failure to report for military duty, of cowardice in battle,

46

Above 45. Oath stone (*lithos*) at the front of the Royal Stoa.

Left 46. Boundary stone of the Agora, ca. 500 B.C.

of impiety or mistreatment of their parents, for instance, as well as young men who had not yet fulfilled their military service.

On the ridge southwest of the Agora a new meeting place was laid out on the Pnyx Hill, to accommodate the new assembly (*ekklesia*), which now was part of the legislative process. Here the full citizen body was entitled to meet about every ten days to consider any legislation proposed by the senate (*boule*), and most Athenian decrees indicate that they were passed by both bodies. Though the citizen body numbered in the tens of thousands it seems that their meeting place on the Pnyx accommodated between 8,000 and 13,000 people (see figs. 147, 148). Only the slightest traces and a boundary stone survive from this earliest phase of the Pnyx.

THE PERSIAN WARS

In 499/8 the Athenians sent help to the Ionian Greeks on the west coast of Asia Minor, who were in revolt against Persia. The Greeks were successful at first and burned the provincial capital of Sardis, but in 494 the revolt was suppressed after the crushing loss of a sea battle at Lade and the destruction of Miletos. The Persian king then turned his attention to punishing Athens and Eretria, the two mainland Greek cities which had participated. In 490 a Persian fleet sailed across the Aegean, took Eretria in a matter of days, and put in at the Bay of Marathon. Guiding the Persians—and hoping to be reinstated once the battle was won—was Hippias, the tyrant who had been expelled twenty years earlier, now an old man.

The Athenians marched out to confront the Persians and camped in the sanctuary of Herakles at the south end of the plain. After several days' delay, battle was joined, and the Persians were routed, suffering tremendous casualties by the great marsh at the north end of the plain. Herodotos (6.102–20) describes the battle and records that 6,400 Persians were killed but only 192 Athenians. The Battle of Marathon, often considered a turning point in the history of Western civilization, resulted in an enormous boost to Athenian morale and prestige. Alone, except for a small contingent of allies from Plataia, the Athenians had defeated the army of an empire of almost inconceivable size and resources. Monuments to commemorate the great victory proliferated. 47

At Marathon itself, the dead were cremated and buried where they fell on the battlefield and a huge mound, or *soros*, 9 meters high and almost 50 meters across, was heaped up over their remains. The hero of the battle, the general Miltiades, dedicated a bronze helmet at Olympia as a thank offering to Zeus, and he, too, was eventually buried on the battlefield. 48, 49

The thousands of Persian dead were treated more casually. A German topographer in the nineteenth century reported a loose scatter of human bones throughout the north end of the plain, corresponding to the account of Pausanias (1.32.4):

> The Athenians assert that they buried the Medes because it is a sacred and imperative duty to cover with earth a human corpse, but I could find no grave; for there was neither a barrow nor any other mark to be seen. They just carried them to a trench and threw them in pell-mell.

Just south of the marsh is a medieval tower in which were found several marble column drums and an Ionic capital datable to the early fifth century B.C., with cuttings to carry sculpture on top. This almost certainly is the trophy, set up at the turning point (*trope*) of the battle, where the enemy suffered the greatest number of casualties. It was a source of great pride to the Athenians, and a number of ancient writers refer to it, describing it as a column of white marble. Several drums are now missing, but it is possible to estimate the original height at more than 10 meters.

Another burial associated with the battle is more controversial. In the late 1960s a tumulus (burial mound) was found near the museum at Vrana. Half of it was excavated, producing eleven graves, all dated to the early fifth century B.C. and all males. One man was aged between thirty and forty, and there was a boy of about ten; the rest were all in their twenties. The suggestion has been made that this was the tomb of the Athenian allies, the Plataians, who fought at Marathon and were also buried on the field of battle, as recorded by Pausanias (1.32.3):

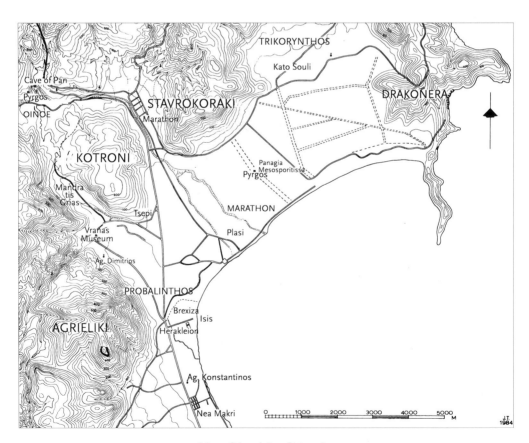

47. Map of the plain of Marathon.

Above 48. The soros, or burial mound, of the Athenian dead at Marathon, 490 B.C.

Left 49. Bronze helmet dedicated by Miltiades at Olympia after the Battle of Marathon.

In the plain is the grave of the Athenians, and over it are tombstones with the names of the fallen arranged according to tribes. There is another grave for the Boiotians of Plataia and the slaves; for slaves fought then for the first time. There is a separate tomb for Miltiades, son of Kimon.

Against the identification is the location of the tomb, 2.5 kilometers from the soros and the battlefield, and the fact that none of the skeletons show signs of wounds. In addition, the tumulus covers eleven individual graves, whereas in most military multiple graves (*polyandreia*) the bodies were all neatly laid out in rows, like sardines in a tin: at Thespiai (424 B.C.), in the Kerameikos at Athens (403 B.C.), and at Chaironeia (338 B.C.). Finally, two nine-

50. Ionic marble column capital of the trophy for the Battle of Marathon.

teenth-century travelers, Leake and Clarke, each saw a second, smaller tumulus near the soros during their visits to Marathon. The location of the tomb of the Plataians, therefore, remains an open question.

Various deities were worshiped after the battle in thanks for the help they were thought to have provided. In particular, the horned, goat-footed god of Arcadia, Pan, received special attention, according to a story in Herodotos (6.105):

> The generals sent as a herald to Sparta Pheidippides, an Athenian, one who was a runner of long distances and made that his career. This man, as he said himself and told the Athenians, when he was on Mount Parthenian above Tegea met Pan, who calling Pheidippides by name told him to say to the Athenians, "Why do you take no thought of me, who is your friend, has been before, and will be again?" This story the Athenians believed and when they succeeded, they founded a sanctuary of Pan below the Acropolis and sought the god's favor with yearly sacrifices and torch races.

According to both Pausanias and Lucian, Pan's sanctuary was on the northwest slopes of the Acropolis. It is associated with one of the shallow caves there which have rock-cut niches designed to receive votive reliefs, several of which were found lower down on the slopes (see fig. 112). This sanctuary was not an isolated phenomenon; other caves throughout Attica show signs of cult activity in honor of Pan, all beginning in the first half of the fifth century B.C. Evidence for his worship takes the form of inscriptions, votive plaques in marble, and terra-cotta statuettes of the god and his companions, the nymphs.

One of the most impressive caves, only partially excavated, is located at Oinoe near Marathon itself. Other caves sacred to Pan and the nymphs have been found on Mounts Parnes, Pentele, Hymettos, and Aigaleos, as well as at Eleusis. The cave on Hymettos is the most ornate. A man from Thera (Santorini) by the name of Archedemos, who described himself as a *nympholept* (one seized by the nymphs), covered the walls of the cave with reliefs and dedicatory inscriptions. Miltiades also dedicated a statue of Pan at Marathon; the dedicatory inscription on the base is said to have been composed by Simonides (*Anth. Pal.* 16.232):

Miltiades erected me, goat-footed Pan, the Arcadian, the foe of the Medes, the friend of the Athenians.

Herakles had already been popular in Athens for years, showing up on numerous black-figured pots and, as noted, on several of the sculptural groups on the sixth-century Acropolis. He had a particular association with Marathon, however; the spring there called Makaria was named after his daughter, and the people of Marathon claimed to have been the first to worship him as a god. When they marched out to confront the Persians, the

51. The "tomb of the Plataians" at Vrana (Marathon), early 5th century B.C.

Athenians camped in Herakles' sanctuary at Marathon before the battle, and after the victory they instituted special games in his honor. Two fifth-century inscriptions found not far from each other allow us to identify the general area of his sanctuary at the south end of the plain.

52   In Athens a new temple was laid out to house Athena on the Acropolis. Unlike the two sixth-century limestone temples, this one was to be of Pentelic marble and represents the earliest substantial exploitation of the quarries on Mount Pentele. Before this, when marble was required, the Athenians imported it from the Cycladic islands of Naxos and Paros. A huge platform of limestone was constructed south of the old temple of Athena (on the site of the future Parthenon), and large blocks and drums of marble were hauled
53 up the hill. Several dozen column drums were brought up and put in place, but, as a result of the continuing war with Persia, the building was never finished. Although no ancient source specifies the connection, it has been generally accepted that this predecessor to the Parthenon was started soon after 490 B.C. and was intended to commemorate the victory
54 at Marathon.

A fragmentary inscription of the year 485/4 provides some information about the Acropolis at this time, though its interpretation is uncertain (*IG* I³ 4B). It consists of a series of regulations about what may not be done up there, such as lighting fires and dumping dung. The areas where these things may not take place are defined by monuments: around or between the temple, the altar, the Kekropion (grave or sanctuary of Kekrops), and a structure—perhaps a temple—known as the Hekatompedon. The word *hekatompedon* (100-footer) is often used to describe a large temple, though some think it may simply refer to a part of the Acropolis. The inscription also refers to *oikemata* (rooms or structures) in the Hekatompedon, which treasurers are to open every ten days to ensure that the treasure kept therein is safe. The inscription is carved on a reused metope (part of the frieze) of the mid-sixth-century temple, so we know that the early limestone temple with lion and bulls (see figs. 25, 26) had been dismantled by the mid-480s, presumably to make way for a new temple. Unfortunately, it is not clear which temple succeeded it, the one with the marble gigantomachy built around 510–500 on the foundations south of the Erechtheion (see figs. 40, 41) or the marble temple started after 490 on the site later occupied by the Parthenon.

Several years later the Athenians added a colossal bronze statue of a fully armed Athena Promachos (Champion) to the Acropolis. A work of the sculptor Pheidias, it was paid for with the spoils from Marathon, according to Pausanias (1.28.2). It stood just inside the gateway, and Pausanias tells us it was so large that

> the head of the spear and the crest of the helmet of this Athena are visible to mariners sailing from Sounion to Athens.

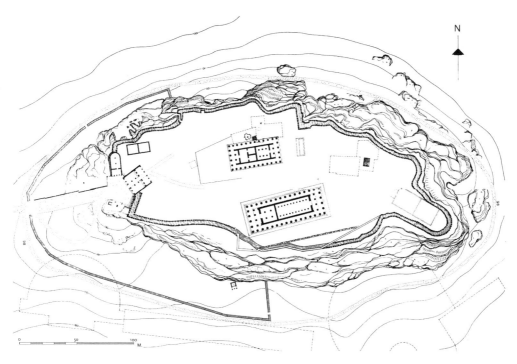

52. Plan of the Acropolis, ca. 480 B.C., with the old temple of Athena at the top (north) and the predecessor to the Parthenon (unfinished) at the bottom (south).

Representations of the statue are found on Athenian lamps and coins of the Roman period; the statue itself was carried off to adorn Constantinople in the fifth century A.D. and was eventually destroyed in the early thirteenth century. A Byzantine writer, Niketas Choniates (738 B), describes the statue as he saw it in the forum of Constantine, before its destruction:

In stature it rose to the height of about 30 feet, and was clothed in garments of the

53. Unfluted marble Doric column drum from the unfinished predecessor of the Parthenon, 490–480 B.C.

54. The Acropolis as it would have appeared in 480 B.C., with the old temple of Athena (ca. 510–500 B.C.) on the left and the half-finished older Parthenon (started ca. 490 B.C.) on the right. (Watercolor by Peter Connolly)

same material as the whole statue, namely, of bronze. The robe reached to the feet and was gathered up in several places. A warrior's baldric passed round her waist and clasped it tightly. Over her prominent breasts she wore a cunningly wrought garment, like an aegis, suspended from her shoulders, and representing the Gorgon's head. Her neck, which was undraped and of great length, was a sight to cause unrestrained delight. Her veins stood out prominently, and her whole frame was supple and, where needed, well-jointed. Upon her head a crest of horsehair "nodded fearfully from above." Her hair was twisted in a braid and fastened at the back, while that which streamed from her forehead was a feast for the eyes; for it was not altogether concealed by the helmet, which allowed a glimpse of her tresses to be seen. Her left hand held up the folds of her dress, while the right was extended toward the south and supported her head.

At Cape Sounion, the southernmost tip of Attica, a Doric temple was begun, in limestone, dedicated to Poseidon. Its unfinished, unfluted column drums may be seen built into the platform which surrounds the later Classical temple. At Rhamnous, just north of Marathon, a small Doric temple with two columns on the front was built, while a huge piece of Parian marble, said to have been brought by the Persians in the confident certainty that it would be made into a trophy, was eventually carved by the sculptor Agorakritos into a statue of Nemesis. And at Apollo's sanctuary in Delphi, the victory of Marathon was commemorated by the Athenians with the construction of a marble treasury decorated with sculpted scenes of the labors of Herakles and Theseus. In addition, bronze statues depicting Athena, Apollo, several early Athenian kings, and the general Miltiades were set up on the sacred way in the sanctuary.

The appearance of Hippias with the Persian army at Marathon made the Athenians extremely nervous. They had become accustomed to their democratic form of government, and the possibility of a renewed tyranny was distasteful. Statues of Harmodios and Aristogeiton, the slayers of Hipparchos, had been set up in the Agora soon after Hippias' departure, and the two were worshiped as the Tyrannicides—a personal feud quickly taking on the guise of political heroism, according to Thucydides. Soon after Marathon, therefore, a new procedure, known as ostracism, was instituted. Once a year all the citizens gathered in the Agora and voted on a simple question: was anyone in the city becoming so powerful that he represented a threat to the democracy? If a majority voted yes, then the Athenians met two months later, again in the Agora, each one bringing with him an *ostrakon* (potsherd) on which he had scratched the name of the man whose power and influence were

55. A selection of ostraka cast against Aristeides, Themistokles, Kimon, and Perikles, 485–440 B.C.

too great. The man with the most votes was exiled for ten years. Early in the fifth century most of Athens' leading statesmen took this enforced vacation at one time or another. The ballots, useless immediately after the vote, were used to fill potholes in roadways and the like, and close to ten thousand of them have been found in the excavations of the Agora and the Kerameikos.

At first the ostracisms were aimed at friends and supporters of the Peisistratids, but soon they became a weapon in the arsenal of skilled politicians. The first man to be ostracized who was not a friend to tyranny was Xanthippos, the father of Perikles, in 484. His opponent seems to have been Themistokles, one of the most astute and effective leaders of early Athens. Convinced that the victory at Marathon did not mean the end of the Persian threat, Themistokles championed a long-term policy to turn Athens into a naval power. He fortified the Peiraieus and persuaded the Athenians to build a huge fleet. Thucydides describes the Themistoklean wall of the Peiraieus (1.93):

> Following his advice they built the wall around the Peiraieus of the thickness that may still be observed; for two wagons carrying the stones could meet and pass each other. Inside, moreover, there was neither rubble nor clay but stones of large size hewn square were laid together, bound to one another on the outside with iron clamps and lead.

The line of this early wall has been recognized, though most of what survives today is dated to later rebuilding. In 484/3 B.C. a large deposit of silver was found in the mining district of Laureion in south Attica. The public revenues of this discovery amounted to some two hundred talents, a huge sum of money: 1.2 million drachmas at a time when the drachma was worth roughly a day's wage. At the urging of Themistokles, the Athenians did not distribute the money among themselves in the usual fashion but used it to build a fleet of two hundred warships (triremes), a decision which made Athens the primary Greek naval power in the Mediterranean. Intended for use against the neighboring island of Aigina, these ships proved essential in the next phase of the Persian Wars.

The Persians, though thwarted at Marathon, did not abandon their plans for the conquest of Athens and ten years later, in 480/79, they returned, led by King Xerxes himself, this time with both a large fleet and a huge land army. After beating the Spartans and their allies at the narrow pass of Thermopylai, the Persians broke into southern Greece. The Athenians, faced with this vast army, took the decision to abandon Athens. Women, children, and the elderly were transported to the island of Salamis and to Troizen in the Peloponnese, while the men manned the triremes, determined to oppose the Persians at sea. The Persians occupied Athens, taking the citadel against only a token defense, plundered the temples, and burnt the Acropolis. According to Herodotos and Thucydides, hardly a building was left standing as the Persians sacked and burned the city in retaliation for the destruction of Sardis in 498. Herodotos writes of the Persian general Mardonios,

> He burnt Athens, and utterly overthrew and demolished whatever wall or house or temple was left standing. (9.13)

Thucydides' account is similar:

> Of the encircling wall only small portions were left standing, and most of the houses were in ruins, only a few remaining in which the chief men of the Persians had themselves taken quarters. (1.89.3)

The archaeological record seems equally compelling. The temples and buildings which adorned Athena's sanctuary on the Acropolis were all destroyed: the old temple of Athena, the unfinished marble predecessor of the Parthenon, the early temple of Athena Nike, and the little treasury-like buildings. The dozens of korai and other statues now in the Acropolis Museum all bear witness to the deliberate destruction of the sanctuary and its offerings, and excavations have recovered numerous small fragments of high-quality red- and black-figured pottery, dedicated to Athena, showing clear signs of the effect of the fire.

Excavations in the Agora and elsewhere also attest to the almost complete destruction of the lower city. Seventeen wells excavated in the Agora were filled with the debris from the private houses they once supplied with water, and all of the Archaic public buildings show signs of grave damage. Works of art were carried off: the statues of the Tyrannicides to Susa (Arrian, *Anabasis* 3.16.8) and a bronze statue of a water bearer commissioned by Themistokles to Sardis (Plutarch, *Themistokles* 31.1). The clear break seen in Greek art between the Archaic and Classical periods is punctuated in Athens by the total devastation of the city, requiring a completely new start in 479/8.

The devastation extended to Attica as well. The small Archaic temple at Rhamnous, the unfinished temple of Poseidon at Sounion, and the Telesterion at Eleusis were all destroyed. Pausanias (3.16.8) tells us also that the cult statue of Artemis from Brauron was carried off to Susa by the Persians.

Following the burning of the Acropolis, a great naval battle was fought and won against the Persians off the island of Salamis, in 480. The victory, due in large part to Themistokles and the Athenian fleet, established the preeminence of Athens as a naval power among the Greek city-states. With the destruction of the Persian land army at Plataia in 479, the Greek mainland was freed from the Persian threat, and the focus of the war shifted to the eastern Mediterranean. As a result of the victories at Salamis and Plataia, two cities laid claim to the hegemony of Greece: the Athenians at sea and the Spartans on land. Their rivalry marks the rest of the fifth century.

4

Classical Athens

After the Persian Wars the Athenians returned to rebuild their shattered city. The first concern was a new defensive wall, which was built despite Spartan opposition. Themistokles held the Spartans off with foot-dragging diplomacy, having instructed the Athenians in the meantime,

> [that they should raise] the wall to such a height as was absolutely necessary for defense; and that the whole population of the city—men, women, and children—should take part in the wall building, sparing neither private nor public edifice that would in any way help to further the work, but demolish them all. (Thucydides 1.90.3)

Thucydides describes the result as follows (1.93.1–2):

> It was in this manner that the Athenians got their wall built in so short a time, and even today the structure shows that it was put together in haste. For the lower courses consist of all sorts of stones, in some cases not even hewn to fit but just as they were when the different workers brought them, and many stelai from grave plots and worked stones were built in. For the circuit wall of the city was extended in every direction, and for this reason they laid hands on everything in their haste.

The German excavations at the Kerameikos in the area of the Dipylon and nearby dramatically confirm this account. A number of handsome pieces from Archaic funerary

56. Archaic grave stele recut for use as a building block in the Themistoklean wall of 479 B.C.

monuments—some almost intact, many crudely trimmed—were found built into the lowest courses of the city wall. The new circuit, some 6.5 kilometers in length, became the basic line of fortified defense for Athens, in use until the third century A.D. The line of this so-called Themistoklean wall has been traced at numerous points underneath the modern city, as well as the location of at least fifteen gates.

After the walls, the Athenians began to rebuild the rest of the city. Left untouched, however, were the temples and sanctuaries destroyed by the Persians. Before the Battle of Plataia the Greeks are said to have taken an oath not to rebuild the sanctuaries but to leave them in ruins as permanent memorials of the Persian barbarism. A version of the oath is preserved in a speech by the fourth-century orator Lykourgos (*Against Leokrates* 81):

I will not hold life dearer than freedom nor will I abandon my leaders whether they are alive or dead. I will bury all allies killed in the battle. If I conquer the barbarians in war I will not destroy any of the cities which have fought for Greece, but I will consecrate a tenth of all those who sided with the barbarians. I will not rebuild a single one of the shrines which the barbarians have burnt and razed but will allow them to remain for future generations as a memorial of the barbarians' impiety.

Although the historicity of the oath of Plataia has been questioned since antiquity, the archaeological record seems to confirm its account; the temples of the Acropolis and elsewhere in Attica were left in ruins, not replaced for almost a generation. Eventually the pieces of the two great sixth-century temples were built into the north wall of the Acropolis. A long stretch of the architraves, frieze, and cornices of the old temple of Athena were set in their correct positions relative to one another at the top of the wall, and, farther east, many unfluted column drums from the half-finished older Parthenon were incorporated. Seen from the Agora, they remain on display even today, a constant reminder of the destruction of the Acropolis in 480.

In the 470s the Athenians and the Greeks continued to prosecute the war against the Persians, though the scene shifted to the east. An alliance was formed with Athens as leader, by virtue of the large fleet the city controlled. The Greek allies had the option of contributing either money or ships to the fight. Most contributed money, which the Athenians used to build and maintain their ships. The treasury of the alliance was originally located on the island of Delos, Apollo's sacred island and a traditional center of the Ionian Greeks; we know the alliance therefore as the Delian League. Over time this league evolved gradually into an Athenian empire as Athens was able to compel the various cities to pay tribute. Thus throughout the middle years of the fifth century B.C. Athens grew to be a large, rich, and dominant city-state, in control of many sources of revenue.

The old leaders of the war against Persia passed on. Miltiades, the hero of the Battle of Marathon in 490, had died soon after the battle. Themistokles, architect of Athenian naval power and hero of the victory at Salamis, was ostracized around 472. A cache of 190 ostraka all bearing his name but written by only a few individuals suggests that his fall was engi-

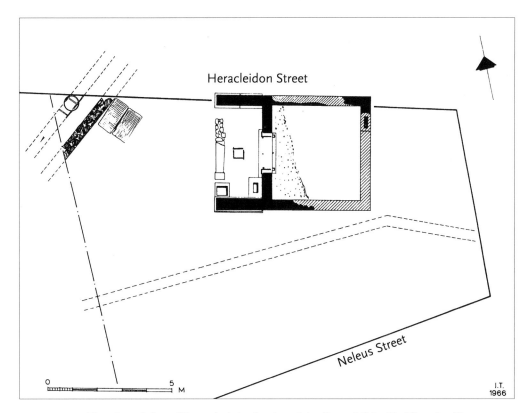

57. Temple and altar of Artemis Aristoboule, originally established by Themistokles.

57

58. Column marking the tomb of Themistokles at the entrance to Peiraieus harbor.

neered by intense party politics of the sort he had himself used a dozen years earlier to remove Xanthippos. One of the things which had annoyed the Athenians, according to Plutarch (*Themistokles* 22), was his dedication of a temple to Artemis Aristoboule (Best Counsel), an unsubtle reference to his advice and leadership during the Persian invasion. Remains of this little sanctuary in the deme of Melite have been found west of the Agora. It consisted of a small temple, no more than 6 meters long, facing west, like many other temples to Artemis (Ephesos, Magnesia, and Sardis).

Pursued by various enemies while in exile, Themistokles eventually made his way to Asia Minor and won the favor of the Great King. He died in Magnesia, which claimed to have his tomb; other sources suggest that his remains were brought back and buried, appropriately enough, in Peiraieus:

> Diodoros the Topographer, in his work "On Tombs," says, by conjecture rather than from actual knowledge, that near the large harbor of the Peiraieus a sort of elbow juts out from the promontory opposite Alkimos, and that as you round this and come inside where the water of the sea is still, there is a platform of good size, and the altarlike structure on top is the tomb of Themistokles. He thinks that the comic poet Plato is a witness in favor of his view: "The tomb is mounded in a fair and sightly place; the merchantmen shall ever hail it with a glad cry; it shall behold those outward and inward bound, and all the rivalry of racing ships." (Plutarch, *Themistokles* 32.4–5)

Pausanias (1.2) also claims to have seen the tomb there:

> When Themistokles was appointed archon he made Peiraieus the port of Athens, because it seemed to him to lie more conveniently for navigation and to

have three harbors instead of the single one at Phaleron. And there were ship sheds there down to my time, and beside the largest harbor is the grave of Themistokles. For they say that the Athenians repented of what they had done to Themistokles, and his kinsmen took up his bones and brought them back from Magnesia.

At the westernmost tip of the Akte Peninsula, on the right as one enters the largest harbor, Kantharos, there are the remains of foundations of squared blocks and rock-cut tombs. Immediately adjacent were found eight drums of a large unfluted stone column, and early 58 in the nineteenth century the traveler Edward Dodwell saw part of an Ionic capital. The column has been re-erected near the foundations, which stand on the property of the Naval Academy, and these remains are thought to be from the tomb of Themistokles.

KIMON

Coming to the fore in the 470s was Kimon, son of Miltiades and the descendant of a rich family. During his period of prominence he used his money and influence to rebuild

59. The Agora and the northwest suburbs of Athens, showing the roads and general location of the Academy. The Panathenaic Way, at upper right, leads out to the Dipylon Gate; the road continued some 3 kilometers to the Academy (upper right-hand corner). The Painted Stoa is at the extreme right. (Watercolor by Peter Connolly)

60. Ancient clay water pipes in the alley behind the Stoa Poikile, looking southwest. The large pipe at the right leads toward the Academy and is dated ca. 470–460 B.C.

and refine Athens as a city. The oath of Plataia precluded rebuilding temples, so Kimon's energies were directed elsewhere, to public buildings, defenses, and new facilities for the citizens:

> He was also the first to adorn the city with those spacious and elegant places of public resort, which not long after became popular to the point of abuse; he did this by planting the Agora with plane trees and by transforming the Academy from a parched and barren wilderness into a well-watered grove, which he provided with shady paths to walk in and clear tracks for races. (Plutarch, *Kimon* 13.7–8)

The Academy, which takes its name from the sanctuary of a local hero, Hekademos, lay outside the city to the northwest. A broad street, lined with tombs, led out to it, about 2.5 kilometers from the city walls. Here a gymnasium had been founded, which, as the Plutarch passage suggests, was greatly improved by Kimon. Several stretches of the aqueduct which brought fresh water out to the groves of the Academy have been excavated; the water line is made up of terra-cotta sections, carefully collared at the joints to fit together tightly. The Academy itself lies largely under the modern city, and though some excavation has been carried out in the area, little can be associated for certain with the original buildings. The general area is identified, thanks to the discovery in 1966 of a stone in situ carrying the inscribed text: "boundary of the Hekademeia" written in early letters.

Kimon was a successful general, and several of his campaigns—in Thrace, in Skyros, and at the Eurymedon River—resulted in further adornment of the city. Large building proj-

61. Head of a herm, found by the Stoa Poikile, ca. 470 B.C.

ects were funded with the proceeds of enemy spoils taken in battle. After defeating the Persians in Thrace and capturing land along the Strymon River, Kimon was allowed to set up three herms, which carried epigrams recording his success though not mentioning him by name (Plutarch, *Kimon* 7). 61, 62 Herms were primitive statues, used by the Athenians to mark entrances. In fully developed form a herm consisted of a plain square shaft carved halfway up with a set of male genitalia, with a portrait of the god Hermes at the top. Sculpted herms go back well before the time of Kimon, but the placement of these three, with their verse inscriptions, seems to have been particularly influential. They were set up at the northwest entrance to the Agora, which thereafter became the preferred venue for other herms. Indeed, so concentrated were they that the whole area became known as "the Herms." Nearby was built a stoa (colonnaded building) where such monuments may have been displayed; it was called, in any case, "the stoa of the herms." It is first referred to by the fifth-century orator Antiphon and then in several Hellenistic inscriptions down to the third century B.C.; its remains have not yet been recognized.

Kimon's next campaign, the capture and Athenian settlement of the island of Skyros, resulted in the recovery of the bones of Theseus, as recounted by Plutarch (*Kimon* 8.5–6):

On learning that the ancient Theseus son of Aigeus had fled in exile from Athens to Skyros, but had been treacherously put to death there by Lykomedes the king, Kimon eagerly sought to discover his grave. For the Athenians had once received an oracle bidding them bring back the bones of Theseus to the city and honor him as became a hero, but they did not know where he was buried since the Skyrians would not admit the truth of the story nor permit any search to be made. Now, however, Kimon set to work with great ardor, at last discovered the hallowed spot, had the bones taken on his own trireme, and with great pomp and show

62. Red-figured fragment showing three herms.

brought them back to the hero's own country after an absence of about four hundred years.

The bones were installed in a sanctuary, the Theseion, which lay, according to Pausanias (1.17) and Plutarch (*Theseus* 36), in the middle of the city. It has not been excavated, but inscribed lists of victors in the games held in honor of Theseus suggest the general area of its location in Plaka, several hundred meters east of the Agora. Pausanias describes the paintings which decorated the walls of the sanctuary, executed by Polygnotos and others recognized as the best painters of their day. The scenes are appropriate to Theseus: two showed great battles in which he participated, the Amazonomachy and the Centauromachy, and a third depicted him recovering King Minos' ring from the sea.

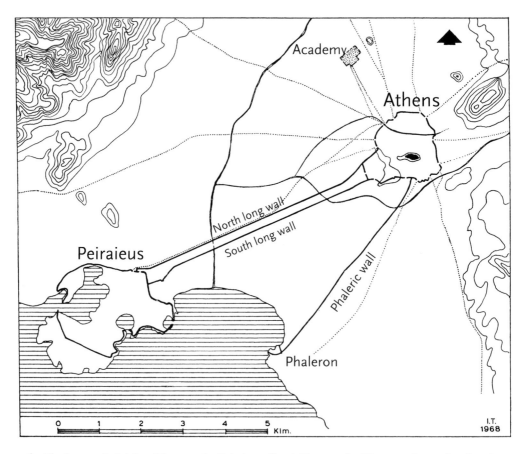

63. The long walls joining Athens to the Peiraieus, first laid out under Kimon and completed under Perikles, 460–440 B.C.

After his third great victory, at the Eurymedon River in the 460s, Kimon provided Athens with sufficient funds from the booty to undertake further major fortification of the city:

By the sale of captured spoils the people were able to meet various financial needs and in particular they constructed the south wall of the Acropolis with the considerable resources obtained from the expedition. And it is said that, though the building of the long walls, called "legs," was finished later, their first foundations, where the work was obstructed by swamps and marshes, were stabilized by Kimon, who dumped vast quantities of rubble and heavy stones into the swamps, meeting the expenses himself. (Plutarch, *Kimon* 13.6–8)   63

The new fortification of the Acropolis was a considerable undertaking, for the citadel is in fact a sharp spine of rock, falling steeply on the south side. The south wall, then, had to serve as a massive retaining wall, holding up huge amounts of fill to create the broad, level top we see today. The fabric of this early wall survives, though deeply embedded in the accretions of later times. The long walls to the Peiraieus, completed later under Perikles, were

64. The Stoa Poikile, built along the north side of the Agora during Kimon's tenure, ca. 475–460 B.C. (Watercolor by Peter Connolly)

65. Inscribed bronze shield taken from the Spartans at Pylos in 425/4
B.C., displayed at the Stoa Poikile.

an important element in Athenian naval strategy, securely joining landlocked Athens to the three fortified harbors of its port. Though largely hidden under modern suburbs, numerous sections of these two walls have been traced as they make their way to the sea. They were built of well-cut squared blocks and run parallel to each other about 180 meters apart.

Still other buildings are associated less directly with Kimon or can be shown on archaeological grounds to have been constructed during the period of his leadership. Along the north side of the Agora square a large stoa was built, originally named after Peisianax, Kimon's brother-in-law. It was of the Doric order, with Ionic columns inside, built of hard limestone, sandstone, and marble. Its westernmost end has been discovered and the rest is under excavation in 2001. Soon after its construction it was decorated with a series of handsome panel paintings done by the best artists of the day, Polygnotos, Mikon, and Panainos, and it became known thereafter as the Painted Stoa (Stoa Poikile). The paintings showed scenes of

64   Athenian military exploits, both mythological and historical: the Greeks at Troy, the Amazonomachy, the Athenians defeating the Spartans at Oinoe in the Argolid, and—most famous of all—the Battle of Marathon. The paintings were executed between 470 and 460, and more than six hundred years later Pausanias could still describe four of them. By A.D. 400 the paintings had been carried off by a Roman proconsul, as we learn from Synesios, who was bitterly disappointed not to find them still in the stoa during his visit to Athens (*Epist.* 54 and 135).

For centuries the Painted Stoa served as something like a modern museum. In addition to depictions, actual mementos of Athenian victories were displayed at the building as well: Pausanias describes bronze shields from the fifth century B.C. still hanging on the
65   stoa, covered in pitch to protect them from the ravages of time. One such shield has been found in the excavations, carrying a punched inscription, "The Athenians from the Lakedaimonians at Pylos," a relic of one of Athens' greatest victories in the Peloponnesian War in 425 B.C.

This stoa was a true public building, designed for no specific magistrate, group, or function. It served as a *lesche,* or place of leisure, open to all Athenians; anyone could pass the time of day there. It was therefore a popular meeting place, and those whose trade required a large crowd or audience were to be found there on a daily basis: jugglers, sword-swallowers, beggars, and fishmongers are all specifically attested to. Among those attracted to the stoa were the philosophers of Athens, in particular Zeno, who came from Cyprus in about 300 B.C.; he so preferred this colonnade as his classroom that he and his followers became known as Stoics, taking their name from the Painted Stoa.

The Tholos, or *Skias,* also was constructed in the Agora during Kimon's administration, probably around 470. It was a large round building which served as dining hall and headquarters for the senate (boule). Each tribal contingent of fifty men served in rotation as the *prytaneis* (executive committee) for a period of thirty-five or thirty-six days, directing the business conducted by the full senate of five hundred Athenians. During their time in of- 66

66. Southwest corner of the Agora in the late 5th century B.C., with the Tholos at left (ca. 470), the Old Bouleuterion at right (ca. 500), and the New Bouleuterion behind (ca. 415). The temple on the hill at upper right is the Hephaisteion (ca. 460–415). (Watercolor by Peter Connolly)

fice, these fifty committee members were fed at public expense in the Tholos, which lay next to the Bouleuterion (senate house). In addition, one-third of the committee was expected to sleep in the building, available to deal with any emergency which might occur at night. In a sense, the Tholos represents the heart of the Athenian democracy, where at least seventeen citizens serving as senators could be found on duty at all times.

Considering its primary function as a dining room, the round form of the building is puzzling. Generally we think of Greeks as reclining on couches at meals, and there is no good way of fitting such couches into the Tholos. It may be, however, that dining while reclining was largely an aristocratic pursuit; there is evidence that many Greeks ate sitting up. If this is the case, perhaps a bench was placed around the inner wall of the building to accommodate fifty seated diners with ease. Another problem presented by the round form is the roof, which was covered with custom-made diamond-shaped tiles. These look fine around the outer part of the roof, but they become increasingly cumbersome near its center. It is possible to calculate that sixteen rows of tiles were needed, yet no example from higher than the ninth row from the top has ever been recovered, raising the possibility that the center of the Tholos was unroofed and open to the sky. This solution would allow sufficient light and air into the building, though the lack of any provision for drainage inside is troublesome.

In addition to its primary function as a dining room, the Tholos housed an official set of weights and measures and thus served also as the bureau of standards. A set of official weights in bronze was found in a well nearby. They were inscribed with their weight and the words *demosion Athenaion* (public property of the Athenians) and were decorated with relief representations of a knucklebone (for a stater, 795 grams), a shield (for the quarter-stater), and a sea turtle (for a third-stater), by which the illiterate or hurried user could tell the weight. These weights were thrown down the well in 500 B.C. and thus predate the Tholos itself. Other similar, later versions of official weights in lead have been found elsewhere in the Agora.

Another building generally dated to the time of Kimon is a substantial subterranean fountain house on the northwest slope of the Acropolis. Pausanias knows it as the Klepsydra (literally, water thief), and other sources tell us that originally it was named after the nymph Empedo. It is also said that the water ran underground all the way to the coast

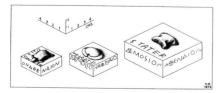

67. Set of official bronze weights found in a well in the Agora, ca. 500 B.C. A similar set was kept in the Tholos.

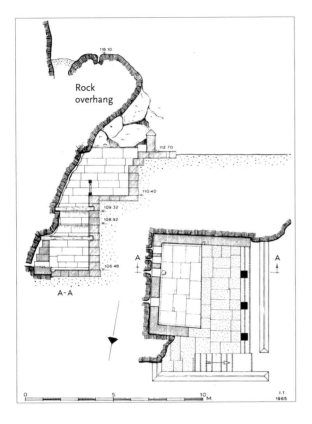

68. Cross-section drawing and plan of the Klepsydra on the northwest slopes of the Acropolis, ca. 470 B.C.

near Phaleron, some 5 kilometers away. Aristophanes paints a lively picture of the daily scene at a fountain house, probably at this one, in his play *Lysistrata* (ll. 326 ff.):

Rising at dawn I had the utmost trouble to fill this jar at the fountain. Oh, what a throng there was and what a noise! What a rattling of water pots! Servants and slave girls pushed and crowded me! However, here I have it, full at last!

The fountain itself takes the form of a stone-built basin set deep into a cleft in the Acropolis rock, where water poured in from the underground spring. A walkway on the north and west sides originally gave access to the basin. Subsequent collapses of the overhanging rock made it increasingly difficult to draw water, but the convenience of such an abundant, reliable source of water so close to the Acropolis led the Athenians to maintain some sort of access for centuries, until the end of antiquity.

In Attica we have little evidence for activity immediately following the Persian Wars. Many of the excavated sites, of course, are sanctuaries and therefore did not receive much attention as long as the provisions of the oath of Plataia were in force, prohibiting the rebuilding of the temples burned by the barbarians. At Eleusis one of the many phases of the fortification wall has been dated to the years of Kimon's leadership. One of the many versions of the Telesterion has also been called Kimonian, but this seems unlikely and has recently been called into question.

Despite his military successes and numerous improvements to the city, like so many before him, Kimon eventually fell afoul of Athenian popular opinion. Seen as too friendly toward the Spartans, he was ostracized in 461, opening the way for the next great Athenian statesman, Perikles.

PERIKLES

At the time of the ostracism of Kimon there were several months of civil strife. A man called Ephialtes stripped the old aristocratic Council of the Areopagos of much of its power, transferring it to the boule and the law courts. Although we have little information about them, his reforms were apparently a significant step in the development of a full democracy. Ephialtes was assassinated soon thereafter, and Perikles, son of Xanthippos, succeeded him as the leading statesman of Athens. A skillful politician, Perikles guided the fortunes of the city almost continually for a generation, from 461 until his death in 429. His time in power coincided with a period of Athenian political and economic dominance as well as a time when art, theater, philosophy, and democracy flourished to a degree not seen before and only rarely since. Athens at the time of Perikles represents the high point of the Classical period (480–323), setting a standard against which all subsequent expressions of Western civilization have been measured.

The Athenians suffered a reverse in 455 when a fleet sent against the Persians was wiped out in Egypt. The following year the treasury of the Delian League was transferred from Delos to the Acropolis of Athens, ostensibly for the safe-keeping of the funds. Long lists of the annual tribute paid by the allies were inscribed on huge stone stelai, recording the one-sixtieth of each annual payment which was given to Athena for her guardianship of the money. At about the same time the long walls linking Athens to the Peiraieus started by Kimon were finally brought to completion:

> For the long walls, concerning which Sokrates says he himself heard Perikles introduce a measure, Kallikrates was the contractor. Kratinos pokes fun at this work for its slow progress in these words: "Since ever so long now Perikles has pushed the thing in words, while in fact he does not budge it." (Plutarch, *Perikles* 13)

At some time in the middle years of the fifth century, perhaps as early as 463 or as late as 449, a peace of some sort was made with Persia, known as the Peace of Kallias, after the Athenian ambassador. With this peace, the professed reason for the Delian League ceased to exist. The Athenians, however, had become used to their allies' contributions, and they were strong enough to enforce their continuation. Perikles therefore proposed that the oath of Plataia be nullified and the allies' money be used to rebuild all the temples burned by the

Persians, most of which happened to be in Athens or Attica. During the third quarter of the fifth century, magnificent marble temples were built on the Acropolis, in the lower city of Athens, and throughout Attica, ostensibly replacing Archaic structures left in ruins by the Persians in 480/79. The program was costly and the financing ethically questionable, the money largely extorted from reluctant allies; both allied objections and intense domestic opposition had to be overcome.

> But that which brought most delightful adornment to Athens, and the greatest amazement to the rest of mankind, that which now alone testifies for Greece that her ancient power and splendor, of which so much is told, was no idle fiction—his construction of sacred buildings—this more than all the public measures of Perikles his enemies maligned and slandered. They cried out in the assemblies, "The people have lost their fair reputation because they have removed the money of the Hellenes from Delos into their own keeping, and that best of all excuses it had against its accusers—that out of fear of the Persians they had moved the public money from that sacred island and were now guarding it in a stronghold—of this Perikles has robbed them. Surely Greece is insulted and manifestly subject to tyranny when she sees that, with their enforced contributions for the war, we are gilding and decorating our city which, like a wanton woman, adds to her wardrobe precious stones and costly statues and temples worth their millions. (Plutarch, *Perikles* 12)

In what was essentially a referendum, Perikles' chief opponent Thucydides, son of Melesias (not the historian), was swept aside in an ostracism in 443. Here one sees the inherent flaw of ostracism: if the strongest man in the state is powerful enough, ostracism becomes a useful way to remove opposition. The building program, in any case, was submitted to popular judgment and approved. Plutarch, writing six centuries later, describes as well as anyone the impact and effect of these great buildings.

> [Perikles] boldly laid before the people proposals for immense public works and plans for buildings, which would involve many different arts and industries and require long periods to complete, his object being that those who stayed at home, no less than those serving in the fleet or the army, might have an excuse to share in the national wealth. The materials to be used were stone, bronze, ivory, gold, ebony, and cypress, while the arts or trades which wrought or fashioned them were those of carpenter, modeler, coppersmith, stonemason, dyer, worker in gold and ivory, painter, embroiderer, and engraver, and besides these

were the carriers and suppliers of the material such as sailors and pilots by sea, and wagon makers, trainers, and drivers by land. There were also ropemakers, weavers, leatherworkers, road builders, and miners. . . . So the buildings arose, as imposing in their sheer size as they were inimitable in the grace of their out-lines, since the artists strove to excel themselves in the beauty of their work-manship. And yet the most wonderful thing about them was the speed with which they were completed. Each one of them, men supposed, would take many generations to build, but in fact the entire project was carried through in the high summer of one man's administration. . . . . It is this above all which makes Perikles' works an object of wonder to us—the fact that they were cre-ated in so short a time and yet for all time. Each one possessed a beauty which seemed venerable the moment it was born, and at the same time a youthful vigor which makes them appear to this day as if they were newly built. (*Perikles* 12–13)

The Parthenon, the Erechtheion, the Nike temple, and the Propylaia were built when Athens was at the height of its power—both economic and military—and able to afford the best craftsmen, artists, and materials available. As anticipated by both Thucydides and Plutarch, the temples of the Acropolis remain the most visible legacy of Classical Athens.

THE PARTHENON

Centerpiece of the program and one of the earliest buildings to go up was the Parthenon, a huge marble Doric temple with an unusual monumental arrangement of eight columns on the front and seventeen along the sides. Some of the building accounts are preserved on stone, and these record that construction began in 447 and that the work had progressed sufficiently for the gold-and-ivory statue of Athena to be dedicated in 438, only nine years later. Further work, primarily on the ornamental sculpture of the temple, continued until 433/2, so the entire building took some fifteen years to complete. The names of the architects said by ancient sources to have been responsible for the building are Iktinos (named by Pausanias, Plutarch, and Vitruvius), Kallikrates (Plutarch), and Kar-pion (Vitruvius).

The Parthenon is generally and correctly regarded as the outstanding expression of Greek architecture and particularly of the Doric order. Yet certain features of its construc-tion, though important, are not unique. It is big, but by no means the largest Greek temple; in Athens alone the temple of Olympian Zeus is larger. It was built entirely of marble, rather than the far more common limestone used even on such important temples as those at Olympia and Delphi, but this too can be paralleled in Athens and throughout the eastern Aegean. Three elements in particular set the building apart from all others: the plan, the architectural refinements, and the sculptural decoration.

The plan exhibits a sophistication of design not found in most Doric temples. A basic ratio of four to nine is incorporated and repeated throughout, creating a unity among the various parts of the building: width to length, height to width, column spacing to column height. In addition, the outer colonnade consists of eight columns across the front rather than the canonical six, resulting in a grandeur not encountered in other Doric buildings. The architect has designed a temple which seems monumental without greatly increasing the scale of the columns and other individual architectural elements, a device used with only limited success in other large Doric temples. This extension of the width and length of the outer colonnades also affords more interior space. The interior is divided into four parts: a front porch (*pronaos*) with six Doric columns; the "hundred-foot" cella, or sanctuary proper (*hekatompedos naos*); a separate back chamber, known in antiquity as the Parthenon; and a back porch (*opisthodomos*), also with six Doric columns. Within the cella the great

69. The Parthenon, seen from the northwest, 447–432 B.C.

70. Plan of the Parthenon.

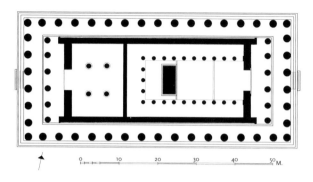

width of the building allowed another innovation. The two interior
colonnades of superimposed Doric
columns which supported the
ceiling across the huge span of the
chamber were connected to one
another by a third colonnade at
the back of the room, providing an unprecedented architectural frame and backdrop for the
statue of Athena Parthenos. Hitherto in Doric temples the interior colonnades had simply
run the length of the cella. Thus the plan of the Parthenon allowed innovations and improvements in the design of both the exterior and interior of the temple.

The second exceptional feature of the Parthenon is the extensive use of architectural
refinements. These are slight adjustments in the construction of the building—some
shared with other temples, some unique to the Parthenon—which free the temple from
the severe horizontal and vertical lines of the Doric order. There are, in fact, no straight
lines in the building. Some of the refinements are fairly clear, even to the naked eye. The
column shafts, for instance, taper upward on a curved rather than straight line, swelling
slightly, somewhat like a cigar. The stepped platform on which the columns rest is not horizontal. The steps bow up in the middle and are lower at the ends, in a refinement known
as curvature of the stylobate. Along the short ends the steps bow up about 0.065 meters,
and along the long sides the difference is around 0.12 meters.

Other refinements are more subtle and can be detected only by measurement. The
corner columns, seen against the background of the sky rather than the mass of the building, are one-fortieth larger in diameter than the other columns (a difference of 0.06 meters) and are set somewhat closer to their neighbors (0.25 meters) than is required by structural considerations. The columns are not vertical; all of them incline inward, leaning
slightly toward the center of the building. The inclination is about 0.07 meters for columns
just over 10 meters in height.

The purpose of these refinements is not entirely clear in all instances. They cannot be
simply to correct possible optical illusions. Some, such as the inclination, exaggerate the
perspective and make the building seem higher and grander than it is. There may be a de-
sire on the part of the architect to set up an internal aesthetic tension in the viewer between
what he or she expects to see and what is actually there. Whatever their function, which

may vary from case to case, the refinements required a degree of precision in construction which would be hard to match today. The total effect is a building which flows, freeing the Parthenon from the static quality inherent in Doric architecture. These refinements, unparalleled in their complexity, carry the temple far beyond all other buildings of Classical antiquity.

The third element which sets the Parthenon apart from other temples is its sculptural adornment. Many Greek temples carried sculpture, but none had as much as the Parthenon. The themes of the sculpture are particularly appropriate to the building and illuminate its varied roles in projecting the city's image. The man responsible for the sculptural program of the temple was Pheidias, the leading sculptor of the day and, according to Plutarch, the general overseer of the entire Periklean building program. Although he probably worked personally on some of the figures, literally dozens of sculptors must have been needed to do them all. A close examination of the carving shows almost ninety hands at work.

There were four main groups of sculpture: the pediments, the exterior Doric frieze, the Ionic frieze, and the gold-and-ivory (chryselephantine) statue inside. In the pediments the scenes depicted concern Athena, to whom the Parthenon was dedicated. A drawing made in the seventeenth century, before many of the pieces fell or were removed from the building, gives us some idea of the arrangement of the figures, and Pausanias describes the scenes (1.24.5):

> All the figures in the pediment over the entrance to the temple called the Parthenon relate to the birth of Athena. The back pediment contains the strife between Poseidon and Athena for possession of the land.

The birth of Athena decorated the eastern end, therefore. According to the story, Athena's father, Zeus, had intercourse with Metis, goddess of wisdom, and then—afraid that she would give birth to a god or goddess more intelligent than himself—he swallowed her. Nine months later he found himself with a terrible—literally splitting—headache. Summoning his son Hephaistos, god of the forge, Zeus commanded him to strike him on the head with an ax to relieve the terrible pressure and pain. Hephaistos did so, and out popped Athena, fully armed, from the head of her father. Zeus sat enthroned in the center of the pediment, with a full-grown Athena standing in front of him. Beyond her was Hephaistos, holding his ax and falling back in amazement. The wings of the pediment on either side of the center were filled with a gathering of Olympian gods watching this wondrous event. The west pediment showed the contest between Athena and her uncle Poseidon by which the goddess won the right to be patron deity of Athens. In the center were Athena with her

71. East end (entrance) of the Parthenon.

olive tree and Poseidon, about to strike the rock of the Acropolis with his trident. The olive tree and a well of salt water, which sprang up where the trident struck, were the tokens of the contest, the exact nature of which is uncertain. On either side of the central figures were two-horse chariot groups, and in the wings were the legendary royal families of early Athens.

All ninety-two metopes of the Doric frieze running around the outside of the temple were sculpted as well. Although the metope reliefs of the east, north, and west sides were systematically hacked away by early Christians, and the south central metopes were destroyed in the explosion of 1687, the subject matter of the four sides is certain. Each side tells a different story, yet all are bound thematically. The east end showed gods fighting giants, the south side Greeks fighting centaurs, the west end Greeks fighting Amazons, and the north side Greeks fighting Trojans. The theme that unites all four sides is the triumph of civilization over barbarians, and we are intended to see here a symbolic reference to the triumph of Athens over the barbarian Persians. Historical scenes on public buildings are

72. Detail of the northwest corner of the Parthenon showing the western metopes with the Amazonomachy at right.

still rare at this period, and the war is therefore alluded to only in mythological terms. In some sense the Parthenon should be seen as a long-delayed victory monument for the epic struggle against the Persians, which in the eyes of Classical Athenians took on the superhuman dimensions of legend, one more chapter in the conflict between East and West which has so often been played out in the eastern Mediterranean.

Ringing the building on top of the two porches and the solid side walls was a sculpted Ionic frieze facing outward toward the exterior colonnades. The scene here is usually interpreted as a version of the Panathenaic procession, the huge formal parade which made its way from the lower city to the Acropolis to present the cult image of Athena with a newly woven robe. Two streams of action began at the southwest corner and ran in opposite directions, meeting over the eastern doorway. The frieze was a celebration of the people of Athens. Much of the space was given over to the cavalry: handsome, aristocratic young men mounting up and riding out on spirited steeds. At the head of the parade came the sacrificial victims (both sheep and bulls), bearers of the sacrificial paraphernalia, musicians, and elders. Over the center of the doorway was an enigmatic scene involving the peplos (robe), watched by the gods and goddesses of Olympos, who are seated on low stools.

The final element of the sculptural program was the colossal chryselephantine statue of Athena, described in the second century A.D. by Pausanias (1.24.5–7):

The image is made of ivory and gold. Its helmet is surmounted in the middle by a figure of a sphinx . . . and on either side of the helmet are griffins wrought in relief. . . . The image of Athena stands upright, clad

73. Parthenon frieze, west end.

in a garment which reaches to her feet; on her breast is the head of Medusa wrought in ivory. She holds a Victory (Nike) about 4 cubits [2 meters] high, and in the other hand a spear. At her feet lies a shield, and near the spear is a serpent, which may be Erichthonios. On the base of the statue is carved in relief the birth of Pandora.

Numerous later copies on a much smaller scale in marble, terra-cotta, and gold bear out this description, though it seems that the serpent once coiled up the other side of the goddess, and the column often shown under her right hand was an addition, not part of the original design. The statue was dedicated in 438 B.C. The flesh would have been carved of ivory, and the drapery in sheets of gold, attached to a wooden or metal armature. The gold was regarded as part of the state treasure of Athens and could be removed if necessary. Pheidias was the sculptor, and it is clear that his masterpiece made a great impression in antiquity; the statue must have been literally awe-inspiring, standing more than 9 meters high, gleaming in the huge dark cella of the Parthenon.

The sculptural program of the Parthenon defines Perikles' and Pheidias' view of Athens. The cult image and pediments honor Athena, patron of the city, in all her glory, the recipient of this most perfect and ornate of all Greek temples; the Doric frieze refers symbolically to Athenian triumphs over the Persians; and the Ionic frieze depicts and celebrates the Athenians themselves, fortunate citizens of Greece's foremost city. In many ways the Parthenon is a victory monument for Athens as an imperial force, built at

74, 75

74. Marble Roman copy of the Athena Parthenos, Pheidias' gold-and-ivory statue in the Parthenon, 2nd century A.D.

75. Clay token dating ca. 400–375 B.C., preserving the earliest representation of the Athena Parthenos.

the height of the city's powers and paid for out of funds unwillingly contributed by its allies in the Delian League. Although the building housed a statue, it need not be thought of as an expression of Athenian religious fervor; there is no known priestess of Athena Parthenos, and no altar was built to accompany the temple. Throughout antiquity the focal point of cult activity on the Acropolis was to be found on the north side, the area occupied in the fifth century by the building known as the Erechtheion.

The Parthenon served also as the repository of state funds and other offerings belonging to the Athenians; it was, in effect, a huge treasury. Special boards of treasurers were appointed to render an exact yearly accounting of the funds available as well as of the value and weight of the offerings stored there. These accounts make fascinating reading, for they give a picture of objects of precious metals which have not survived because the gold or silver was plundered, melted down, and reused. They also describe materials which do not readily withstand the effects of time, such as wood and ivory. The range of objects is extraordinary and makes the Parthenon sound rather like a crowded attic or antiques store: vessels of gold and silver, coins, carved gemstones, small statues, jewelry, furniture, musical instruments, gold wreaths, weapons, and armor.

Some objects show up in the accounts year after year, sometimes for as many as twenty-three consecutive years. Here is a partial list of what was in the Parthenon in 434/3 B.C.: a gold wreath, five gold *phialai* (libation bowls), two nails of gilded silver, six Persian daggers, twelve stalks of golden wheat, two gilded wooden baskets, a gilded wooden box and incense burner, thirty-one bronze shields, seven Chian couches, ten Milesian couches, nine sabers, four swords, fourteen breastplates, six thrones, four stools, a gilded lyre, three ivory lyres, four wooden lyres, and thirteen bronze feet for couches. Not everything kept on the Acropolis and listed by the treasurers was of great value: "eight and a half boxes of rotten and useless arrows" show up for years (*IG* I³ 343–346, 350–359). The detail of the accounts is impressive; one example gives some idea of the splendor of the decoration of the doors leading into the cella of the Parthenon, in disrepair after several decades:

> The doors, the ones into the Hekatompedon [cella], are lacking these parts and are not complete. Around the lion's head is missing one of the leaves, and around the front part of the ram five of the smaller leaves are missing. Around the front part of the gorgon's head a strip of molding about eight dactyls long is missing. The nails in the lowest row of the door lack three poppy heads, two on one side, one on the other. These are in the care of the treasurers in the transfer. Starting from the first nail of the right door some gold has fallen off, the length of ten dactyls, eleven dactyls across, and two dactyls in depth. (*IG* II² 1455)

And the bureaucratic mentality of the treasurers may be glimpsed in the following crabby heading of an account:

> Gold wreaths, which were handed over to us by the treasurers in the archonship of Euxenippos [305/4 B.C.], who recorded neither the archon in the year they were dedicated nor the names of the dedicants. (*IG* II² 1486)

Since antiquity, the Parthenon has survived many vicissitudes. The interior of the building was badly damaged in the Roman period, and the interior colonnade had to be replaced. The date of this damage and subsequent repairs has been much debated. In the sixth century A.D., apparently, the building was converted to a Christian basilica, then used as a Roman Catholic cathedral in the Frankish period and as a mosque during the Turkish domination. Various changes were made to the building, but the basic structure survived until 1687, when the Venetians under Francesco Morosini were besieging the Turks on the Acropolis. Numerous artillery shots hit the temple, and one fell through the roof, ignited the powder stored there, and blew up the building. A mosque was built into the ruins at the east end in about 1700, and in 1800–1801 Lord Elgin's agents stripped the Parthenon of many of its sculptures and sent them to England.

THE PROPYLAIA

The next building to go up on the Acropolis after the Parthenon was the Propylaia, the
76   monumental gateway to the citadel. It is one of the most remarkable Greek buildings extant, though its state of preservation and unusual plan make it difficult for modern visitors to appreciate at first glance. Pausanias describes the building as follows (1.22.4–7):

> There is but one entrance to the Acropolis; it admits of no other, being everywhere precipitous and fortified with a strong wall. The Propylaia has a ceiling of white marble, and for the beauty and size of the blocks it has never yet been matched. . . . On the right of the gateway is a temple of Wingless Victory. . . . On the left of the portal is a room containing pictures.

Plutarch provides further information (*Perikles* 13.7):

Opposite 76. The Propylaia as it would have appeared during a Panathenaic procession.
(Watercolor by Peter Connolly)

The Propylaia of the Acropolis was brought to completion in the space of five years; Mnesikles was their architect.

Some of the original building accounts also survive, and these confirm that the Propylaia took only five years to construct, from 437 to 432. Work began after the major construction of the Parthenon was completed in 438 and stopped with the outbreak of the Peloponnesian War against Sparta in 432/1.

There are indications that the building was never completely finished. In designing the complex structure, as detailed study of the remains has shown, the architect, Mnesi-   77

kles, drew up several plans before construction began. The basic design of the building consisted originally of five parts: a large central hall with projecting wings off the four corners. Though the two eastern wings were laid out, they were never built, leaving only the two western wings to flank the columnar facade of the entrance. Both wings have symmetrical facades of three small Doric columns set at right angles to the main facade, but there the similarity between them ends. The northwest wing served as a picture gallery as early as the second century B.C., as we learn from the traveler Polemon. Pausanias, writing several centuries later, also saw paintings and describes several portraits and a variety of mythological scenes on display: Diomedes and Odysseus at Troy, Orestes killing Aegisthus, the sacrifice of Polyxena, Achilles and Odysseus on Skyros, and Perseus and Medusa. The facade of three columns and the irregular placement of the door and two windows behind it has puzzled architectural historians, and several theories have been put forward to explain the unusual arrangement. The southwest wing has no comparable chamber behind the columns, just a solid wall; this truncated arrangement served primarily to allow access westward to the top of the bastion which carries the temple and altar of Athena Nike, or "Wingless Victory" as Pausanias names her. Despite these differences in function, the

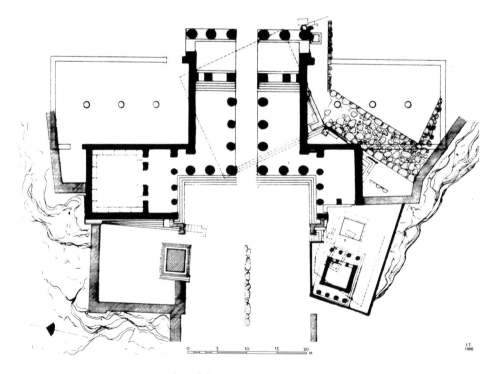

77. Plan of the Propylaia, 437–432 B.C.

matching facades of the two wings gave the impression of symmetry to anyone approaching the building from below. It is only when one gets near the top of the ramp that one realizes that the building is so irregular in plan.

A second feature, easily appreciated, gives further insight into the ingenious mind responsible for the design of the Propylaia. The massive columns of the main facade sit on four marble steps, and the total height of the steps works in planned and correct proportion to the diameter and height of the columns they carry. The columns of the wings are far smaller, however, and yet the four steps of the central facade had to be carried around the corner to the facades of the wings. Structurally, Mnesikles was tied to four steps, though the total height of the four was too large, aesthetically, for the smaller diameters and heights of the columns of the wings. His solution was to make the lowest step of each wing out of gray limestone rather than white marble, thereby erasing it from the mind's eye so that the three marble steps above work in correct proportion with the smaller columns of the wings. Note 78 that this problem was anticipated and solved before a single block of the superstructure was laid.

The central chamber marks the actual entrance onto the Acropolis. Six large Doric columns face west and give access to a deep hall with two rows of three Ionic columns. The ceiling Pausanias so admired is made up of huge white marble beams close to 6 meters long, carried on the columns; the ceiling slabs are cut back in a series of recessed squares known as coffers. This deep cutting of the coffers reduced their weight, which was clearly a matter of concern to Mnesikles; for additional strength he inserted long iron bars into the upper surfaces of the supporting beams. The decorative effect of the carved coffers was greatly enhanced by the use of bright paints and gilding: the innermost squares of the coffers were decorated with stars or floral ornaments.

The east side of the hall is the actual door-wall, approached by a flight of four steps. The wall is pierced by five doorways, each aligned on one of the five intercolumnar spaces of the east and west facades. The central doorway is the largest and was approached by a ramp (for the procession) rather than stairs, while the pairs of flanking doors decrease in size on either side of the main door. The threshold of the small northernmost door shows by far the greatest wear, suggesting that at some periods it was the principal means of access, with the other doors usually kept shut. After passing through the door, the visitor 79, 80 stands in the Doric portico of the east facade, looking out on the Acropolis itself.

It is along this eastern side that one can best make out the evidence that the building was unfinished, both in its early stages and at the end. As noted, two large wings were planned for this side as well. The foundations were laid for the northeast wing, and even as the central building rose to the cornice, provisions were made to incorporate the ceilings and roofs of both wings, even though no other work was done on them above ground level.

78. The Pinakotheke (picture gallery) at the northwest of the Propylaia. Note the gray limestone bottom
step on the wing and the marble step across the facade at right.

Mnesikles had to abandon his original plan at an early stage, but he clearly hoped to be able
to construct the wings at some point.

For evidence of the lack of completion in the final stages, we can start with the
columns of the central chamber. These rest in what appear to be recessed panels a centimeter or so lower than the rest of the stylobate, the course which carries the columns.
They sit, in fact, on the intended final surface, which had to be finished before the columns
were placed. Elsewhere a protective thin layer of marble was left to minimize damage during construction. We know from various sources that in Greek buildings the outer colonnades were erected first, and then the interior walls went up. Dragging large wall blocks between the columns could easily have damaged the stylobate had a protective surface not
been left. Had the building been completely finished, the protective surface would have
been dressed down to the same level already prepared around the columns.

In addition, the wall blocks of the eastern wall all still have their lifting bosses (see fig.
79). These are square knobs of marble which protrude several centimeters from the faces

79. The Propylaia from the east. Note the wider central intercolumniation for the ramp and processional way, and how each of the five doors aligns with an intercolumniation. Note also the lifting bosses left on the wall blocks beyond the colonnade. The base for the statue of Athena Hygieia is against the column at far left.

80. Cutaway view showing the Acropolis seen from the Propylaia, with the Athena Promachos of Pheidias to the left of center.

81. Detail of the protective surfaces on the eastern stylobate of the Propylaia.

of the blocks, near the center of gravity. They were intended to provide purchase for ropes or crowbars when the blocks were maneuvered into place during construction. Once the building was finished, the bosses would have been chiseled away. Structurally, the building functioned for centuries; we are speaking here only about details of the architectural finish, which allow some insight into the process of construction and the care with which the Propylaia was built.

Plutarch tells a story about the Propylaia which shows that Athena herself approved of the new work on her sanctuary:

> A wonderful thing happened in the course of building [the Propylaia], which indicated that the goddess was not holding herself aloof but was a helper both in the beginning and in the completion of the work. One of the craftsmen, the most active and zealous of all, lost his footing and fell from a great height; he lay in a sorry plight, despaired of by the physicians. Perikles was much cast down by this, but the goddess appeared to him in a dream and prescribed a course of treatment to use so that he quickly and easily cured the man. In commemoration of this he set up

82. Base for the Statue of Athena Hygieia, ca. 430 B.C., signed by the sculptor Pyrrhos.

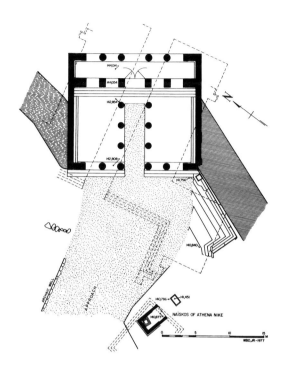

83. Plan of the early propylon and temple of Athena Nike at the entrance to the Acropolis.

the bronze statue of Athena Hygieia [Health] on the Acropolis near the altar of that goddess which they say was there before. (*Perikles* 13.7–8)

Against the southernmost columns of the east facade can be seen what appears to be the base for this statue, apparently marking the spot where the unfortunate workman fell (see fig. 79). It is a cylindrical piece of marble with moldings at top and bottom. On top are cuttings for the attachment of the feet of a bronze statue, and an in- 82 scription in handsome letters of the fifth century B.C. runs across the face: "The Athenians to Athena Hygieia. Pyrrhos the Athenian made it" (*IG* I³ 506). A few meters to the east is the altar mentioned by Plutarch.

An unusual and important feature of the Propylaia is its relation to the Parthenon. At this early period, Greek sanctuaries often developed in a haphazard fashion, with the individual buildings taking little cognizance of one another. That is emphatically not the case on the Acropolis, and the three connections between the Propylaia and Parthenon are among the easiest associations to appreciate. The Propylaia, as laid out, was intended to be almost exactly as wide as the Parthenon is long. The ratios used in the Propylaia (3:7) are almost identical to those of the Parthenon (4:9). And the two buildings, though not on the same axis, are set on the same orientation. These and similar associations among the buildings on the Acropolis must have been part of the overall design of the entire program, which, as noted, was under the general supervision of a single individual, Pheidias.

Traces of the predecessor of the Propylaia survive just south of the main hall. These consist of a stylobate with an anta of limestone and marble, and part of a marble side wall. This earlier propylon faces more toward the southwest, on a different orientation from the

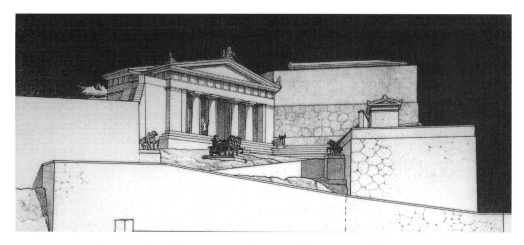

84. Elevation of the entrance to the Acropolis in pre-Periklean times.

83, 84   Periklean building. Close analysis of the architectural details indicates that there were several phases in this earlier gateway.

In later times, when access to the Acropolis was restricted, the Propylaia was incorporated into a more extensive defensive system. As early as the third century A.D. a supplementary gate was built on the slopes below (see fig. 219), and numerous additional walls
and gateways were in use throughout the medieval period. When Athens fell to the Franks
in 1204, the Propylaia was converted into a palace for the dukes of Athens (see figs. 234,
235).

THE TEMPLE OF ATHENA NIKE

The third building to go up on the Periklean Acropolis was the marble temple of
85   Athena Nike, which stood just outside the Propylaia on the right (south) as one ascended
the slope (see fig. 76). As noted, the cult of Athena goes back at least to the middle years of
the sixth century, to judge from an inscribed altar found beneath the later sanctuary. The
bastion on which it stands dates to the Late Bronze Age and was said by Pausanias to be the
spot from which Aigeus threw himself into the sea when he mistakenly thought that Theseus had been killed by the Minotaur.

By the middle years of the fifth century the sanctuary consisted of an altar and a very
small, simple temple, both of limestone, whose remains survive deep beneath the later

temple. Once the huge marble Propylaia was built immediately adjacent, these modest monuments would have looked sadly out of place, and a grander, marble temple was planned for Athena Nike while the Propylaia was still under construction. Space in the sanctuary was limited, and the new temple was still much smaller than the other buildings of the Periklean Acropolis. Of the Ionic order, it had columns only on the front and back, four at each end, in an arrangement known as amphiprostyle. The columns at the back may have been added for aesthetic reasons: the Acropolis is entered from the west, and the temple would otherwise have presented a blank back wall to the approaching visitor. The columns are about half the size of those used in the interior of the Propylaia and are similar in style.

There was also a sculpted Ionic frieze on all four sides of the Nike temple. Part of this remains in Athens, while other slabs are now in the British Museum. The east side has an assembly of deities standing in repose; battle scenes make up the other three sides. Two of them (north and south) show Greeks fighting Persians, which makes them among the earliest specifically historical reliefs we have. The fourth (west) side shows Greeks against

85. Temple of Athena Nike, 435–420 B.C., from the east.

Greeks and may depict a battle against the Corinthians at Megara in the mid-fifth century. The statue of Athena Nike (Victory) which stood inside the temple is described by several sources (Pausanias, Harpokration, the Souda): it was made of wood and showed the goddess with a pomegranate in her right hand and a helmet in her left. The concept of victory is usually depicted in Greek sculpture and painting by a winged female figure; but this statue is of Athena and therefore had no wings; the sanctuary and cult are often referred to accordingly as those of the Wingless Victory.

The start of construction must have been the late 430s. The cult goes back at least a century earlier, so there is no need to seek a specific Athenian victory as the impetus for the dedication of the marble temple, the third sacred structure (at least) to occupy the site. An inscription of 424/3 records provisions for payments of fifty drachmas to the priestess of Athena Nike; this is often taken as evidence that the new building and its associated altar were ready for business in that year. Another inscription dating to the years around 400 is the gravestone of a certain Myrrhine (*Supplementum Epigraphicum Graecae* [Leiden and Amsterdam], XII 80), who is described as

86

the "first woman chosen from all the Athenians to serve as priestess of Athena Nike." Late in the century a parapet of marble was added around the edge of the bastion, decorated with exquisite reliefs of Nikai (winged female figures representing victory) preparing to sacrifice bulls to Athena, who is seated near a trophy. The north face of the bastion has pairs of cuttings suitably placed for the attachment of bronze shields, common booty after battles and an appropriate dedication to Athena as goddess of victory.

The temple was dismantled at the time of the Venetian siege of 1687, and all the blocks were used to build a bastion in front of the Propylaia. This in turn was dismantled in 1835, and the Nike temple was reconstructed soon thereafter.

86. A Nike from the parapet around the Athena Nike temple bastion.

THE ERECHTHEION

Occupying the north side of the Acropolis was the last temple on the citadel to be built under Perikles. This was the temple of Athena Polias, patron deity of the city of Athens. It is also usually identified and referred to as the Erechtheion, the building Athena shared   87 with Erechtheus, though several scholars in recent years have argued that the two are separate buildings; our primary source, Pausanias, is somewhat ambiguous (1.26–27), describing the two cults in succession. What he does make clear is that this temple rather than the Parthenon is the sacred building of the Acropolis. Pausanias is especially interested in religious matters, and whereas it takes him only two sentences to describe the Parthenon, he needs two pages to describe the Erechtheion-Polias area:

> There is also a building called the Erechtheion. In front of the entrance is an altar of Zeus Hypatos, where they sacrifice no living thing; but they lay cakes on it and having done so they are forbidden by custom to make use of wine. Inside the building are altars: one of Poseidon, on which they sacrifice also to Erechtheus in obedience to an oracle; one of the hero Butes; and one of Hephaistos. On the walls are paintings of the family of the Butadai. Within, for the building is double, there is sea water in a well . . . and there is the mark of a trident in the rock. These things are said to have been the evidence produced by Poseidon in support of his claim to the country.
>
> The rest of the city and the whole land are equally sacred to Athena, for although the worship of other gods is established in the demes, the inhabitants nonetheless hold Athena in honor. But the object which was universally deemed the holy of holies many years before the synoicism of the demes is an image of Athena in what is now called the Acropolis but what was then called the city. The legend is that the image fell from heaven, but whether this was so I shall not inquire. Kallimachos made a golden lamp for the goddess. They fill the lamp with oil, and wait until the same day the next year and the oil suffices for the lamp during all the intervening time, though it burns day and night. . . .
>
> In the temple of the Polias is a wooden Hermes, said to be an offering of Kekrops, but hidden under myrtle boughs. Among the ancient offerings which are worthy of mention is a folding chair made by Daidalos and spoils taken from the Persians, including the corselet of Masistios, who commanded the cavalry at Plataia, and a sword said to be that of Mardonios. . . . About the olive they say nothing except it was produced by the goddess as evidence in the dispute over the country. They say that the olive was burned down when the Persians torched

Athens, and that it sprouted the same day to a height of 2 cubits [1 meter]. Contiguous to the temple of Athena is a temple of Pandrosos.

The architect of the Erechtheion, committed to a site only a stone's throw from the Doric Parthenon, wisely chose not to invite direct comparisons and built his temple in the Ionic style. The distribution of the two main architectural orders, Ionic and Doric, is a geographical rather than chronological one. The Ionic order developed in the eastern Greek world of Ionia and the islands of the Aegean, the Doric order in the Peloponnese and the western Greek world. The Athenians, who lived at the juncture of the two areas, were comfortable with both orders and often used them together in a single building, as in the Propylaia.

Just as the Parthenon is regarded as the outstanding example of the Doric order, so the Erechtheion stands as a high point of the lighter, more ornate Ionic. A quick glance at the two buildings shows the major differences. The Ionic columns are far thinner than their Doric counterparts and are provided with profiled bases and elaborately voluted capitals. In general, the Erechtheion carries far more carving on its numerous decorative moldings than the more severe, unadorned Parthenon.

88
89   The plan of the building is unique. There are six columns in a prostyle arrangement at the east and four columns incorporated into the line of the west wall. An immense Ionic

87. Restored view of the Erechtheion from the northwest. (Watercolor by Peter Connolly)

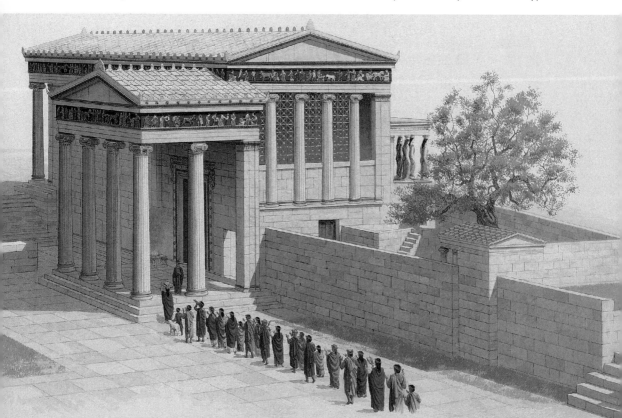

88. Detail of the carving of the architectural moldings at the east end of the south wall of the Erechtheion; note the frieze course of Eleusinian gray limestone at upper right.

porch projects from the west end of the long north wall, while a small porch with sculpted maidens serving as columns decorates the south wall. The position and prominence of the porches is so peculiar that the architectural historian Vitruvius (4.8.4) describes the temple as having "all the features which are customarily on the front transferred to the flanks." The interior plan is obscured by later rebuildings, but it is clear that there were several rooms and more than one floor level.

90

The unusual design was clearly influenced by two factors. First, the architect had to build on steeply sloping ground: the west end is more than 3 meters lower than the east end. Second, he may have been required to replicate in some fashion the arrangement of the rooms in the old temple of Athena, which had been destroyed by the Persians and whose ruins lay immediately to the south. The oddities of the plan of the Erechtheion may also result in part from the fact that the building looks exactly like what it probably was: a temple built by committee. From Pausanias' account and other sources it is clear that the architect had to respect or include numerous preexisting cult spots or monuments, and the design is a complex attempt to satisfy everyone. Among the cult monuments known to have been in the area were an altar to Zeus, an altar to Poseidon/Erechtheus, an altar to Hephaistos, an altar to the hero Butes, a statue of Athena, a statue of Hermes, marks of the trident, a well of sea water, a sacred olive tree, the tomb of Kekrops, and the sanctuary of Pandrosos. At the west end of the Erechtheion, in particular, it appears that major adjustments had to be made during the course of construction to ensure that the building did not encroach on some of these sacred spots.

We have no precise evidence for when construction began on the building; presumably it was conceived of with the other monuments, but actual work may not have begun until the late 430s and possibly later. It was certainly under construction during the Peloponnesian War, though the work was not continuous. We have an inscription (*IG* I³ 474)

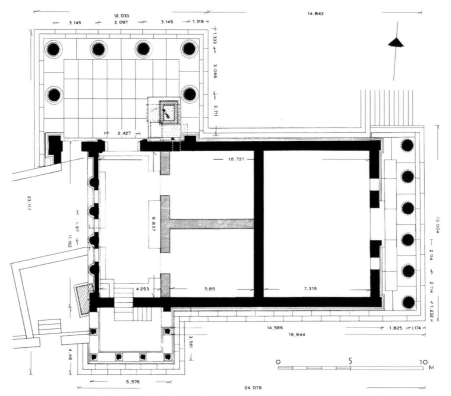

89. Plan of the Erechtheion, late 5th century B.C.

which describes the situation in 409/8, when it was decided to resume work after a period of abandonment. It reads in part:

> The commissioners of the temple on the Acropolis in which is the ancient statue—Brosynides of Kephisia, Chariades of Agryle, Diodes of Kephisia, architect Philokles of Acharnai, secretary Etearchos of Kydathenaion—recorded as follows the state of the work on the temple, in obedience to the decree of the people proposed by Epigenes, listing whether they found it complete or incomplete, in the archonship of Diokles, when Kekropis held the first prytany [chairmanship], in the session of the council for which Nikophanes of Marathon was first to serve as secretary.
>
> The following parts of the building we found unfinished: At the corner toward the Kekropion, four wall blocks not placed, 4 feet long, 2 feet wide, 1½ feet

thick; one *maschaliaia* (?) 4 feet long, 3 feet wide, and —— feet thick; five blocks of the wall-crown, 4 feet long, 3 feet wide, 1½ feet thick; one corner block, 7 feet long, 4 feet wide, 1½ feet thick; one molded block not placed.

After presenting a wonderfully detailed account of the state of the building, completed almost up to the roof for the most part, the commissioners go on to record payments made to bring the building to completion (*IG* I³ 476):

Two talents of lead were bought for the fastening of the sculptures, from Sostratos, living in Melite: 10 drachmas.

Two leaves of gold were bought for gilding the two eyes of the column, from Adonis, living in Melite: 2 drachmas.

Stonework. For fluting the columns at the east end, by the altar: the column next to the altar of Dione, Laossos of Alopeke, Philon of Erchia, Parmenon, son of Laossos, Karion, son of Laossos, Ikaros: 110 drachmas. The next column, the sec-

90. South side of the Erechtheion, with the caryatid porch at the left.

91. Pentelic marble figures from the Erechtheion frieze.

ond one, Phalakros of Paia-nia, Philostratos of Paiania, Thargelios, son of Phala-kros, Gerys, son of Pha-lakros: 110 drachmas. . . .

Sum total of pay-ments to sawyers: 46 drachmas. To painters in encaustic, for painting the cymation on the inner epistyle, at 5 obols a foot, contractor Dionysodoros, living in Melite, 30 drachmas. To gilders, for gilding rosettes . . . [text breaks off here].

From these accounts we learn much about the economics of temple building and a fair amount about the social structure of the workforce. It took, for instance, five men twenty-two days to flute a column, and each man was paid a drachma a day. It is also clear that full Athenian citizens, resident aliens from other Greek cities, and slaves all worked side by side on the building, performing the same tasks for the same daily wage. From the accounts, we have the names of more than 110 different workmen who built the Erechtheion. Their professions cover many of the skills listed by Plutarch in his general description of the building program: masons, carpenters, sculptors, painters, and laborers, as well as providers of gold, wood, and lead.

The temple carried two sculpted friezes, one around the top of the building and a separate one above the north porch. They were unusual in that their backgrounds consisted of slabs of dark gray marble to which were pinned relief figures of white marble. The result was a clear contrast between the figures and the background, allowing the sculptures to be understood from below, an effect usually obtained with paint. Several fragments of the fig-91 ures have been recovered, and the accounts give payments for figures carved. Despite these tantalizing hints, we do not know the subjects of the sculpted scenes:

> To Phyromachos of Kephisia, the youth beside the breastplate: 60 drachmas.
> To Praxias, living in Melite, the horse and the man appearing behind it and striking it on the flank: 120 drachmas.

Antiphanes of Kerameis, the chariot and the youth and the two horses being harnessed: 240 drachmas.

Phyromachos of Kephisia, the man leaning on a staff beside the altar: 60
drachmas.

Iasos of Kollytos, the woman with the little girl leaning against her: 80
drachmas. (*IG* II² 374)

In addition to the friezes, the other major sculptural adornment of the building appears on
the south porch. Here, instead of columns, six voluminously draped maidens, known as
Caryatids, are used to support the roof. Their design was carefully worked out. The outer leg   92
(the right one for the three western figures, the left for the eastern ones) is straight, with the
folds of the drapery falling vertically in a fashion reminiscent of the flutes of a column and
giving the impression of strength and support. The inside leg of each figure is bent in a re-
laxed pose, suggesting that the maidens are not overwhelmed or strained by their task. The
tradition of using women as columns goes back at least to the sixth century; there are several
Ionic treasuries at Delphi which employ them. The identity of the Erechtheion maidens is
uncertain, though it has been suggested that they represent the daughters of Kekrops; the
building accounts and construction anomalies indicate that his tomb lay at the southwest corner of the Erechtheion, near or even under the porch, though no actual tomb has been found.

Soon after it was finished, or even perhaps while it was still under construction, the
temple caught fire. Xenophon begins his account of the year 406/5 as follows:

In the ensuing year—the year in which there was an eclipse of the moon one
evening, and the old temple of Athena at Athens was burned, Pityas being now
ephor at Sparta and Kallias archon at Athens . . . (*Hellenika* 1.6.1)

Stone buildings can and do burn. One has only to imagine the offerings inside, including
the many wooden objects like those listed in the Parthenon accounts, to picture fuel for a
good fire. If the fire were big enough, the flames could reach the wooden ceiling and roof
beams, and the building would be seriously damaged.

The exact extent of the damage to the Erechtheion is uncertain, but it was repaired or
rebuilt over a period of several years. Further repairs were apparently necessary early in the
Roman period, and a major remodeling took place in the seventh century A.D., when the
building was converted into a Christian basilica. This involved tearing out all the interior
walls, which explains our uncertainties concerning the original plan (see fig. 232). The
columns of the north porch were walled up in the Turkish period, when the building was
used as a house. One of the Caryatids was taken by Lord Elgin and is in the British Mu-

92. Caryatids from the south porch of the Erechtheion viewed from the southeast.

seum; the others were removed from the building in the 1970s and are now displayed in the Acropolis Museum.

With the Erechtheion, the Periklean rebuilding of the Acropolis was complete, and the citadel of Athens was provided with three temples to Athena and a magnificent marble gateway into the sanctuary. Centuries later it remains a magnet for all those seeking to appreciate the artistic achievements of the Classical period.

THE LOWER CITY

The Odeion of Perikles

The lower city was not neglected in the Periklean building program, nor was the rest of Attica. Below the Acropolis on the southern side a great hall was built just east of the theater in the sanctuary of Dionysos (see figs. 114, 242). It was called the Odeion, which means a roofed concert hall; in time it became known as the Odeion of Perikles to distinguish it from the two *odeia* of Roman Athens, the Odeion of Agrippa and the Odeion of Herodes Atticus. Plutarch gives the fullest ancient account, describing both the building and its use for musical events:

The Odeion, which was arranged internally with many rows of seats and many columns and had a roof which sloped down from a single peak, was an exact replica of the Great King's tent, so they say, and this too was built under the superintendence of Perikles. . . .

Desirous of honor, Perikles then for the first time decreed that a musical contest be held as part of the Panathenaic festival; he was elected director and set the manner in which people played the flute, sang, or played the kithara. Then and in later times these contests were performed in the Odeion. (*Perikles* 13)

One tradition records that Themistokles built an early version of the tent using timber from the Persian ships captured off Salamis in 480. Most sources, however, indicate that the building went up in the mid-440s, about the time Perikles succeeded in having his main opponent Thucydides, son of Melesias, ostracized. It would seem that the actual tent of Xerxes, captured from the Persians at the Battle of Plataia in 479, was displayed in Athens as part of the Athenian share of the spoils; about a generation later, Perikles had the replica made in stone and timber.

The Odeion has been only partially excavated, and the details of the plan are obscure, though the broad outline is clear. It was a large square building, measuring close to 60 meters on a side, consisting of a forest of internal columns set in either nine or ten rows of nine columns each. It is not clear whether there were any exterior walls, though awnings of some sort could presumably have been used. Appropriately enough, this huge hypostyle hall finds its best parallels in the audience chambers of the great palaces of Susa and Persepolis. When Xerxes went on the road, he evidently took with him a full-scale portable version of his palace. The only Greek buildings which bear any resemblance to this hall are the Telesterion at Eleusis and a later meeting hall of the Arcadians in Megalopolis. As the Odeion derived from war booty and conformed to no regular type of Greek building, it had no obvious function. As we have seen, it was used as a concert hall, but it also saw service at one time or another as a law court, grain dispensary, marshaling area for the cavalry, lecture hall for philosophers, and rehearsal hall for the plays performed in the Dionysia.

The original tent was set up in the sanctuary of Dionysos, with the theater immediately adjacent, and it has been suggested that the building may have had some influence on the design of Greek theaters. The Greek word for a scene-building, *skene,* means "tent," and it may well be that Xerxes' tent was used as the backdrop for early fifth-century performances, many of which had an Eastern setting. This suggestion becomes more compelling when we note that the stone scene-building eventually built for the theater is almost exactly the same length as the tent, if we can judge the length of the latter from the size of the Periklean Odeion.

The Hephaisteion

A second prominent monument in the lower city built during the mid-fifth century,
93   although it was not strictly part of the rebuilding program, was the Hephaisteion, the marble Doric temple which dominates the hill west of the Agora. The best-preserved ancient
temple in Greece, the Hephaisteion serves as a model for the Doric order. There is a peristyle, with six columns across the front and thirteen down the sides, and within this frame
of columns the building is divided into three parts, the *pronaos* (front porch), cella, and
opisthodomos (back porch). Unusual in a peripteral temple of this sort is the emphasis on
the eastern end, an effect carried out by the placement of the sculptural adornment. On the
east facade, the ten metopes of the frieze are sculpted with scenes of the Labors of Herakles. On the long north and south sides, only the four easternmost metopes are sculpted,
94   showing the labors of Theseus. Where they stop, the third columns in from the facade on
both north and south carry a huge beam surmounted by a continuous "Ionic" frieze which
runs across the pronaos. Thus the east end is essentially framed with sculpture in front of
the pronaos on all four sides. This contrasts with the west end, where the outer metopes are
not carved. In addition, the columns of the opisthodomos do not line up with the third
flank column on the sides, and the frieze of the opisthodomos is thus confined to the width
of the interior structure only, rather than extending the full width of the temple, as is the
case at the east.

The identification of the building as the Hephaisteion is based both on the account of

93. The Hephaisteion, above the Agora, mid-5th century B.C.

94. Detail of the southeast corner of the Hephaisteion, showing Theseus fighting the Minotaur.

Pausanias and on the fact that metalworking establishments were found in the area. Hephaistos was the god of the forge, and he appears as the master metalworker in the *Iliad*, responsible for the shield of Achilles and for Agamemnon's scepter. His cult may have been brought to Athens from the volcanic island of Lemnos, one of his original places of worship, which became an Athenian dependency. Hephaistos was worshiped in the building together with his sister Athena (as Athena Hephaistia), and statues of the two would have stood inside. Early on, the building was identified as the Theseion (still its popular name today) because of the sculpted scenes of Theseus' labors; other identifications have been proposed as well.

The carved moldings, associated pottery, and some structural considerations suggest that the temple was laid out before the Parthenon, perhaps in the decade 460–450. Differences in the moldings and clamping systems in the lower and upper parts of the building indicate that work was abandoned for some time, perhaps because the workers were needed on the Acropolis, and then resumed in the last quarter of the century. Inscribed accounts also suggest that work on the two cult statues was carried out between 421 and 415 (*IG* I³ 472). When work resumed it was decided, apparently under the influence of the plan of the Parthenon, to add an interior colonnade to frame the statues. This was done by laying additional interior foundations and setting the cella walls on the outermost edge of their foundations; even so, it must have been a squeeze.

Excavations around the building have highlighted a feature common to all Greek sanctuaries. In contrast to the present day, when archaeological sites are often the hottest and dustiest places in antiquity, sanctuaries were well watered and shaded by trees and shrubs. Around the Hephaisteion several rows of planting pits, some with large terra-cotta flower pots still in situ, indicate the laying out of a garden in the third century B.C.

Like its counterparts on the Acropolis, the Hephaisteion was converted into a Christian church, probably in the seventh century A.D. (see fig. 231). Doors were cut into the south and west walls of the cella, and an apse was built into the eastern end as the orientation of the building was shifted 180 degrees to conform with early Christian church architecture. The pagan sculpture had to be dealt with as well, and in the metope of Theseus and the Minotaur we find some insight into the early Christian mind: Theseus has lost his head, but the Minotaur has not; pagans were apparently worse than monsters.

95. Landscape planting pits along the south side of the
Hephaisteion, 3rd century B.C.

The Hephaisteion, though dating to Periklean
times, is perhaps not technically a full member of
the Periklean program, in that we have no evidence
for an immediate predecessor destroyed by the Persians. Two other buildings in the lower city were also
probably conceived of and planned under Perikles
and have an association with the Persian Wars, but,
as with the Hephaisteion, there is no evidence of an
earlier structure burnt in 480/79.

The Stoa of Zeus Eleutherios

Within the Agora itself, a stoa was built and dedicated to Zeus Eleutherios (Freedom).
96   The epithet is said to derive from the freedom the Greeks won at the Battle of Plataia, the final victory over the Persians on Greek soil. Zeus Eleutherios had an altar near the battlefield, and sacrifices and a festival were still being celebrated there by all the Greeks as late
as the time of Plutarch, around A.D. 120, some six hundred years after the battle. The stoa
in Athens is unusual in that it is dedicated to Zeus but takes the form of a civic or public
building rather than a temple. It was set along the west side of the Agora square, a colonnade of marble in the Doric order. The facade has projecting wings at either end, an innovation found also in a contemporary stoa built for Artemis at Brauron (see figs. 118, 249).
Architectural details suggest that the building should be dated to the years around 430–
420 B.C. Decoration of the stoa consisted of paintings on the walls, four of which are described by Pausanias (1.3.3–4):

> Behind is built a stoa with paintings of the so-called twelve gods. On the wall op-
> posite is painted Theseus, and also Demokratia and Demos. . . . Here is also a
> picture of the Athenians sent to help the Lakedaimonians at Mantineia [362
> B.C.]. . . . In the picture is a cavalry battle, in which the most notable figures are,
> among the Athenians, Grylos the son of Xenophon, and in the Boiotian cavalry,
> Epaminondas the Theban. These pictures were painted for the Athenians by
> Euphranor, who also made the Apollo Patroos in the temple nearby.

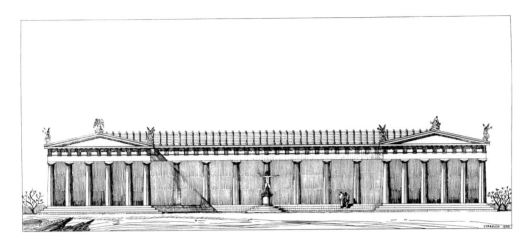

96. Reconstruction of the Stoa of Zeus Eleutherios in the Agora, 430–420 B.C.

Appropriately enough, the stoa served as the repository of the shields of those who died fighting to preserve the freedom of Athens. Pausanias writes of two such inscribed memorials from the early third century B.C. They were taken from the building by Sulla's soldiers after he took Athens in 86 B.C.

The Sanctuary of Artemis Agrotera

Another deity associated with victory over the Persians was Artemis Agrotera (Huntress); several ancient sources (Aelian, Aristophanes, Plutarch, and Xenophon) refer to the large number of goats sacrificed to her each year in celebration of the victory at Marathon. The hunter Artemis was a rural deity, and Pausanias saw her sanctuary well out of town, southeast of the city (1.19.6):

> When you have crossed the Ilissos there is a place called Agrai and a temple of
> Artemis Agrotera; here they say Artemis first hunted after coming from Delos,
> and for this reason the statue has a bow.

Her sanctuary has been identified with a high degree of probability with a small Ionic temple which stood above the banks of the Ilissos River until as recently as the eighteenth century. It was incorporated into a little Byzantine chapel which had been abandoned and sold off for building material by 1768. Fortunately, two British architects, J. Stuart and

97. Drawing done by J. Stewart and N. Revett in the 1750s showing the temple on the Ilissos River embedded in a Byzantine chapel (dismantled 1778–1779).

97   N. Revett, had studied and drawn the temple in detail between 1751 and 1753. Only the slightest traces of some foundations of the retaining wall for the terrace it occupied survive on the site today.

The plan is very close to that of the Athena Nike temple: amphiprostyle with four columns at either end. The architectural details are similar as well, and for that reason it is usually assumed to have been designed by the same architect and to be close in date to the Nike temple, perhaps a few years earlier (445–435 B.C.). Several slabs of the sculpted frieze survive, in Vienna, Berlin, and Athens.

Thus at least four substantial buildings in the lower city of Athens were constructed or planned during the administration of Perikles. Although there is no good evidence for any predecessors burnt by the Persians, three of the four have attested associations with victory over the Persians and, in a general sense, they should probably be considered part of Perikles' plans for the architectural renovation of the sacred spaces of the city.

ATTICA

Several important sanctuaries in the scattered demes of Attica were part of the Periklean program as well, with new temples erected over the ruins of pre-Persian predecessors at Eleusis, Sounion, Rhamnous, and perhaps Thorikos and Brauron.

At Eleusis, the famed Hall of Mysteries, or Telesterion, with its central chamber, had been in use for decades and had already been through several building phases by the time the Persians arrived and destroyed it. Herodotos refers to its destruction in his account of the Battle of Plataia, when he writes (9.65),

Herein is a marvelous thing, that though the battle was fought near the grove of Demeter there was no sign that any Persian was killed in the precinct or even entered it. Most of them fell near the temple on unconsecrated ground. And I judge—if it is not a sin to judge divine matters—that the goddess herself denied them entry, since they had burned her temple, the Anaktoron at Eleusis.

The Periklean reconstruction called for a huge building, square in plan, with rows of interior columns and stepped benches along the walls to accommodate participants (see fig. 256). The cult at Eleusis was different from most Greek cults, which required the sacrifice of animals on an altar outside the temple. A temple was needed to house the statue and to store votives, but it was not the venue of the actual liturgy or religious activity. Demeter's cult, however, was a mystery, open only to initiates; so well-kept was its secret that even today we are not certain what was said or done. What is clear is that the rites were nocturnal, held inside, and very popular. Hence the large building, which could accommodate thousands of worshipers indoors. The construction project was a huge one, taxing more than one architect, as we learn from Plutarch:

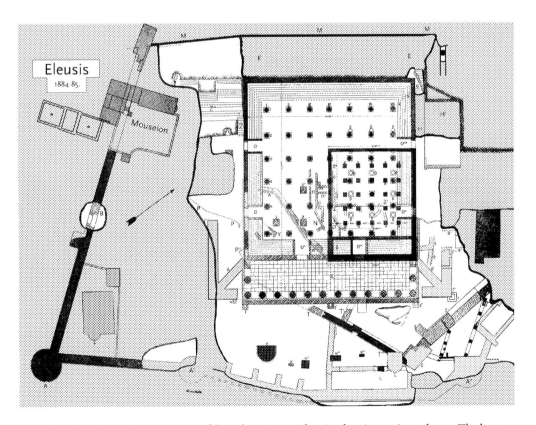

98. Plan from the early excavations of the Telesterion at Eleusis, showing various phases. The large porch was added in the 4th century B.C.

99. Interior view of the Telesterion. (Watercolor by Peter Connolly)

> Koroibos began to build the Telesterion at Eleusis, and he set the columns on
> the floor and joined their capitals with architraves; but on his death Metagenes
> of Xypete set the frieze course and the upper colonnade, and Xenokles of Chol-
> argos set the clerestory over the Anaktoron. (*Perikles* 13)

With the Periklean building phase the Telesterion comes close to its greatest extent, though
a massive porch was added in the fourth century B.C., and the building was slightly enlarged in the Roman period.

The Poseidon and Athena Temples at Sounion

At Cape Sounion, a new temple was constructed for Poseidon. The unfinished late
Archaic limestone building was replaced by a Doric temple in marble (see fig. 266). It is

usually dated somewhere in the 440s, and there is no evidence which allows more precision. In plan it is close to the Hephaisteion, with six columns by thirteen. The marble was   101
heavily veined local stone from the Agrileza quarries, a few kilometers to the north. Until
recently the old road could be followed easily from the temple back to the quarries, where
the traces of the removal of column drums can still be made out. At Sounion several bat-   102
tered slabs survive, carrying indistinct traces of a frieze showing a boar hunt, a gigantomachy, and a centauromachy; these apparently decorated the pronaos. The sanctuary was   103
also provided with a handsome small marble propylon and a stoa, both in the Doric order.

On a lower hill to the northeast a second temple was built, apparently dedicated to
Athena Sounias. Its plan is most unusual. Of the Ionic order, the temple has colonnades on
only two adjacent sides, the east and south (see figs. 268, 269). There are ten columns   104, 105
across the front (east) and twelve down the long side. This arrangement is unique in Greek
architecture, and Vitruvius (4.8.4) takes note of it, including it with the Erechtheion as a
building where the elements that usually appear on the front have been shifted to the side.
There is no obvious reason for this arrangement, though columns on the facade only
would be no surprise. The flank colonnade on the south in effect serves as a stoa for the

100. Aerial view of the sanctuary and temple of Poseidon at Sounion from the south, ca. 440–430 B.C.
The Hellenistic catapult tower is at upper right. (Cf. fig. 163)

101. South colonnade of the temple of Poseidon from the southeast.

sanctuary, providing shade in summer and shelter from rain and the northerly wind in winter. Within the almost square cella, the supports for four interior columns as well as the bedding for the cult statue can be made out. The Ionic capitals are beautifully carved, with light stippling on the moldings, presumably intended to help the painted decoration adhere (see fig. 185). The style of the column capitals indicates that this temple should be dated to the years around the middle of the fifth century or slightly earlier.

The evidence suggests that the temple of Athena was largely down by the first century A.D., while only the roof trim of the Poseidon temple was missing. This may explain Pausanias' confusion in describing only one temple on the cape and identifying it as

Left 102. Quarry at Agrileza showing traces of the removal of column drums for the temple of Poseidon at Sounion.

Right 103. Ionic frieze block with a centauromachy from the temple of Poseidon.

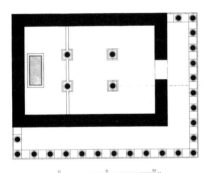

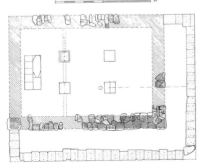

Above 104. Foundations of the temple of Athena at Sounion, viewed from the east: cella with four column supports at center rear, east and south colonnades in foreground and at left, ca. 450 B.C.

Left 105. Plan of the temple of Athena.

that of Athena. The Poseidon sanctuary is identified on the basis of an inscription found on the site, the temple of Athena by Vitruvius' description of its unusual plan.

Cape Sounion has always been a common stopping place for ships, providing good shelter in the deep harbor below, with its sandy beach. Visitors through the ages have scratched their names in the marble of the temple of Poseidon, including Lord Byron, whose inscription may be made out on the northeast anta. Other visitors helped themselves to column drums, as either souvenirs or ballast, and pieces of the temple have been recognized in England and Italy.

The Sanctuary of Nemesis at Rhamnous

At Rhamnous, on the northeast coast of Attica, the sanctuary of Nemesis was also provided with a new temple. Like the temple of Poseidon at Sounion, it was of the Doric order, of local marble, and close in plan to the Hephaisteion, though somewhat smaller (see figs. 263, 264). It was peripteral, with six columns by thirteen. The carved moldings suggest that work was being done on the temple in the 430s and perhaps the 420s, though it was clearly left unfinished. The columns are not fluted, nor were the protective panels on the steps carved away. The usual assumption is that the outbreak of the Peloponnesian War and the annual invasions of Attica by the Spartans which started in 431 caused the work to be abandoned. Though the final tooling was not carried out, the building was roofed, and it functioned for years. It housed a statue carved either by Pheidias or his pupil Agorakritos. Pausanias' account of his own visit to the temple includes this description (1.33.1 ff.):

> Just 60 stades [12 kilometers] from Marathon is Rhamnous, on the road that runs beside the sea to Oropos. The dwellings of the people are by the shore, but a little above the sea is a sanctuary of Nemesis, who of all deities is the most implacable toward the proud. It appears that the barbarians who landed at Marathon incurred the wrath of the goddess; for, thinking it an easy task to capture Athens, they brought with them Parian marble to make a trophy, as if the victory were already won. Of this very marble Pheidias made a statue of Nemesis. On the head of the goddess is a crown ornamented with deer and small Nikai [Victories]; in her left hand she carries an apple bough, in her right a bowl, on which are worked figures of Ethiopians.

After digressions on Ethiopians and Nemesis, Pausanias goes on to describe the sculpted base of the statue:

> I will now describe the figures on the base of the image, but for the sake of clarity will preface the following observation. They say that Nemesis was the mother of Helen but that Leda suckled and reared her. As for Helen's father, the people of Rhamnous agree with the rest of the Greeks that he was Zeus, not Tyndareus. Pheidias, acquainted with these legends, has represented Helen

106

107

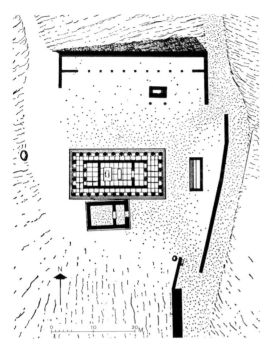

106. Plan of the sanctuary of Nemesis at Rhamnous, 430–420 B.C.

brought by Leda to Nemesis, and has shown Tyndareus and his sons, and a man named Hippeus standing by with a horse. There are also Agamemnon and Menelaus and Pyrrhos, son of Achilles.

The excavations have brought to light many fragments of both the statue and its base. The fragments are small and bat- 108 tered; it is clear that someone destroyed the statue deliberately. Nonetheless, these pieces represent one of our few original fifth-century cult statues, most of which are known only from descriptions, and they have been painstakingly reassembled and studied. The statue itself is indeed of Parian marble, as the story told by Pausanias requires, and shows a standing draped female figure about 3 meters high. Only part of the head survives, now in the British Museum. While Pausanias, Zenobios, and Pomponius Mela identify the sculptor as Pheidias, Pliny (*Natural History* 36.17) and Strabo (396) attribute it to Agorakritos, a pupil of Pheidias' who was from Paros himself. Modern scholars tend to favor Agorakritos.

Equally rare is the sculpted base. Again, few examples survive, though a number are described in the accounts of Pausanias and other writers. Of interest is the use of white marble for the die of the base, with dark gray Eleusinian limestone for the crowning

107. Detail of the unfluted, unfinished column drums of the temple of Nemesis.

108. Artist's rendition of the interior of the temple of Nemesis showing the cult statue of Parian marble on its sculpted base and a cult table in front. Fragments of the statue, sculpted base, and table have all been recovered.

element. We have seen this use of contrasting gray and white stone also on the Erechtheion frieze, but it seems to be especially favored for Athenian cult statue bases of the second half of the fifth century. In addition to the temple of Rhamnous, it was used in the Hephaisteion, the Parthenon, the temple of Apollo built by the Athenians on Delos, and for the statue of Zeus built by Pheidias at Olympia.

The Stoa at Thorikos

One other deme, Thorikos, has a building which also should perhaps be assigned to the Periklean program. Down in the plain below the town site a large marble colonnaded building was constructed in the second half of the fifth century (see fig. 271). It has been excavated several times after repeated reburials by the heavy alluviation in the valley. The building has an unusual form, and interpretation is further complicated by the fact that it is unfinished. It consists of a peristyle with seven columns along the short sides and fourteen columns down the long sides. There is a gap on each of the long sides, which essentially divides the building into two separate halves, a most unusual feature. The steps carrying the colonnades simply stop, and the space between the columns on either side of the gap indicates that there was little, if any, structural connection between the two halves. The remains look rather like the peristyle for a temple, though the gaps are without parallel. Within the colonnade are the foundations of a single wall running lengthwise down the middle of the building.

109, 110

What is clear is that the building, of local marble, was a fine one, for the column capitals are very well done. As at Rhamnous, the column shafts were unfluted, except where they rest on the topmost step, and the steps still have their protective surfaces; no traces of architrave or frieze have ever been recognized: clearly the structure was never finished. The quality of workmanship is so high that it seems likely that the building was religious in nature. No deity can be assigned it with certainty, however, though Demeter

109. Unfinished Doric "stoa" of Thorikos, ca. 430 B.C., in a nineteenth-century photograph. Note the gap in the foundations.

has been favored on the evidence of a boundary stone found somewhere in Thorikos and from the tradition that she landed at Thorikos on her way to Eleusis (*Homeric Hymn to Demeter*, ll. 123–128).

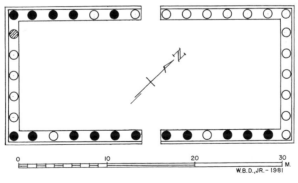

110. Plan of the "stoa."

The Athena Temple at Pallene

At least one other peripteral Doric marble temple of Periklean date was built in Attica. Paradoxically, we have the temple but not its original foundations. Early in the Roman period it was taken down stone by stone, moved into the Agora, re-erected on new foundations, and dedicated to the war god Ares. Fragments of step blocks, column shafts and capitals, frieze, and cornice survive, each marked with letters of early Roman date to guide their correct placement in the reconstruction. Protective surfaces and lifting bosses have been left on the steps, suggesting that the temple, like the Propylaia, the temple of Nemesis at Rhamnous, and the building at Thorikos, was never completed.

Its original location in Attica is unknown and has been a matter of some debate. The most common suggestion is the large northern deme of Acharnai, where a cult of Ares is attested to. An inscription from Acharnai does record the foundation there of an altar (and therefore of the cult?) in the fourth century, that is, later than the marble temple. Furthermore, the assumption that the cult would have been transferred along with the architecture is not necessarily justified: just because the material was reused for a temple of Ares it does not follow that the original building was also dedicated to him. A more likely place of origin

III. Marble blocks from a 5th century B.C. Doric temple, reused in the Agora for a temple of Ares in early Roman times.

for the temple architecture has only recently come to light. A set of temple foundations in search of a superstructure has been found near modern Stavro, between Pentele and Hymettos, at the spot where we would expect to find the venerable sanctuary of Athena Pallenis. This was the cult center for a small group of demes (Pithos, Gargettos, Acharnai, and Pallene) which were affiliated in a manner similar to the demes of the old Marathonian Tetrapolis.

Thus, in all, more than a dozen marble cult buildings were put up in Athens and Attica between 460 and 430 under the guiding hand of Perikles, in a program which transformed the city forever and which still serves as a permanent reminder in architecture and sculpture of the acme of Athenian achievement.

THE PELOPONNESIAN WAR

The Periklean building program came to an abrupt halt in the late 430s with the outbreak of the Peloponnesian War, which pitted Athens and its empire against Sparta and its allies. Several monuments—the Propylaia, the Rhamnous temple, the building at Thorikos—show signs even today of having been left unfinished; other buildings, such as the Erechtheion, the Hephaisteion, and the Telesterion at Eleusis, took years to complete because the work was delayed.

Thucydides and Xenophon give vivid and detailed accounts of the war, which raged all over Greece and the eastern Mediterranean for a generation, from 432/1 until 404/3. In addition to the difficulties of war, the Athenians suffered also from the effects of a devastating plague which ravaged Athens in 429 and 427/6, carrying off thousands of Athenians, including Perikles himself. Conduct of the war thereafter passed into the hands of other generals: Demosthenes, Kleon, Nikias, and Alkibiades. The war was halted for a nominal peace from 421 to 415, but resumed with the disastrous loss of a large Athenian fleet in Sicily in 414/3. Thereafter the Athenians suffered from poor leadership and political turmoil; the loss of another fleet at Aigospotamoi in the Hellespont in 404 spelled the loss of the war as well.

During the war, work on most of the great marble temples of the Periklean program seems to have been halted or curtailed. Religious monuments, however, continued to be built, though not on the lavish scale we have just been studying. A major impetus for cult activity seems to have been the outbreak of the plague; its apparently random choice of victims left the Athenians searching for additional sources of divine help. Thucydides gives a long, detailed account of the symptoms and course of the plague, describing the dead bodies in the temples and the dying crawling in the streets or—driven by a raging thirst—massed around the fountain houses.

The outbreak of the disease was exacerbated by Athenian policy at the start of the war. Perikles had persuaded all those living in Attica to abandon their homes, take refuge within the walls of Athens, and prosecute the war by sea:

> After the Athenians had heard his words they were won over and began to bring their children and wives from the fields, as well as their household furniture, pulling down even the woodwork of the houses themselves; the sheep and draft animals they sent over to Euboia and the adjacent islands. And this move was a hard thing for them to accept, because most of them had always been used to living in the country. (Thucydides 2.14)

The huge influx of population led to severe crowding in Athens:

> When they came to the city, only a few of them were provided with dwellings or places of refuge with friends and relatives; most of them took up residence in the vacant places of the city and the sanctuaries and shrines of the heroes, all except the Acropolis and Eleusinion or any other precinct which could be securely closed. And the Pelargikon, as it was called, at the foot of the Acropolis—although it was under a curse that forbade its use for residence and was prohibited also by the closing line of a Pythian oracle ("The Pelargikon is best left unoccupied")—nevertheless under the stress of the emergency was completely filled with buildings. (2.17)

The reference to the Pelargikon, at the foot of the Acropolis, as land best left unoccupied reminds us that it was not the top of the citadel alone that was holy; various important cults were accommodated on its lower slopes as well. Pausanias lists many of these, and excavations have shown that the Acropolis was ringed with cults. As most were functioning during the war, we will consider them all here, starting at the western entrance and taking them in clockwise order.

At the entrance to the Acropolis, Pausanias describes several cults and their shrines (1.22.3):

> The worship of Aphrodite Pandemos and of Peitho [Persuasion] was instituted by Theseus when he gathered the Athenians from the towns into a single city. In my time the ancient images were gone, but the existing images were by no

obscure artists. There was also a sanctuary of Ge Kourotrophos [Nurturing Earth] and Demeter Chloe [Green]; the meaning of these epithets may be learned by inquiring of the priests.

Several inscriptions referring to these three goddesses have been found clustered around the west end of the Acropolis, just below the Nike temple bastion, suggesting that their shrines should be located in the immediate vicinity. In the case of Aphrodite Pandemos an inscription of the 280s B.C. (*IG* II² 659) instructs the *astynomoi* (city magistrates) to carry out several specific tasks at the time of the goddess' festival: provide a dove to purify the sanctuary, anoint the altars, put pitch on the roof of the temple, wash the statues, and supply a specified amount of purple dye (see fig. 114J). Another inscription is written on the architrave of what must have been Aphrodite's temple. It is tiny (only 3.17 meters wide) and decorated with reliefs of doves (*IG* II² 4596).

On the northwest slopes we encounter first the Klepsydra fountain (see fig. 68), whose tutelary nymph was Empedo, and above that several shallow caves, one of which was given over to Pan after the victory at Marathon, according to Pausanias (see figs. 114A, 114C). Sculpted reliefs found on the slopes below depicting Pan and the Nymphs presumably came from the niches cut into the rock of the easternmost cave. Two statues of Pan were also found in the area.

One of the caves has strong associations with Apollo (see fig. 114B), who is said to have raped Kreusa there, resulting in the birth of Ion, progenitor of the Ionian Greeks. Kreusa later exposed the child in the same cave. Euripides tells the story in the opening lines of the *Ion,* written in the late fifth century B.C., and later refers to the area:

O haunt of Pan and neighboring rock near the caves of the long cliffs, where the feet of the three maidens, Aglauros' daughters, tread the green levels in dance before the shrine of Pallas, to the ever-changing

112. Votive relief, perhaps from the cave of Pan, showing Hermes, the Nymphs, and the infant Dionysos, dedicated by Neoptolemos, son of Antikles of Melite, ca. 330 B.C.

113. Dedicatory plaque for Apollo Hyp'Akrais from the cave on the northwest slope, Roman period.

sound of the music of pipes when you, Pan, pipe in your sunless caves. There an unfortunate maiden bore a child to Phoibos and left him out to the fowls of the air for food, a bloody meal for wild beasts, the shameful fruit of a cruel union. (*Ion*, ll. 492–505)

Despite this early version of the story associating the caves, Apollo, Pan, and the long cliffs (*makrai*) there is no certain sign of cult activity in honor of Apollo until well into the Roman period. Starting in the first century A.D. the rock face received numerous thin votive plaques of marble dedicated by magistrates to Apollo Hypoakraios (Apollo Below the Heights), Hyp'Akrais, or Hypo Makrais.

Farther east, excavations have uncovered a small open-air sanctuary of Aphrodite and Eros, with rock-cut dedications and niches, going back to the fifth century B.C. (see fig. 114D). Eastward still, there are several niches cut into the Acropolis rock, but they have no certain association with any deity.

At the easternmost end of the Acropolis there is a large cave which produced little material when excavated in 1936. On the slopes below, however, a complete stele of the mid-third century B.C. was found, carrying an honorary inscription for a priestess of Aglauros (see fig. 114E). According to its publication clause (the clause at the end of the inscription explaining where the stele was to be set up, that is, made available to the public), the decree was to be placed in the sanctuary of Aglauros, which many scholars believe therefore to be the area of the slopes just below the cave, though Herodotos' account of the final Persian assault on the citadel would seem to place the sanctuary farther to the west, along the north slopes of the Acropolis (8.53):

In front of the Acropolis, and behind the gates and the way up to them, there was a place where no one was on guard for no one would have thought that any man would ascend that way; here certain men mounted near the shrine of Kekrops' daughter Aglauros, though the way led up a sheer cliff.

Proceeding around the slopes to the south side of the Acropolis, one comes first to the Odeion of Perikles and then to the sanctuary of Dionysos Eleuthereus (see fig. 114F, 114G).

The ancient cult statue of Dionysos was brought to Athens from Eleutherai, a town on the 114
Athenian-Boiotian border, and the Athenians recognized Dionysos as an import from Boiotia. Every year they reenacted the bringing of the cult statue to Athens with a magnificent procession from the Academy to the sanctuary on the south slopes of the Acropolis. The old statue and the first temple go back at least to the late sixth century, but additions and improvements were also made in the fifth. A chryselephantine statue of the god was made by Alkamenes, while the wealthy statesman Nikias is said to have financed lavish choral performances. The focal point of the festival of Dionysos, the theater, does not survive in its fifth-century form. Only a few fragments of inscribed seat blocks of limestone remain from the great period of Attic theater, when the tragedies of Aischylos, Sophokles, and Euripides, as well as the comedies of Aristophanes, were first produced.

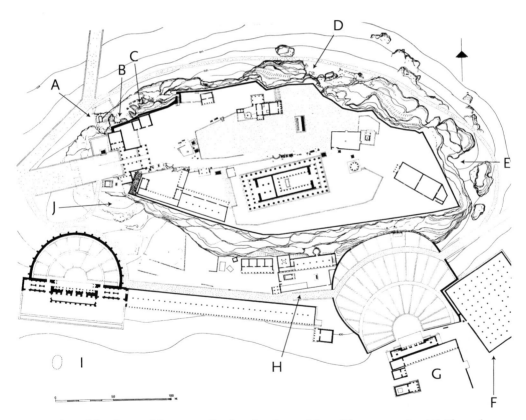

114. Plan of the slopes of the Acropolis, showing the position of the sanctuaries: (A) Klepsydra; (B) Cave of Apollo; (C) Cave of Pan; (D) Aphrodite and Eros; (E) Cave of Aglauros (?); (F) Odeion of Perikles; (G) Sanctuary of Dionysos; (H) Asklepieion; (I) Shrine of Nymphe; (J) Aphrodite Pandemos.

115. Votive relief from the Asklepieion at the base of the Acropolis showing Asklepios, Hygieia, and worshipers, 4th century B.C.

One of the most important shrines of the lower city lay just west of the theater of Dionysos. This was the Asklepieion (see fig. 115 149), which was founded during the Peloponnesian War, perhaps as a direct consequence of the plague (see fig. 114H). Asklepios was the son of Apollo and Koronis, a mortal woman. Born human, he acquired divine honors as a hero, and eventually became a full-fledged god. (Only he, Herakles, and Amphiaraos seem to have managed this transformation.) Asklepios came originally from Thessaly and was honored as the principal healing deity in the Greek pantheon; 116 he was immensely popular, and virtually every Greek city had an Asklepieion. His most important sanctuary was at Epidauros, in the Peloponnese, and it was from here that his cult was introduced to Athens. His worship was imported by a private individual, one Telemachos, and only later, in the mid-fourth century B.C., did the state take over the administration of his cult.

We have a fragmentary account inscribed on stone of his introduction to Athens (*IG* II² 4960 and 4961); this indicates that the god arrived in the form of a sacred snake in 421/0. The so-called Peace of Nikias (during the Peloponnesian War, between 421 and 415) perhaps afforded the city its first opportunity after the plague to deal with Epidauros. The inscription records some sort of objection by other priests to both the establishment of the cult and its location, but no details are given. The inscribed block is crowned with reliefs on all four sides. On one side are Asklepios and his daughter Hygieia (Health); on the other an unusual scene depicting a wall and a doorway, with a statue next to the door. Beyond the wall is the upper part of a tree, with a stork in its branches. The Greek word for stork is *pelargos,* which seems to be a clear punning reference to the Pelargikon, which must in some way relate to the Asklepieion.

West of the Asklepieion, Pausanias reports a temple of Themis and the grave of Hip-

116. Votive relief from the Asklepieion in Peiraieus, showing Asklepios healing a sleeping patient, 4th century B.C.

polytos, son of Theseus. Somewhat lower down the slope, excavations have also brought to light a simple enclosure dedicated to Nymphe (see fig. 114I), with a rectangular altar of unworked stones dating to 650–625 B.C., the earliest altar yet known from Athens. Athenian brides dedicated the vessels containing the water for their bridal bath in this sanctuary, and thousands of fragments of these vases (*loutrophoroi*) were found here.

This completes our circuit of the lower slopes and a tour of the virtually contiguous sanctuaries around the Acropolis. Many, if not all, fall within the limits of the old Pelargikon, which is usually dated to the Bronze Age and was apparently defined by a wall at least until the time of the Persian sack. The full extent of the area is not known, as no trace of the original wall has been recognized, though the northwest slope was certainly part of it. In any case, the disorderly occupation of the area because of the war seems to have prompted the Athenians to reassert their control over the Pelargikon and its venerable cults. Following an inscribed law concerning Eleusinian matters we find a rider appended by one Lampon (*IG* I³ 78, ll. 54–59):

> The king archon is to set the boundaries of the sacred places in the Pelargikon, and in the future no altar is to be established without the boule [senate] and the demos [people], nor is any stone to be quarried from the Pelargikon, nor is earth or stone to be taken away. If anyone transgresses this, let him be fined 500 drachmas and let the king archon prosecute him before the boule.

A possible remnant of the results of this rider can be seen today. Along the south side of the Acropolis, between the Asklepieion and the temple of Themis, there is a small fountain house. It is poorly preserved, the western half having been cut away by the construction of a vaulted reservoir in the sixth century A.D. It takes the form of a rectangular stone-lined basin sunk deep into the ground. The handsome polygonal masonry of the lining suggests an Archaic date, in which case a late Archaic Doric capital of limestone found nearby may be associated. Some 24 meters south of this fountain there is a short stretch of wall made of large blocks of Acropolis limestone set in a trapezoidal arrangement (see fig. 149). Incor-

117   porated into this wall is a marble boundary stone, which reads, "boundary of the spring"
(*IG* I³ 587). The letters are consistent with a date in the second half of the fifth century, and
it is tempting to see here the hand of the king archon, fulfilling his instructions to reestab-
lish and mark out the limits of the Pelargikon and its old shrines. The circumstances that
the rider appears on a decree concerning Eleusinian matters and that the Eleusinian priests
(the Kerykes) objected to some aspect of Asklepios' installation suggest that the Pelargikon
also extended along the north slopes of the Acropolis.

In addition to concern over reestablishing the Pelargikon and the laying out of the
Asklepieion, other cult activity may be attributed to the outbreak of the plague as well. In
the Agora, a statue by Kalamis was dedicated to Apollo Alexikakos (Averter of Evil) for his
help in stopping the epidemic (Pausanias 1.3.3), and another to Herakles Alexikakos was set
up in his sanctuary near the Agora (schol. Aristophanes, *Frogs* 501; see fig. 116). The cult of
Asklepios was introduced to the port of Peiraieus as well, as was that of Bendis, a healing
deity from Thrace.

The traditional bringer of plague was
Apollo, together with his sister Artemis.
An attempt was made to appease Apollo at
his major sanctuary on the island of Delos,
which was under Athenian control. In 426
all the burials on the island were dug up
and transferred to neighboring Rheneia; it
was forbidden to give birth or die on Delos; and a festival with games and choruses in honor of Apollo was reestablished
(Thucydides 3.104 ff. and Diodoros Siculus 12.58). Plutarch describes a particularly lavish chorus at Delos paid for by the
wealthy general and statesman Nikias.
And to the years around 425 can be dated a
fine Doric amphiprostyle marble temple
built by the Athenians.

It may be that Apollo's sister Artemis
received similar attention at her main Attic sanctuary, Brauron. For the most part,

117. Boundary stone of the fountain on the
south slopes of the Acropolis, 5th century B.C.

there is little sign of building activity in Attica during the war, hardly surprising since the Athenians had abandoned the countryside for the city, the Spartans were invading regularly, and the war was consuming resources. We have already seen that fancy buildings in Thorikos and Rhamnous were left unfinished, probably because of the war. Against this bleak background in Attica generally, the situation at Brauron calls for special notice. Here a Doric stoa was built in limestone with marble trim. It had a central colonnade, along with 118 two flank colonnades which were planned, partially built, and never finished. Behind the central colonnade were several large dining rooms, a common feature of many sanctuaries. The consumption of the meat of the sacrificed animals was a major element in most festivals from the time of Prometheus, who persuaded the gods that while they liked the smell of roasting meat, they did not really care what happened to the meat itself.

The stoa was also used to display many of the statues and reliefs set up by thankful parents after a successful childbirth. A close analysis and study of the architecture of the 119

118. Aerial view of the sanctuary and stoa of Artemis at Brauron from the east, ca. 425 B.C. The dining rooms are to the right of the colonnade, and the poorly preserved foundations of the temple lie under the tree at upper left.

building suggests that it was built in the years around 425, an unusual time for building activity in Attica. The impetus for this stoa must therefore have been strong, and clearly the plague would represent a suitable motive, particularly when we remember that the foundation legends suggest that the sanctuary or some of its cult practices were instituted specifically to allay the goddess' anger at the time of a plague.

Other buildings at the sanctuary may also have been built at the same time. A bridge over the Erasinos River almost certainly was. We have the indirect testimony from Pausanias (3.16.7–8) that the Persians plundered the sanctuary in 480; it seems virtually certain that they destroyed the old temple, especially when we recall the damage they did at Rhamnous to the north and Sounion to the south. One phase of the temple should probably be dated to the latter part of the fifth century, therefore, and the surviving foundations are suitable for an amphiprostyle plan similar to that favored by the Athenians for other temples built at this time: Nike on the Acropolis, the Ilissos temple, the Apollo temple on Delos, and, after a fashion, the Erechtheion. A later inscription calling for the repair of no fewer than seven buildings in the sanctuary at Brauron refers to them as follows:

> [Buildings] which the city, having built them, dedicated to the goddess for the saving of the people of Athens.

Although this has a formulaic ring to it, the phrase may well reflect a whole program of improvements to the sanctuary, carried out by the Athenians at the time of the plague, when they were paying similar attention to Apollo's sanctuary at Delos.

One more healing deity came to prominence in Athens during the war, presumably because of the plague: Amphiaraos. Originally a hero (one of the warriors from Argos known as the Seven against Thebes), Amphiaraos lost his life in the war which erupted between the sons of Oedipus. He and his chariot were swallowed up by the earth, after which he became a healing deity. His principal sanctuary was in the territory of the small city of Oropos, on the northeast frontier of Attica (see fig. 276). Wedged in between the

119. Votive relief from Brauron showing Artemis, deer, and worshipers, 4th century B.C.

120

120. Votive relief for Amphiaraos, a local healing deity from nearby Oropos, 4th century B.C. (Cf. fig. 276)

two great states of Athens and Thebes, Oropos was something of a political football, and both neighbors exerted their influence and direct control over the city whenever possible. It was Athenian during the early years of the Peloponnesian War, when the sanctuary first began to take on monumental form with the construction of a small temple and two altars. As in the case of Asklepios, the plague may have induced the Athenians to ingratiate themselves with a known healing deity.

Aside from these various cult installations, the Athenians continued to build within the city throughout the war, though the emphasis shifted from religious needs to civic concerns. The buildings are much more modest structures than the great marble temples of the Acropolis, with walls of sun-dried mudbrick and floors of packed clay. In the Agora a new bouleuterion (council chamber) was built for the senate (*boule*) of five hundred. It lies on the west side, just west of its predecessor (see fig. 66), in an area quarried out of the slopes of the hill. The bouleuterion has been plundered down to its foundations, and there is little about the plan or interior arrangement which can be understood with certainty; as is the case with other early council chambers, however, it seems likely that it had a level seating area rather than banked rows of seats. The date, based on scraps of associated pottery and literary sources, seems to be between 416 and 409.

Also constructed in the Agora was a long colonnaded building known as South Stoa I. Facing north along the south side of the square, it had a Doric outer colonnade, with a row of Ionic columns inside and sixteen rooms at the back. Off-center doors and a characteristic raised border indicate that several, perhaps all, of the rooms were equipped with couches and used as dining rooms. It is clearly a public building, and dozens of coins and an inscription suggest that it served a commercial function. An inscription (Agora I 7030) indicates that the officials in charge of weights and measures (*metronomoi*) were housed in the stoa. Other small boards and commissions charged with the orderly running of the economy of the city may also have held office and been fed at public expense in the build- 121 ing. Pottery from beneath the floor suggests that the stoa was built around 430–420. It is modest in construction, composed in part of reused wall blocks supporting a superstructure of mudbrick. It was properly maintained, however, and only went out of use some 275 years later, when it was deliberately dismantled to make way for a replacement.

In the second half of the war, after the collapse of the Peace of Nikias, the Spartans changed their tactics. Instead of annual invasions during the campaigning season, they now fortified Dekeleia, one of the northeastern demes of Attica, which they garrisoned year-round. The site chosen has a commanding view of the entire plain. Slight remains of what is believed to be the fort can be made out on the hill which now serves as the cemetery of the Greek royal family, at modern Tatoi. This garrison, suggested to the Spartans by Alkibiades, the Athenian general in exile in Sparta, put tremendous pressure on the Athenians. It cut off the land route through Oropos to the island of Euboia, where the Athenians had sent much of their cattle, and it provided a place of refuge for runaway slaves working at the silver mines at Laureion in south Attica. The year-round occupation allowed the Athenians even less access to Attica than formerly. It provided, in effect, a form of economic warfare, and the Athenians had to respond to protect Attica. The western approaches were already fortified: Eleusis, of course, had been strongly walled since the sixth century, and the northwesternmost deme, Oinoe, had also been fortified before the beginning of the war:

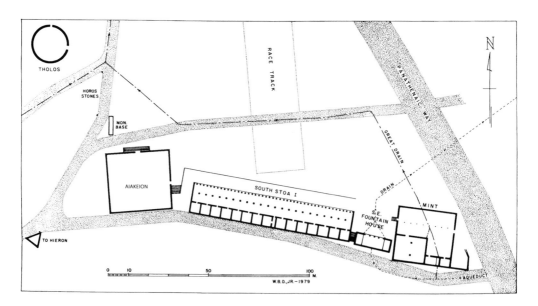

121. South side of the Agora, showing the layout and position of South Stoa I, ca. 430–420 B.C.

122. Mudbricks used for upper parts of walls of South Stoa I.

Meanwhile the army of the Peloponnesians was advancing [431 B.C.], and the first point it reached in Attica was Oinoe, where they intended to begin the invasion. And while they were establishing their camp there, they prepared to assault the wall with engines and otherwise; for Oinoe, which was on the border between Attica and Boiotia, was walled and was used by the Athenians whenever war broke out. (Thucydides 2.18)

After 413 other demes on the east coast (see fig. 248) were also fortified, to protect the sea route to Euboia and the Black Sea, source of so much imported grain: Sounion in 412 (Thucydides 8.4), Thorikos in 411 (Xenophon, *Hellenika* 1.2.1), and Rhamnous, probably around 412 as well.

In 407 Alkibiades, returned to Athens from exile, defied the Spartan occupation he himself had advocated:

As his first act he led out all his troops and conducted by land the procession of the Eleusinian mysteries, which the Athenians had been conducting by sea on account of the war. (Xenophon, *Hellenika* 1.4.20)

The procession, some 21 kilometers from Athens to Eleusis, was an important part of the yearly festival. The processional road, known as the Sacred Way, has been traced for much of its route, and Pausanias has a description of the numerous 124 tombs and shrines which lined it (1.36.3–1.38.5). The partici-

123. Early photograph of a tower at the fortified deme of Oinoe.

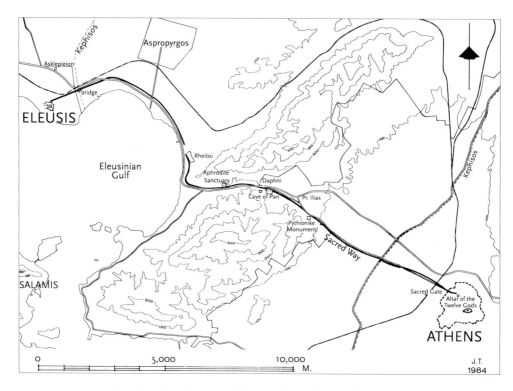

124. Map showing the route of the Sacred Way from Athens to Eleusis.

pants left Athens by the Sacred Gate, just south of the Dipylon, and made their way northwest to a low pass through Mount Aigaleos and on into the Thriasian Plain around Eleusis.
The monastery of Daphni in the pass seems to occupy a shrine of Apollo, noted by Pausanias
in his account of the route. The roadway itself was cobbled and is marked with wheel ruts.
125   Just beyond Daphni the route passes a shrine of Aphrodite. This takes the form of a walled
open-air enclosure set against the face of a low outcrop. Numerous niches and dedications
are carved onto the rock face, like those in the sanctuary of Aphrodite on the north slopes of
126   the Acropolis. Excavations have recovered several votives, including inscribed marble doves.
Farther on, near the plain of Eleusis itself, one of the shallow lakes known as the Rheitoi was
bridged in 421 in order to carry the processional route:

> Resolved by the boule and demos: to bridge the Rheitos near the city, using
> stones from the destroyed old temple at Eleusis, those blocks left over from
> building the wall, so that they may carry the sacred things to the rites as safely as
> possible; making the width 5 feet, so wagons may not pass, but those going on

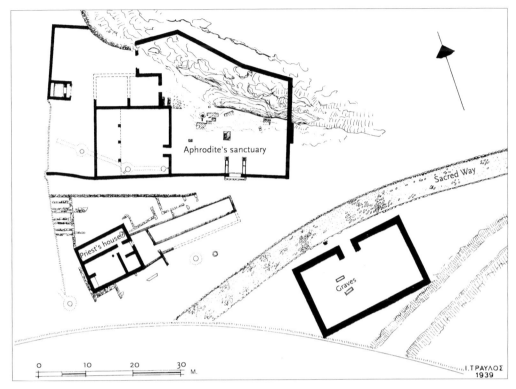

125. Plan of the sanctuary of Aphrodite along the Sacred Way.

foot to the rites. The architect Demomeles is to cover over the channels of the Rheitos with stones according to the specifications. (*IG* I³ 83)

Despite the successful staging of the procession, Alkibiades was later held responsible for a naval loss at Notion in 407 and withdrew from Athens once again. Other generals or admirals were exiled or put to death in 406, when, after a victory at Arginoussai, they failed to retrieve their own shipwrecked sailors because of stormy seas.

Finally, the loss of a huge fleet in the Hellespont in 404 led to the siege and eventual capitulation of Athens and the

126. Inscribed marble doves dedicated to Aphrodite, 4th century B.C.

end of the Peloponnesian War. Under Spartan influence, the democracy was disbanded and thirty conservative Athenians were chosen to run the city as an extreme oligarchy, in which only three thousand men were to have full rights. The Athenians were required to tear down long stretches of their fortification walls, and the dozens of ship sheds which housed the huge Athenian fleet in the Peiraieus were dismantled as well.

The Thirty Tyrants, as they came to be known, were not in power long enough to initiate any serious building projects, though they are associated with a change in orientation at the old meeting place of the Assembly, the Pnyx:

127   Therefore it was too that the *bema* [speaker's platform] in the Pnyx which had stood so as to look off to sea, was afterward turned by the Thirty Tyrants so as to look inland [see figs. 147, 148], because they thought that rule of the sea fostered democracy, whereas farmers were less likely to be bothered by oligarchy. (Plutarch, *Themistokles* 19)

127. The speaker's platform (*bema*) (at right) on the Pnyx. (Cf. figs. 147, 148)

The rule of the Thirty Tyrants was harsh. Undoubtedly understanding its significance as an administrative center, they set up headquarters in the Tholos, former seat of the *prytaneis* (executive committee) of the democratic boule. From here and from the Stoa Poikile (Diogenes Laertius 7.1.5) they condemned hundreds to death:

> They put many people to death out of personal enmity, and many also for the sake of acquiring their property. They resolved, in order to have money for their guards, that each one should seize a resident alien, put him to death and confiscate his property. (Xenophon, *Hellenika* 2.3.21)

Numerous democrats went into exile, finding refuge in neighboring Thebes. During the winter of 403, a small band returned with Thrasyboulos and seized the border fort of Phyle on Mount Parnes. There is still today a handsome, well-built fort at Phyle, occupying a steep crag. The word used by Xenophon to describe Phyle, however, *chorion,* can mean either a fort or simply a naturally defensible site, and many scholars believe that the fort should be dated somewhat later than the famous events of 403. The oligarchs marched out to confront the democrats but were defeated and then driven back by a snowstorm. More democrats made their way to Phyle, and when their numbers reached a thousand they seized the port of Peiraieus, and a full-scale civil war erupted. The Spartans sent troops to help the oligarchs, and several were killed in the ensuing skirmishes and battles. These fallen Spartans were buried at Athenian state expense in a prominent location in the great burial ground which lined the road leading from the Dipylon Gate to the Academy. The monument takes the form of a long walled enclosure, within which thirteen bodies were neatly laid out side by side, several of the skeletons showing clear signs of wounds. Part of an inscription (*IG* II² 11678) has been found, carrying the first two letters of the word Lakedaimonians, as well as the names of two of the generals, Chairon and Thibrachos, written in the Spartan rather than Athenian alphabet. The identification is certain, thanks also to Xenophon's account, which mentions the tomb and these same two officers by name:

128

129, 130

> In this attack Chairon and Thibrachos, both of them polemarchs [generals] were killed, and Lakrates the Olympic victor and other Lakedaimonians who lie buried in the Kerameikos in front of the gates of Athens. (*Hellenika* 2.4. 33)

The inscription on the grave runs from right to left, or retrograde, a common enough occurrence in the sixth century, but rare this late. Since the monument lies on the right of the road as one approaches the city, it is clear that the inscription was laid out to be easily read

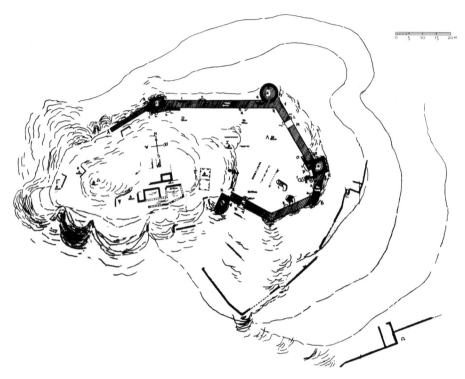

128. Plan of the fort at Phyle, ca. 400 B.C.

130. Inscription from the tomb of the Lakedaimonians, with the names of the polemarchs (generals) Chairon and Thibrachos in Lakonian letters.

by those entering Athens rather than those leaving. The primary goal was to impress and inform the visitor, not the local Athenians.

The democrats eventually prevailed in this war, the extreme oligarchs were exiled, the democracy was reinstated, and a general amnesty was declared. Despite all the turmoil, some building was undertaken in the last decade of the century. One example is a poorly preserved square building at the southeast corner of the Agora thought to have served as the mint in later times. It was built around 400, to judge from the pottery, and water basins, pits, and assorted debris indicate that industrial activity took place there. It must originally have produced items other than coins, because bronze coinage seems not to have been introduced to Athens until around the middle of the fourth century B.C. The building's location close to South Stoa I (see fig. 121) suggests that it may have produced items necessary for managing the marketplace, such as the pair of inscribed official bronze measures found in a nearby well.

A second building dating to the years around 400 is the Pompeion, described by Pausanias as soon as he passed through the gates into Athens (1.2.4):

> When we have entered the city we come to a building for the preparation of the processions which are conducted at yearly and other intervals.

The building takes its name from the Greek word for a procession (*pompe*) and has been identified with the remains of a large structure which was squeezed into the irregularly shaped area between the Dipylon and Sacred Gates (see fig. 246B). It takes the form of a peristyle court with rooms equipped for dining built off the north and west sides; six rooms provide space for sixty-six diners. The walls of the building are mostly simple limestone blocks, and the columns of the colonnades are unfluted shafts of limestone; they are spaced far enough apart to suggest that the upper elements were of wood. The general impression of economy is mitigated only at the east side, where a handsome marble propylon

Opposite 129. Tomb of the Lakedaimonians in the Kerameikos, 403 B.C., from the east (church of Aghia Triada visible above). (Cf. fig. 246)

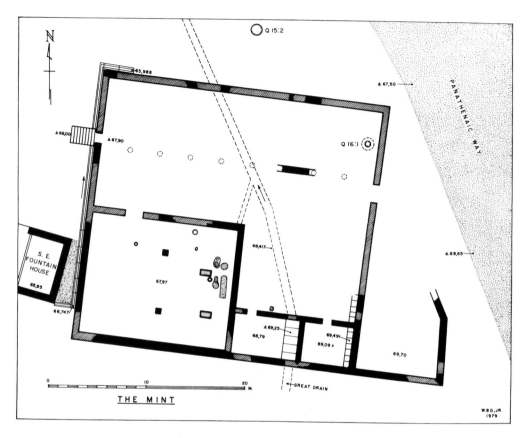

131. Plan of the Mint, ca. 400 B.C. (Cf. fig. 121 for location)

gave access to the building. This gateway is shifted as far north as possible on the east wall, so that any person or procession leaving the Pompeion would have stepped almost directly onto the great Panathenaic Way. A highlight of the Panathenaic procession was the conveyance to the citadel of a new, ornately woven robe, which was displayed as though it were a sail, hanging from the mast of a wheeled ship. Heavy wheel ruts through the propylon

may reflect the passage of the ship as it set out from the

132. The Pompeion in the Kerameikos, ca. 400 B.C., from the southeast.

Pompeion on its voyage to the Acropolis, though as the Pompeion was used also to store grain, much of the wear may derive from supply carts. The Panathenaia also involved the sacrifice of dozens of animals, whose meat was then divided among the citizens for a huge feast, said to have taken place in the Kerameikos. Presumably most of the throng picnicked outside, and the Pompeion dining rooms may have been reserved for priests and other high officials in charge of the festival.

Literary sources indicate that the building was decorated with statues and paintings, including those of famous comic poets. An inscription on the marble dado of the eastern wall reads, "Menandros," presumably the label of a portrait of Menander painted on the wall above. Other inscriptions nearby seem far less formal; they are the names of youths, some grouped under the heading "friends." Similar informal graffiti are found scratched on the walls of assorted gymnasia throughout the Greek world, the ancient equivalent of carving one's name on one's desk. At various times the Pompeion apparently accommodated bored young Athenians waiting to take their part in the processions which originated in the building.

THE FOURTH CENTURY

Soon after 400 the Athenians were once again embroiled in war against Sparta, this time with Persian support at sea and in alliance with Corinth, Thebes, and Argos on land. Much of the fighting took place around Corinth, and the struggle is often referred to as the Corinthian War (395–387 B.C.). During a skirmish at Corinth in 394, five Athenian cavalrymen were killed. As was the custom, they were buried at state expense in the public burial ground (Demosion Sema) outside the city walls. The crowning block of their collective tombstone has been found, along with a relief commemorating them (*IG* II² 5221, 5222). In addition, the family of one of the knights, Dexileos of the deme of Thorikos, set up a separate sculpted monument in the family burial plot outside the Sacred Gate. The relief   133 shows a mounted horseman riding down a fallen warrior. An inscription on the base reads,

> Dexileos, son of Lysanias, of Thorikos. He was born when Teisander was archon [414/3 B.C.] and died when Euboulides was archon [394/3]. One of the five knights who died in Corinth. (*IG* II² 6217)

What is notable about this text is the fact that it gives the birth and death dates of Dexileos. Although such information is standard on gravestones today, it is almost without parallel in antiquity. There are well over ten thousand grave markers extant from Athens and Attica, and only a handful provide even the age of the deceased; none give the date of birth and death. There must have been some strong motive for the family to have had them inscribed in this particular instance. The best explanation is to be found in the turmoil surrounding the rule of the Thirty Tyrants. Their strongest supporters, and the most conservative element in Athenian society, were the aristocratic knights, and a general animosity toward them as a class had to be controlled by means of an amnesty, though ill will lingered on so tenaciously that many preferred to take up foreign service as mercenaries. By inscribing his birth date, the family invites the viewer to determine that Dexileos was only eleven years old during the events of 404, and thus innocent of any undemocratic tendencies shown at that time by other members of his class.

At sea a Persian fleet commanded by the Athenian admiral Konon defeated the Spartans in 394 off Knidos, in southwest Asia Minor. With Persian help and money, Athens was soon in a position to rebuild the walls torn down at the end of the Peloponnesian War:

Pharnabazos eagerly dispatched him [Konon] to Athens and gave him additional money for the rebuilding of the walls. Upon his arrival Konon erected a large part of the wall, offering his own crews for the work, paying the wages of carpenters and masons, and meeting whatever expense was necessary. There were some parts of the wall, however, which the Athenians themselves, as well as volunteers from Boiotia and from other cities, helped build. (Xenophon, *Hellenika* 4.8.9–10)

Several inscriptions have been found which record payments to contractors for material and labor for different sections of these fortifications. They are dated by

134

133. Grave stele of Dexileos, with inscribed base giving his birth and death dates, 395/4 B.C. (Cf. fig. 246)

134. Building inscription concerning the reconstruction of the walls of Athens under Konon, in the archonship of Philokles, 392/1 B.C.

the year, from 393 to 390, and were apparently actually set into the mudbrick superstructure of the wall. The stretches rebuilt by Konon have been recognized at various places around Athens, along the long walls, and particularly in the circuit around the Peiraieus. The lower part of the wall is a stone socle several courses high (see fig. 136), with the upper parts done in sun-dried mudbrick. There were towers at regular intervals and battlements along the top of the curtain wall.

The Corinthian War ended when peace of a sort was imposed on the Greeks by Persia in 387/6, and in 378 Athens established a new maritime league, which promised far more equality to the allies than the Delian League of the fifth century. Economic prosperity and full recovery, however, did not return to Athens until near the middle of the fourth century. Except for the few modest examples presented above, the first half of the century was a time of limited public building in Athens.

When prosperity returned, it was fueled in large part by the exploitation of the silver mines at Laureion in south Attica. We have already seen how the mines affected Athenian fortunes in the Persian Wars, by allowing the construction of the fleet, and in the Peloponnesian War, when they were a target of the Spartan occupation of Dekeleia. In the fourth century the mines were run in an extremely organized fashion. The mineral rights were owned by the state and leased out to individuals; the cost of a lease varied tremendously, depending on whether it was for a speculative new venture or a well-established, productive mine. Detailed accounts of the leases were kept by the *poletai* (state auctioneers; Aristotle, *Ath. Pol.* 47) and written up on stone stelai. Dozens of these stelai survive to give a vivid impression of the intense activity in the mining district from 367 to 307/6.

> Mines were leased. . . . In the second prytany, that of Antiochis, at Laureion, the same [the Artemisiakon mine] and the cuttings, of which the boundaries are on the north [property of] Diopeithes of Euonymon and the furnace of Demostratos of Kytheros, on the south the workshop of Diopeithes and the wagon road and the ravine of the Thorikioi, the lessee, Kephisodotos of Aithalidai, the price, 20 drachmas. (Agora I 5509)

Well-established mines were named, often after a deity. The mines were worked by slaves, and fortunes could be made from them. Nikias, the Peloponnesian War general, was one such individual. We are told that he consulted diviners and that

> most of his inquiries were made about his own private matters and especially about his silver mines; for he had large interests in the mining district of Laureion, and they were exceedingly profitable, although worked at great risk. He maintained a multitude of slaves in these mines, and most of his substance was in silver. (Plutarch, *Nikias* 4)

Laureion was a district in southern Attica, and several demes fell within its area: Sounion, Besa, Anaphlystos, and Thorikos (see fig. 270). The valleys there are littered with the remains of the mining installations: mine adits and passages, ventilation shafts, workshops (*ergasteria*) where the ore was processed, furnaces to smelt it, and slag heaps.

Several of the ore washeries and furnaces have been excavated. The washeries consist of a large square platform surfaced with lime mortar, with a channel running around all four sides. Crushed ore was placed on the platform and washed into the channels. As the water flowed along the channels, it was slowed by means of settling basins, where the heavier, metal-bearing ore sank, while the lighter soil, gravel, and other impurities were carried on. The ore would be removed from the settling basins and spread on the platform to dry, after which it was ready for smelting.

The procedure required large amounts of water, never a ready commodity in Attica, and every effort was made to recycle and conserve it. Near each washery was a huge cistern, designed to trap and save as much rainwater as possible. The furnaces are usually found down by the coast, removed from the mines and washeries. This may be for reasons of health or, more likely, because the immense amount of wood or charcoal needed for fuel presumably had to be imported by ship, as Attica is also poor in timber.

The silver would then be refined to a high degree of purity; Athenian coins were trusted and circulated widely throughout the Mediterranean. From the beginnings of Athenian coinage, sometime in the sixth century B.C., come small silver coins carrying a wide variety of devices: wheels, amphoras, horses. In the late sixth century a single standard design was adopted, showing the head of Athena in profile on the obverse and an owl with olive sprig and the legend AΘE on the reverse. Once established, this type survived essentially unchanged for several hundred years.

135

In the Hellenistic period, when the sizes of the silver coins were changed, inscriptions and other elements became more prominent, but the head of Athena and the owl still appeared on each side, ensuring that the coin would be recognized as an Athenian product.

135. Athenian silver coins, 5th to 2nd century B.C.

We have not yet found the building in which the silver coins were minted, though it seems to have been in the city; inscriptions have been found referring to it or to its administrative officials, the *epistatai*. The mint excavated in the Agora is not old enough for the earliest Athenian silver coinage, and analysis of material recovered from it suggests that only bronze was processed there.

One of the mining demes, Thorikos, has been under excavation and provides a complementary view of the economy of southern Attica when the mines were being actively exploited in the fourth century. One striking feature of the city's layout is the intermingling of various aspects of daily life. Mine adits, ore washeries, private houses, cemeteries, public buildings, and sanctuaries are all crowded together, side by side (see figs. 271, 272). This higgledy-piggledy urban arrangement can also be seen in an excavated section of the deme of Aixone and in the residential area southwest of the Agora. There is a handsome theater in the town of Thorikos, one of the earliest in Greece and one of the first to be excavated. It was laid out originally in the late sixth century, though only the retaining wall for the orchestra survives from this period. In the fifth century the theater had stone seats; the orchestra is an unusual shape: essentially rectilinear with straight rows of seats that are curved only at the end of each row. In the middle years of the fourth century the auditorium was enlarged, and the seating capacity was more than doubled, to six thousand, a huge number for an average-sized deme. Presumably this is a reflection of a large increase in population during the mining boom.

In foreign affairs, Athens took an important but secondary role in the 370s and 360s as Sparta, Thebes, and Thessaly contended for the hegemony of Greece. The northwest border of Attica was apparently a matter of concern, as powerful Theban and Spartan armies passed by with some frequency. In the 370s, a long wall was constructed across the gap known as the Dema, between Mount Aigaleos and Mount Parnes, in an attempt to close the natural invasion route into Attica from the Eleusinian plain. This is the route followed by King Archidamos during his invasions early in the Peloponnesian War (Thucydides 2.19). The gap was closed by a wall some 6 kilometers long, constructed of polygo-

nal masonry about 2 meters high on the downhill side and pierced with numerous open-
ings to allow flexibility for fighting in front of it.

In the 350s Athens became embroiled in central Greece, where the city's traditional
allies the Phocians were accused of sacrilege for plundering the sanctuary at Delphi. This
sacred war provided the occasion for a new player to enter the political arena in the mainland of Greece: King Philip II of Macedon. Throughout the 340s Macedonia's expanding
power up north was of concern to the Athenians, for it threatened their access to mineral
wealth, to timber for the fleet from Macedonia and Thrace, and to crucial shipping routes
to the Black Sea, source of much imported grain. The continuing pressure of the war and
the Athenian reaction to Philip's successes are documented in a series of speeches, the
Olynthiacs and the *Philippics,* delivered by the orator Demosthenes in the debate over
Athens' priorities and policies. As so often, the choice was expressed in terms of military action versus domestic development:

> Let someone come forward and tell me who but ourselves has made Philip pow-
> erful.
>
> "But," some might say, "if this [foreign policy] goes badly, in the city itself
> things are better." And what would one say was? The battlements which we
> plaster, the roads we are repairing, the fountains, and the trifles? (*Olynthiac*
> 3.29)

In 338 Philip moved south and soundly defeated a combined Theban and Athenian
army at Chaironeia in central Greece. In many ways this defeat was a key turning point in
Greek history, for it marks the beginning of the end of the polis (city-state) as an autonomous,
independent political unit. After Chaironeia, the Greek city-states continued, but they fell under the domination first of Macedonia and then of a succession of Hellenistic monarchs. Im-

mediately after the battle the
Athenians tried desperately to
improve their fortifications.
Demosthenes himself served as
one of the wall builders (*tei-*

136. The city wall of Athens where it
passes through the Kerameikos,
stone socle with mudbrick above,
5th to 4th century B.C.

137. The city wall of Athens, northwest quadrant, with the Sacred Gate (right), the Dipylon Gate (left),
5th century B.C., before the addition of a moat and outer wall in the 4th century. (Watercolor by
Peter Connolly)

chopoios), spending ten talents of public money and three talents of his own to repair his assigned section. The great haste with which this wall went up is reminiscent of the original
Themistoklean circuit, and it is said to have been built in a similar fashion.   136, 137

> Yet men of every age offered their services for the city's defense on that occasion,
> when the land was giving up its trees, the dead their gravestones, and the temples
> their armor. Some set themselves to building walls, others to making ditches and
> palisades. Not a man in the city was idle. (Lykourgos, *Against Leokrates* 44)

And:

> Indeed it is not for surrounding the walls with palisades and not for tearing
> down the public tombs that the statesman of clean record ought to ask for re-
> wards, but for having been responsible for some good to the city. (Aischines,
> *Ktesiphon* 236)

It is perhaps at this time that the outer wall (*proteichisma*) and dry moat were added outside
the original line, impinging on burials made near the wall.

138. The theater of Dionysos, seen from the Acropolis, 4th century B.C., with later additions.

In the end, Philip's terms of settlement were surprisingly mild, and the Athenians made peace with no further hostilities. Following the death of Philip in 336, his son, Alexander, turned his attention and resources to the conquest of the Persian Empire. The third quarter of the fourth century was a relatively prosperous time for Athens, first under the administration of the financial expert Euboulos, who seems to have started various projects, and then under the leadership of the statesman and orator Lykourgos, who brought the projects to completion. Many important new buildings were begun during this period, several of which are specifically attributed to Lykourgos:

> He built the ship sheds, and the arsenal, and the Dionysiac theater, and he finished the Panathenaic stadium, and he equipped the gymnasium of the Lyceum. (Plutarch, *Vit. X Orat.* 852C)

Several of the buildings mentioned in Plutarch's account are known and are well preserved, others still await discovery.

On the south slopes of the Acropolis the great theater of Dionysos was built with limestone seats, the form in which we see it today. Capable of holding some fifteen to seventeen   138, 139
thousand spectators, it replaced the much simpler version that stood on the same spot,
where the plays of Aischylos, Sophokles, Euripides, and Aristophanes had first been produced in the fifth century. The auditorium reached up to the base of the Acropolis rock,
which had to be quarried away in places. Handsome marble thrones (*proedria*) were placed
in a row around the edge of the orchestra for officials, priests, visiting dignitaries, and others honored by the city, all of whom could expect to be awarded front-row seats at the performances. A large colonnaded stone scene-building served as the backdrop for the action
of the plays and choruses, while a huge drain around the edge of the orchestra carried off
rainwater.

The round form of the orchestra is first attested with certainty in this Lykourgan
phase of the 330s, and it is repeated at the great theater of Epidauros. Other evidence from
Attica, however, indicates that round orchestras may be a late development and that originally orchestras were rectilinear (see figs. 258, 272, 273). This is the arrangement we find

139. The theater of Dionysos, seen from the northwest, with the Odeion of Perikles in the background.
(Watercolor by Peter Connolly)

in the theater at Thorikos, which is earlier than the one in Athens. It also seems to be the case at several other early deme theaters: at Euonymon (Helleniko/Trachones), Rhamnous, and even Ikaria, with its traditions of early influence on Attic drama. The seat blocks which survive from the fifth-century theater of Dionysos are also straight rather than curved.

The orchestra is the dancing ground where the chorus performed; in early Greek drama it was the focal point of the action. Over time, after the addition of actors to the performances, the chorus became less significant and the role of the actors greater. This shift in emphasis led to changes in the form of the theater: the orchestra became smaller, and the stage was raised and moved forward toward the auditorium. The orchestra paving and the sculpted frieze of the stage in the theater of Dionysos represent later additions and rebuilding in the Roman period (see figs. 201, 202).

Elsewhere in the sanctuary a second temple was built for Dionysos in the latter part of

140

140. The theater of Dionysos from the east showing seats and thrones (*proedria*) (4th century B.C.), orchestra paving (1st to 2nd century A.D.), and raised stage at left (4th to 5th century A.D.).

the fourth century. Of this temple only the foundations survive, indicating that it consisted of a simple cella with a colonnaded porch on the front end. The foundations of a large base inside presumably held the chryselephantine statue by Alkamenes described by Pausanias.

The plays and the performances of choral lyric in the theater were held as competitions, and the sanctuary was adorned with monuments commemorating victories in these events. Indirectly associated with the theater was the so-called Street of the Tripods, which led from the sanctuary of Dionysos eastward around the Acropolis, toward the Prytaneion. The street takes its name from the dozens of prize tripods put on display along its length. The cost of producing a play or a choral performance in Athens was a form of taxation levied on the rich citizens of the city, who were appointed to pay for salaries, costumes, music, and the like. These wealthy individuals were known as *choregoi* (producers), or the leaders of the chorus. The choregos responsible for the winning production was awarded a tripod, a large bronze cauldron supported on three legs. He would often then build an elaborate little monument to display his prize. Only one monument survives in good condition along the Street of the Tripods, that of Lysikrates. The dedicatory inscription tells us that he won a dithyramb in 335/4:

141

Lysikrates, son of Lysitheides of Kikynna, was the choregos. The tribe of Akamantis won the boys' chorus. Theon played the flute. Lysiades the Athenian directed. Euainetos was archon. (*IG* II² 3042)

The monument takes the form of a small cylindrical building of the Corinthian order, set on a high podium. The Pentelic marble columns represent the earliest use of the Corinthian order on the exterior of a building. The spaces between the columns were originally intended to be open, to display a statue. They were soon closed with curved slabs of Hymettian marble, appar-

141. The monument of the choregos Lysikrates, built to display the bronze tripod won for producing a winning chorus, 335 B.C.

Left 142. Monument of Lysikrates, detail of roof and frieze.

Right 143. Monument of Lysikrates, frieze: a pirate turning into a dolphin.

ently because the great weight of the roof threatened the stability of the monument. Above the columns was a sculpted frieze showing Dionysos, captured by pirates, turning his captors into dolphins. The roof is crowned by an elaborately carved floral finial which supported the tripod itself.

142, 143

Southeast of the city, across the Ilissos River, a natural ravine between two hills was chosen as the site of the Panathenaic stadium (see fig. 247), where many of the athletic contests of the Panathenaic festival were held. Though the natural slopes undoubtedly helped with the seating, the project was nevertheless a huge landscaping operation, as we learn from the following inscription, passed in honor of Eudemos of Plataia in 329 B.C.:

> Resolved by the people; Lykourgos, son of Lykophron of Boutadai proposed it. Since Eudemos in former times announced to the people a gift of 4,000 drachmas for the war if needed, and now has provided for the construction of the stadium and the Panathenaic theater a thousand pairs of draft animals and arranged all things for the procession before the Panathenaia as he promised; resolved by the people to praise Eudemos . . . (*IG* II² 351)

Earlier, both the theatrical and athletic contests seem to have been held in the Agora. The new stadium was similar to many being built in Greece at about this time, with one end open, the other curved and closed. The details of the original construction are obscured by a rebuilding of the stadium in marble in the second century A.D.

With these great buildings Lykourgos provided splendid venues for the two principal festivals of the city, the Panathenaia and the Dionysia. His attention to the Lyceum indicates an interest in the cultural and educational life of the city. The Lyceum was one of several gymnasia in Athens, second in fame only to the Academy and the philosophical school founded there by Plato in the 380s. The Lyceum, originally a grove dedicated to Apollo Lykeios, became almost equally famous as the location of the school founded by Aristotle in 335.

The gymnasia were the natural venues for the education of the youth of the city. Given over to the training of the body since the sixth century, gymnasia gradually became centers for training the mind as well, and lectures, philosophical discussions, and instruction in other subjects were offered. A cluster of objects relating indirectly to the Lyceum found in the area of Syntagma Square and the National Gardens suggests that the great gymnasium should be sought there.

Military installations in the Peiraieus also were rebuilt under Lykourgos, and perhaps under Euboulos as well. In particular, the harbors were lined with ship sheds once again, replacing those dismantled under the Thirty Tyrants in 404/3. These housed the Athenian warships, the triremes. The ships were used during the sailing season, but for much of the year they were pulled out of the water in order to prevent them from becoming waterlogged. The sheds take the form of sloping ramps perpendicular to the shore, with a deep cutting to carry the keel of each ship; rows of unfluted columns running parallel to the cuttings supported the simple sloping roofs that protected the ships. Several representations of triremes survive, but the sheds provide the clearest evidence for size of the ships. The ramps are 30–35 meters long and about 6.5 meters wide. Inscriptions (*IG* II² 1604–1632) describe the condition and strength of the Athenian fleet at various times in the fourth century. From them we learn that there were a total of 372 ship sheds by 325 B.C., 94 in the large harbor of Kantharos, 196 in the war harbor at Zea, and 82 in the small harbor of Mounychia (see fig. 260).

Closely associated with the ship sheds was a great arsenal in Zea, actually a storeroom (*skeuotheke*) for the hanging tackle of the fleet, the ropes and sails. This, too, was finished under Lykourgos, and the architect's name, Philon, survives. It was a huge building, 400 feet long, 55 feet wide, and 30 feet high (120 by 17 by 9 meters). Until recently, all of our information concerning this building came from literary sources and an extraordinarily well-preserved inscription of ninety-seven-lines, which lists the specifications the architect was required to follow—the most detailed description we have of any ancient building. The inscription mentions two architects, Euthydomos and Philon, but Philon wrote a book about

144. Athenian ship sheds, 4th century B.C. The three harbors of the Peiraieus had a total of 372 such sheds. (Cf. fig. 260) (Watercolor by Peter Connolly)

the arsenal, cited by Vitruvius, and history has given him the lion's share of the credit. As noted, Lykourgos finished the building, but these specifications were recorded as early as 347/6 B.C.:

Specifications for the stone skeuotheke for the hanging tackle, by Euthydo-mos, son of Demetrios, of Melite, and Philon, son of Exekestides, of Eleusis. To build a skeuotheke for hanging tackle, in Zea, starting from the propy-

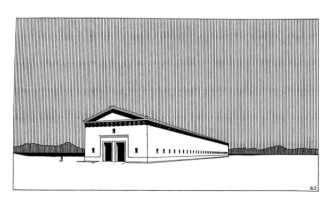

145. Drawing of the arsenal of Philon in the Peiraieus, built to house the tackle of the Athenian war fleet, 4th century B.C.

lon from the Agora behind the ship sheds covered with a single roof, with a
length of 4 *plethra*, a width of 55 feet, including the walls. Excavate the plot to no
less than 3 feet from the highest point, remove the debris, and lay foundations
on firm ground, making them level and straight everywhere, according to the
rule. Lay foundations for the piers as well, at a distance of 15 feet from either
wall, including the thickness of the piers, the number of piers in each row being
thirty-five, thus leaving a passage for the public through the middle of the arsenal 20 feet in width between the piers; the width of the foundations shall be 4
feet, and the stones shall be placed alternately as stretchers and headers. Build
the walls and the piers of the arsenal of stone from *akte* [local Peiraiean poros],
laying a leveling course (*euthynteria*) for the walls of blocks 3 feet wide, $1\frac{1}{2}$ feet
high, and 4 feet long, but $4\frac{3}{4}$ feet at the corners . . . (*IG* II² 1668)

The specifications are precise enough to have allowed the identification of the building in two modern building plots recently excavated (1990s) in the Peiraieus. The two plots
are dozens of meters apart, but one contains foundations which correspond to the description of the doors at the northern end of the building, and the other has pier supports exactly
matching the spacing called for in the specifications. The building is as described: at the
war harbor of Zea, just behind the ship sheds. The complex administration of the navy at
this period is reflected in a series of inscriptions (*IG* II² 1602–1632) recording the condition of individual triremes and their equipment. Proper maintenance was a public service
(*leitourgia*), or form of taxation, and the inscriptions record the handing over of ships, oars,
and tackle from one group of wealthy men to another. Many ships are listed by name, usually feminine and appropriate: Lioness, Victory, Freedom, Peace, Virtue, and an array of female deities, Artemis, Nemesis, Aphrodite.

Concerns for the well-being of the navy were matched by concern for the land army as
well. As noted, many of the border demes of Attica were already fortified by the time of the
Peloponnesian War: Eleusis, Oinoe, Rhamnous, Thorikos, and Sounion. The date of the
fortification of Phyle is uncertain, and Dekeleia was fortified thanks to the Spartans. Other
forts protected the border as well, though they were not associated with a specific deme. 146
Panakton, for instance, was a bone of contention between Athens and Thebes, and the fort
at Eleutherai seems to have changed hands more than once. Numerous other forts and towers, unrecorded in the literature and known only from archaeological investigation, made
up an important part of the defenses of Attica. All these forts and supplementary towers
were maintained and actively used in the fourth century, and new installations were built as
well.

In addition, a program of military training for the youth of Athens, the ephebes, was

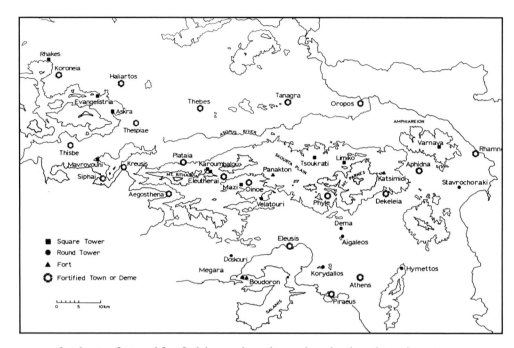

146. Athenian forts and fortified demes along the northern border, 5th to 4th century B.C.

formalized. Young men of eighteen were expected to spend two years in military service. For part of that time they were assigned to duty in one of the big forts: Peiraieus, Eleusis, Phyle, Panakton, Rhamnous, and Sounion. Numerous inscriptions concerning these garrisons have been found at all these forts except Phyle, which is mentioned in other accounts. Aristotle describes the service of ephebes in his *Constitution of the Athenians* (*Ath. Pol.* 42):

> An assembly is held in the theater, and the ephebes give a display of drill before the people and receive a shield and spear from the state; and then they serve on patrols in the country and are quartered at the guard posts. Their service on patrol lasts for two years; the uniform is a mantle; they are exempt from all taxes.

The architect of the arsenal, Philon, is also known for his work at his home deme of Eleusis, where he was awarded the contract for constructing a huge marble porch (*prostoon*) on the east facade of the Telesterion (see figs. 98, 256). The Periklean building, though huge, had no exterior columns. Inscriptions and literary sources again provide considerable information, and the architectural elements are scattered all over the site itself. The column shafts are unfluted, indicating that the trim was never finished, but enough of the frieze and cornice survive to suggest that structurally the porch was completed. From inscriptions it is clear that this work, too, was begun earlier, in the 350s (*IG* II² 1666), and only finished by Lykourgos after 330 (*IG* II² 1671). Vitruvius (7 *praef.* 17) even suggests that the building was not finished until 317–307. Column drums were still being brought from the quarries on Mount Pentele in the 320s. It took thirty-three teams of draft animals three days to drag each column drum from the quarry to the sanctuary (*IG* II² 1673, ll. 66 ff.), a distance of about 33 kilometers, at a cost of about four hundred drachmas per drum.

Between them, Euboulos and Lykourgos were responsible for an impressive program of both new buildings and rebuildings which revived the city after the effects of the loss of the Peloponnesian War. Military, cultural, and religious activities in Athenian life were all provided with suitable structures in the second half of the fourth century. Several other projects undertaken at this time are in all probability associated with their tenure as well, though there are no specific epigraphical or literary sources linking them.

First among these is the refurbishment of the old meeting place of the Assembly, the Pnyx. In use since the years around 500, then reoriented by the Thirty Tyrants in 403, the   147
Pnyx was rebuilt sometime around 345–335. In this third phase a large stepped speakers'

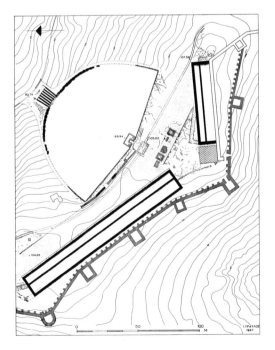

platform (*bema*) was quarried out of the ridge at the southwest. The auditorium was supported on a large curved retaining wall made up of massive trapezoidal blocks, among the biggest ever quarried in Athens. The wall is three courses high, rising to just over 5 meters. It is not clear how much higher it might have gone, but as preserved the wall lies some 8 meters below the level of the base of the bema and could not have supported even a level floor, let alone an auditorium sloping down to the bema. It seems as if this grandiose plan   148
was never fully carried out, perhaps from

147. Plan of the Pnyx and the two unfinished stoas above it, ca. 340–330 B.C.

148. The final (unfinished?) phase of the Pnyx, with the speaker's platform (*bema*) in the center of the long scarp (cf. fig. 127), and the curved retaining wall at left. View from the north, with the Philopappos monument in the background.

lack of funds or because the newly completed theater of Dionysos proved so congenial a meeting place that no other was needed. Two stoas laid out on the ridge above at the same time had their foundation trenches excavated before they, too, were abandoned and never finished.

The Asklepieion, adjacent to the theater, seems to have received special attention in the later part of the fourth century. Laid out, as we have seen, in the fifth century (see fig. 114), the original sanctuary consisted of the sacred spring, an altar, and an enclosure wall; a nearby Ionic stoa with four rooms may also have been part of the early shrine. It is clear from the inventories and references to the priests that the Athenian state took over administration of the cult sometime after its foundation by a private individual, Telemachos. By the end of the fourth century the sanctuary had been provided with a small temple, an altar, and, most imposing, a two-storied stoa.

The stoa was Doric on the outside, presumably with Ionic columns inside. It was set right up against the Acropolis rock, which was quarried back to receive it. On the second

149

floor of its western end it housed a large pit, carefully lined with polygonal masonry. Four column bases still in place suggest that the pit was separately roofed. The pit was empty when excavated, so its function is uncertain, though it would do nicely to house snakes or receive libations. Both are appropriate for a hero, and as Asklepios started out as a hero, the pit may accommodate that aspect of his divinity, while the altar and temple accommodate him as a god. There is a similar juxtaposition of cult installations in his great sanctuary at Epidauros. The stoa otherwise was probably used as a dormitory where those coming to be healed would sleep until the god appeared to them in a dream and brought about a cure. At Epidauros there are dozens of inscriptions recording the miraculous cures of suppliants who slept in the sanctuary there.

Inscribed accounts from the Asklepieion at Athens record the safe-keeping of the god's sacred property. They document either a simple annual transferral of the sacred treasures to the incoming priest or an official record made before the small votives of silver or gold were melted down to make large metal vessels. In the latter case the weights of the objects and the names of the dedicators were carefully recorded for posterity. Asklepios receives the usual range of gifts familiar from other cults, but there is a preference for coins,

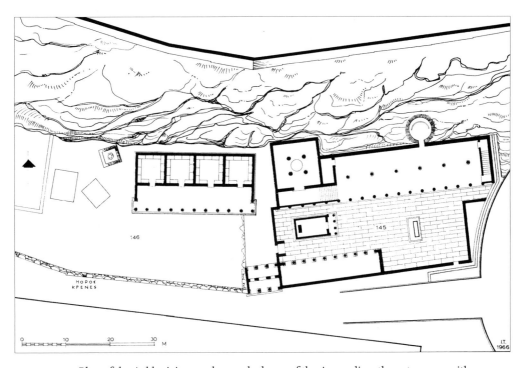

149. Plan of the Asklepieion on the south slopes of the Acropolis, 4th century B.C. with Roman additions.

Top 150. Plan of the Agora in the second half of the 4th century B.C. (Cf. fig. 177)

Bottom 151. Plan of the temple of Apollo Patroos in the Agora, ca. 330 B.C.

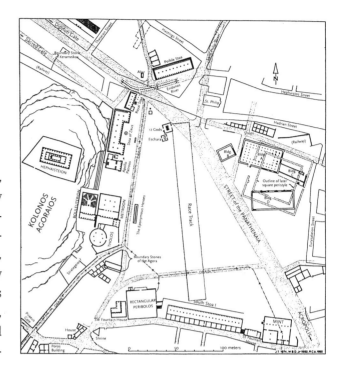

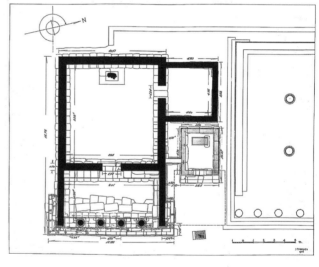

representations of body parts, and small reliefs that usually showed a person praying. Because they were of gold or silver, these objects rarely survive, and they are known primarily from the accounts. Body parts include eyes, heads, torsos, arms, legs, genitalia, jaws, and innards. By far the most frequent type is eyes (in the days before spectacles), followed by torsos. Other dedications listed include jewelry, a silver snake, and a shell carved in Parian marble.

In the Agora, the temple of Apollo Patroos (Ancestral) was built in its present form in the second half of the 150, 151 fourth century. The temple had columns across the front (east) only. It is usually restored with four columns *in antis* (between the spur [antae] walls), but it is equally possible—and perhaps more likely—that there were six columns in a prostyle arrangement. By the time Pausanias visited Athens in about A.D. 150, there were three statues in the temple, sculpted by Euphranor, Leochares, and Kalamis (1.3.4). A monumental statue of Apollo dressed as a kithara player was found nearby and is now on display in the

Stoa of Attalos. It is presumably the one Pausanias saw, done by Euphranor, who worked in   152
the fourth century. Lykourgos may have been associated with this temple as well; he is said
to have concerned himself with an altar of Apollo in the Agora:

> He also made a proposal to crown Neoptolemos, son of Antikles, and to set up a
> likeness of him because he offered to gild the altar of Apollo in the agora in ac-
> cordance with an oracle of the god. (Plutarch, *Moralia,* 843 f.)

This Neoptolemos, friend of Lykourgos, is mentioned as a rich
man in a speech by Demosthenes
and is associated with other religious dedications and public
works. A very fine relief of a scene
in the cave of Pan, found south of
the Agora, carries his name as
dedicator (see fig. 112).

An important Athenian land-
mark, the Monument of the
Eponymous Heroes, was set up   153
along the west side of the Agora in
the third quarter of the fourth
century. Reflecting the tribal
structure created by the Kleisthenic reforms of the late sixth
century, the monument consisted
of a long base carrying statues of
the ten heroes after whom the
ten tribes were named: Hippo-
thoon, Antiochos, Ajax, Leos,
Erechtheus, Aigeus, Oineus, Aka-
mas, Kekrops, and Pandion. Every   154
citizen was enrolled in one of the

152. Marble statue of Apollo Patroos
by Euphranor, ca. 350–330 B.C.

153. View of the Monument of the Eponymous Heroes from the south, ca. 330 B.C.

ten tribes and thereby had an ancestral hero on a par with the aristocrats. The base of the monument served as a public notice board, with announcements concerning members of a given tribe posted on the face of the base beneath the statue of the eponymous hero. The Eponymoi were set up in the Agora as early as the fifth century (Aristophanes, *Peace* 1183–84), and their original base has been recognized in some poorly preserved foundations near the southwest corner of the Agora. The present base was set up just across from the archive building (Metroon) and senate house (Bouleuterion), where Aristotle saw it (*Ath. Pol.* 53.4).

Other political monuments were also built in the fourth century in the Agora. There is reason to suppose that a series of rectangular buildings constructed in the northeast cor-

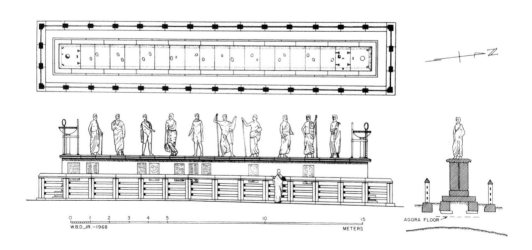

154. Drawing showing the restored Monument of the Eponymous Heroes.

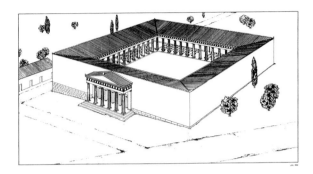

155. Drawing of the square peristyle, identified as one of the law courts of Athens, ca. 300 B.C.

ner of the square served as law courts; one of them preserved a crude container with seven jurors' ballots, and finds of other court equipment cluster in that area. Athenian courts, like our own, were an extremely important part of the government, as they both interpreted and passed on the legality of any new legislation. They were regularly made up of either 201 or 501 jurors and met at a number of locations around the city. Some seem to have convened in the enclosures and colonnades built during the fourth century in the Agora. The latest took the form of a large square peristyle. Like several other projects of the late fourth century, however, it seems not to have been completed.

155

Another structure dated to around this time is a rare one: a monumental water clock (*klepsydra*). It was set up at the southwest corner of the Agora, in a conspicuous location along the road leading toward the Pnyx. Consisting of a large square stone tank about 2 meters deep, it was filled with water and then emptied gradually throughout the day. The falling level of the water was displayed in some way to show the passing hours. Its only known parallel is to be found at Oropos in the sanctuary of Amphiaraos (see fig. 276), which was under Athenian control at this time. The Oropos version is in better condition, virtually intact, and it seems likely that both devices were designed by a single individual. The Athenians were busy with other projects at Oropos at this same time: an inscription (*IG* II² 338) of 333 records a crown for one Pytheas, son of Sosidemos, of Alopeke, for repairing a fountain and seeing to the water system of the sanctuary of Amphiaraos when he was water commissioner.

156

Athens seems to have prospered in the second half of the fourth century despite a serious problem: drought. Several pieces of evidence suggest that water, never plentiful in Attica, was especially difficult to come by during this period. The Athenian response was varied and energetic. A new aqueduct was built to bring water from springs several kilometers away on the lower slopes of Mount Parnes. The channel was carried in an underground tunnel, and a series of inscriptions has been found which allow us to trace its route southward from the area of the deme of Acharnai to the city. In town, two new public fountain houses were built, one beside the Dipylon Gate (perhaps replacing a fifth-century predecessor) and another at the southwest corner of the Agora. Demosthenes' disparaging refer-

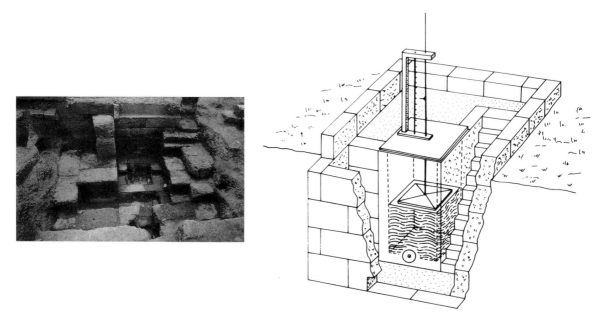

156. Remains and cutaway view of the Agora waterclock, ca. 330–320 B.C.

ence, in *Olynthiac* 3, to fountains may well refer to some of these public measures. As the water table sank and wells ran dry the Athenians started hollowing out rock-cut cisterns, catching whatever rain did fall on the roofs of their houses and carefully saving it. The great cisterns in the mining district at Laureion also reflect concern for the water supply. Numerous honorary inscriptions indicate that the Athenians also worked hard to keep grain coming into the city in abundance and at a reasonable price.

5

Hellenistic Athens

The relative prosperity and peace of Lykourgan Athens came to an end after the death of Alexander the Great in 323. His conquest of Asia led to the eventual spread of Greek culture from Spain to India during the Hellenistic period. Greek language, architecture, and social values were to be found all over this vast area as Alexander's conquests were divided up among his generals and others—Antigonos, Lysimachos, Polyperchon, Cassander, Seleukos, Ptolemy, and Philetairos—into a group of monarchies controlling large amounts of territory. To balance this new political development, individual city-states in Greece were forced to form themselves into leagues in order to collectively match the wealth and size of the new kingdoms.

Like much of the Greek world, Athens was swept up in these wars of succession. An attempt to recover its independence was crushed in 322, and the city fell under the control of a series of Macedonian overlords. In 317 Kassander installed a local philosopher and statesman, Demetrios, son of Phanostratos of Phaleron, as his governor of Athens. During his ten years in office, Demetrios passed various laws, among them sumptuary legislation designed to control ostentatious displays of wealth by aristocrats. The effect was immediate in two areas. The little gems of architecture put up as choregic monuments ceased. The two latest, built near the theater, both date to 320–319, a few years before the legislation was passed.

One was set up just west of the theater of Dionysos. It takes the form of a small Doric temple with six columns across the front. A tripod would have been displayed on top of the pediment, and the dedicatory inscription runs across the architrave (see fig. 219):

Nikias, son of Nikodemos, of Xypete, set this up having won as choregos in the boys' chorus for Kekropis. Pantaleon of Sikyon played the flute. The song was the *Elpenor* of Timotheos. Neaichmos was archon. (*IG* II² 3055)

A second choregic monument, that of Thrasyllos, made use of a natural cave at the top of the auditorium of the theater. A facade of three piers supported a sculpted frieze of wreaths, with the tripod displayed above. According to Pausanias, within the cave Apollo and Artemis were shown shooting down the children of Niobe, though later reuse as a chapel has made it hard to tell whether the scene within the cave was painted or sculpted. The entire facade of the building was intact into the nineteenth century, until it was destroyed during the siege of the Acropolis in 1826–1827. Fortunately, it was drawn by Stuart and Revett and other early travelers before its destruction. The dedicatory inscription reads,

Thrasyllos, son of Thrasyllos of Dekeleia, set this up, being choregos and winning in the mens' chorus for the tribe of Hippothontis. Euios of Chalkis played the flute. Neaichmos was archon. Karidamos son of Sotios directed. (*IG* II² 3056)

The effect of Demetrios' legislation appears on this monument. On the corners were set Hymettian blocks which each carry an inscription:

157. The choregic monument of Thrasyllos, above the theater of Dionysos, 320/19 B.C. The two Corinthian columns above were also built to display prize tripods, in the Roman period.

> The demos was choregos, Pytharatos was archon. Thrasykles, son of Thrasyllos of Dekeleia, was *agonothete*. Hippothontis won the boys' chorus. Theon the Theban played the flute. Pronomos the Theban directed.

And,

> The demos was choregos, Pytharatos was archon. Thrasykles, son of Thrasyllos of Dekeleia, was *agonothete*. Pandionis won the mens' chorus. Nikokles the Ambracian played the flute. Lysippos the Arcadian directed. (*IG* II² 3083 A and B)

The year is 271/0 B.C., and the people of Athens (whether they actually paid or not) are given credit as producers. Thrasykles, son of Thrasyllos, is credited only as an official, the *agonothete,* and allowed to commemorate his office in a far less flashy manner than his father had a generation earlier.

The second piece of sumptuary legislation was far more wide-ranging in terms of its effect on the history of Greek sculpture. A strict limit was put on the type of grave marker which could be erected over tombs. Large and impressive grave markers have a history in Athens going back to the huge funerary urns set up over tombs in the eighth century B.C. Figures of kouroi in the round and sculpted stelai make their appearance in cemeteries in the early sixth century. According to Cicero, several attempts were made thereafter to restrict such ostentatious display. The earliest legislation is attributed to Solon, in the first half of the sixth century:

> Later, when extravagance in expenditure and mourning grew up, it was abolished by the law of Solon. (Cicero, *Laws* 2.25)

Several marble kouroi dating to the second half of the sixth century are known from Attic cemeteries, along with one rare example of a kore (maiden), named Phrasikleia. A second restriction was therefore necessary and was implemented at some unspecified period after Solon:

> Somewhat later, on account of the enormous size of the tombs which we now see in the Kerameikos, it was provided by law that "no one should build one which required more than three days' work for ten men." Nor was it permitted to adorn a tomb with stucco work (?) nor to place upon it a herm, as they are called. (*Laws* 2.64–65)

158. The street of the tombs in the Kerameikos, looking west. Grave plot of Dexileos on left.

This law too, which seems from the lack of grave stelai to have been in effect from the early years of the fifth century, also was abandoned or rescinded by around 425. At that time the Athenians once again began decorating their tombs with elaborate monuments, especially sculpted reliefs of the departed, often shown with members of the family. Over time these stelai became more and more elaborate and larger, with the reliefs becoming deeper and deeper until the figures were virtually sculptures in the round. The stele for Dexileos (see fig. 133) is a good example of the early type, and the Kerameikos excavations have brought to light dozens of late fourth-century examples, now on display in the Kerameikos and National museums. They are among the finest individual pieces of surviving Classical art.

158, 159, 160

They were also expensive and—like the choregic monuments—provided an opportunity for ostentatious display by the wealthy, just the sort of thing sumptuary legislation was meant to curb. A third attempt to restrict such ostentation was undertaken by Demetrios, according to Cicero again:

But Demetrios also tells us that pomp at funerals and extravagance in monuments increased again to about the degree which obtains for Rome at present.

Demetrios himself limited these practices by law. For this man, as you know, was not only eminent in learning but also a very able citizen in the practical administration and maintenance of the government. He, then, lessened extravagance not only by the provision of a penalty for it but also by a rule in regard to the time of funerals; for he ordered that corpses should be buried before daybreak. But he also placed a limit upon newly erected monuments, providing that nothing should be built above the mound of earth except a small column no higher than three cubits [1.5 meters] or a table or a basin, and he created a magistrate to oversee this legislation. (*Laws* 2.66–67)

With the stroke of a pen an entire branch of Athenian art was brought to a halt. Thereafter, funerary monuments were restricted to large rectangular blocks of solid marble (*mensae*), simple low columns (*columellae*) carrying the inscribed name, patronymic, and demotic of the deceased, or plain marble vessels (*labellae*). These simple forms prevailed

161

Left 159. Grave stele of Hegeso, late 5th century B.C.

Right 160. Kerameikos, grave stele of Demetria and Pamphile (cast), late 4th century B.C.

throughout most of the Hellenistic period, in sharp contrast to their elaborate Classical predecessors.

Athens fell under the control of Antigonos the One-eyed and his son Demetrios in 307/6 B.C. and, at first, relations between ruler and ruled were excellent. The new leaders were honored with statues in the Agora, and when that seemed insufficient they were made eponymous heroes; two new tribes were created and named after them. The blocks of the Monument of the Eponymous Heroes show clear traces of the expansion of the base to accommodate twelve statues rather than the original ten. Money, armor, timber, and grain were all provided, and the city walls were repaired to prepare the city for an attack by Kassander in 306/5 B.C. during the so-called Four Years' War (307/6–304/3). In 304 Kassander took Phyle, Panakton, and the island of Salamis and threatened Athens until Demetrios arrived with a fleet of 350 ships, forcing him to withdraw.

Relations between Athens and Demetrios deteriorated soon afterward; he spent a winter in the city, living a lewd life in the Parthenon, and he had himself initiated into the Eleusinian mysteries at the wrong time and without proper preparation. A revolt was put down in 294, and Macedonian garrisons were established in a fort built on the Mouseion

161. Hellenistic grave markers at the Kerameikos Museum: *trapezai (mensae)* in foreground, *columellae* behind.

Hill west of the Acropolis and on Mounychia Hill in the Peiraieus. The Mouseion garrison was expelled in 286, and only slight traces of the outline of the fort survive; the garrison on Mounychia was not expelled until 280. For much of the third century, Athens was occupied with attempts to free itself of Macedonian control, with help from the Ptolemies of Egypt.

The archaeological remains in the city accurately reflect this nadir in the political fortunes of Athens. Many houses in use in the fourth century seem to have been abandoned in the third, and there are virtually no new public buildings which can be dated with confidence to the third century. The assessment of the traveler Herakleides, writing in the third century B.C., is not flattering:

> The city itself is totally dry and not well-watered, and badly laid out on account of its antiquity. Many of the houses are shabby, only a few useful. Seen by a stranger, it would at first be doubtful that this was the famed city of the Athenians. (Pseudo-Dikaiarchos: K. Muller, *Fragmenta historicum Graecorum* [Paris, 1868–1878], II, fr. 59)

A similar decline is notable in Attica as well. The town of Thorikos, so prosperous and busy in the fourth century (see fig. 272), was completely abandoned in the early third century. And a fine little rectilinear theater recently excavated at the deme site of Euonymon seems to have been built in the years around 325 and abandoned within a half a century (see fig. 273). Only the fortified demes show signs of significant activity in the third century, particularly during the 260s, when a concerted effort was made by the Athenians, Ptolemy of Egypt, and some Peloponnesian allies to free Athens from the Macedonians during what is known as the Chremonidean War.

Several fortified camps at various spots in Attica have been recognized as part of the Ptolemaic effort. One, on the east coast of Attica at modern Porto Raphti, has substantial rubble walls, a number of hastily constructed simple shelters, and evidence of a short occupation. Half the coins found on the site were Ptolemaic bronzes, and many of the amphoras are types known primarily in Egypt. The associated pottery from the site all dates to the period of the war as well, providing one of our best fixed points for the chronology of Hellenistic ceramics. 162

A second fort was built on the island of Patroklos, just off the coast at Sounion (see fig. 270); Pausanias records its Ptolemaic connections (1.1.1):

> Sailing on you come to Laureion, where the Athenians once had silver mines, and to a desert island of no great size called the island of Patroklos; for Patroklos built a fort and erected a palisade around it. This Patroklos was an admiral in command of the Egyptian galleys which Ptolemy, the son of [Ptolemy, the son

162. Koroni peninsula, with traces of the
Ptolemaic fort, 260s B.C.

of] Lagos, sent to help the Athenians when Antigonos, [Go-
natas] son of Demetrios, had in-
vaded their country at the head
of an army and was ravaging it
while his ships blockaded the
coast.

Opposite the island, the Athenians expanded and strengthened the fort at
Sounion at about this time. The new
parts of the walls and a huge artillery
tower built to carry catapults show the
characteristic signs of hasty construction: many of the structure blocks come from plundered grave monuments (see fig. 100). From Athens, Eleusis, Rhamnous, and Sounion
come dozens of garrison inscriptions, indicative of the intense military activity which char-
acterizes the third century.

   Athens was freed from Macedonian control in 229 and continued a close association
with the Ptolemies. In 223 the reigning king, Ptolemy III Euergetes, was made an eponymous hero with a new tribe, Ptolemais, named after him, and a new deme named after his
wife Berenike. The Monument of the Eponymous Heroes in the Agora was extended to include his statue as well, as the number of tribes swelled to thirteen (see figs. 153, 154). Pausanias saw statues of several Ptolemies set up in the Agora, and east of the marketplace, in
an area still covered by the modern houses of Plaka, one of the Ptolemies built the Athenians a new gymnasium.

   While Ptolemy was fostering good relations with Athens, the stock of the Macedonians was sinking lower and lower. In 200, after failing to take Athens itself, Philip V took
out his frustration on the cemeteries outside the walls and on the sanctuaries of Attica:

   Afterward, when the Athenians held their men within the walls, Philip, giving
   the signal to retire, pitched camp at Kynosarges, where there was a precinct of
   Herakles and a gymnasium with a grove around it. But Kynosarges, the Lyceum, and all the sacred and pleasant spots around the city were burned; the
   buildings and even the tombs were destroyed, and nothing consecrated to divine or human use escaped his uncontrollable passion. . . .

While he had devoted his former raid to destroying the tombs around the city, in order that he might leave nothing inviolate, he ordered the temples of the gods which the Athenians had dedicated in all the demes to be torn down and burned; and the land of Attica, with its wonderful adornment of works of art and its abundance of native marble and the skill of its artists, offered material for his rage. For he was not satisfied merely with destroying the temples and statues themselves but even ordered the separate stones to be broken up, lest they be left whole on the piles of ruins. After his anger, or rather objects on which to vent his anger, had been exhausted, he retired from enemy territory to Boiotia and did nothing else worth mentioning in Greece. (Livy 31.23–26)

The likeliest place where evidence for these attacks can be detected is at the temple of Nemesis at Rhamnous, which needed extensive repairs to its eastern facade in the Roman period. The sanctuary at Brauron is also left desolate in the Hellenistic period, and Philip's attack may well have been a factor. Fortified sites, such as Eleusis and Sounion, survived intact. One result of his actions was a decree passed by the Athenians:

163. Sounion, artillery bastion built in part out of marble blocks taken from earlier tombs, 3rd century B.C. (Cf. figs. 100, 266)

164. Gilded bronze leg and sword of an equestrian statue of Demetrios, set up ca. 307/6 B.C. and discarded in a well in the Agora ca. 200 B.C.

All statues and pictures of Philip as well as of all his ancestors in both the male and female line should be taken and destroyed; all holidays, rites, and priesthoods instituted in his honor or that of his forefathers should be disestablished; the places too in which a dedication or an inscription of this import stood should be accursed. (Livy 44.4 – 8)

Demetrios and Antigonos ceased to be eponymous heroes, and in inscriptions referring to them their names were carefully chiseled off. Pieces of a bronze equestrian statue thrown down a well in the Agora

164 in about 200 B.C. can almost certainly be identified as a statue of Demetrios; the fact that it was discarded instead of melted down gives some indication of the passionate hatred behind this *damnatio memoriae*.

The benefaction of the Ptolemaic gymnasium for the Athenians was a precursor of the recovery to take place during the second century B.C. Athens was once again adorned with a series of handsome new marble buildings of various types, almost all paid for by foreign potentates. By this time Athens had lost all military, political, and economic preeminence, but in two areas the city was to remain dominant throughout the Hellenistic and succeeding Roman period: as both the cultural and the educational center of the Mediterranean. The great philosophical schools of the Academy and the Lyceum, as well as the Stoics and Cynics, made Athens the place to study, even when Alexandria and Antioch and other great centers of learning arose. As soon as one Hellenistic king made a grandiose gift of a building to the Athenians, the healthy spirit of rivalry which infuses all of Greek life took over, and others felt the need to compete. In addition to the Ptolemies, the Attalids of Pergamon, the Seleucid dynasty of Syria, King Ariobarzanes of Cappadocia, and perhaps others built the Athenians rich buildings of the sort the citizens could never have paid for themselves.

The Attalids of Pergamon fostered particularly close ties with Athens, and they clearly liked to think of themselves as the successors to the Classical tradition. In a series of bitter battles, they subdued the Gauls who crossed over to Asia Minor in 279/8, and they compared their successes to the Athenian triumphs over the barbarian Persians two hundred years earlier. Statues of defeated Gauls were set up in Athena's sanctuary at Pergamon, and Pausanias reports seeing a series of sculptural groups celebrating these same victories on the Acropolis of Athens (1.25.2):

> At the south wall are figures about 2 cubits [1 meter] high, dedicated by Attalos. They represent the legendary war of the giants who once dwelt around Thrace and the isthmus of Pallene, the fight of the Athenians with the Amazons, the battles with the Medes at Marathon, and the destruction of the Gauls in Mysia.

Attalos I was succeeded in 197 by his son, Eumenes II, who continued to favor the Athenians. Along the south slopes of the Acropolis, just west of the theater of Dionysos, Eumenes built a long colonnade, or stoa, to provide shelter for the thousands of people attending the festival and theatrical events (Vitruvius 5.9.1). The steep hillside presented no 165 great challenge to the engineers, who were familiar with the steep slopes which make up the citadel at Pergamon. Behind the back wall of the stoa and hidden by it, a huge retaining wall was built and supported with buttresses; arches spanned the spaces between the tops of the buttresses. The stoa itself consisted of double colonnades on two stories. On the ground floor, the Doric order was used for the outer colonnade and Ionic for the interior; above, the outer colonnade was Ionic, extended to provide a flat panel for parapet blocks. Within, the upper order is a type known as Pergamene, an adaptation of an Egyptian palm-leaf capital. This type was common in northwest Asia Minor in the Archaic period, and two 166 early treasuries at Delphi have similar capitals, identified as having been built by Klazomenai and Massalia (modern Marseille). These capitals become common again in the

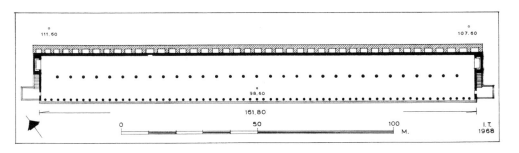

165. Plan of the Stoa of Eumenes on the south slopes of the Acropolis, 196–159 B.C.

166. Column capital from the
Stoa of Eumenes made of
marble from near Pergamon.

Hellenistic period at Perga-
mon and in areas under
Pergamene control, such as
Assos.

An interesting feature
of the stoa of Eumenes is the
evidence for direct influence
in the design and construc-
tion of the building. The Pergamene capitals and
the cornice between upper and lower stories are
of large-crystalled gray marble from the area of
Pergamon itself, and masons' marks characteristic of Pergamon indicate that the blocks were
carved there and shipped to Athens ready to be installed. Clearly the king did not just send a check
when he offered to build the stoa for the Athenians. This same hands-on approach in Attalid dedications is attested to also at Delphi, where workmen and painters were sent from Pergamon to
work on the theater and a stoa.

We can also recognize Pergamene workmanship on a prominent tall statue base erected
167   just to the left before one enters the Propylaia.
The structure is of Hymettian marble, just under
9 meters tall, with courses of alternating heights;
in style it closely matches several bases erected
east of the temple of Apollo at Delphi to carry statues of the Attalid kings and their allies. The

167. Statue base originally built for Eumenes and
Attalos of Pergamon, just outside the Propylaia, later
reused to carry a statue of Agrippa.

Athenian example may have also carried a statue of one of the Pergamene dynasts. The original dedicatory inscription was erased in the Roman period, when the base was reused for a statue of the general Agrippa. This is by far the best-preserved example, but several other tall Hellenistic bases of this type have been recognized in fragments on the Acropolis—one set prominently at the north end of the facade of the Parthenon—and in the Agora as well.

Eumenes' brother, Attalos II, studied in Athens under the philosopher Karneades, and when he became king of Pergamon in 159 he, too, offered the Athenians a stoa in appreciation of his happy college days. The stoa of Attalos lay along the east side of the Agora 168, 169, 170 and served as the principal market building of the city. It had the same arrangement of colonnades as the stoa of Eumenes: Doric outside and Ionic inside on the ground floor, and on the top floor Ionic with a parapet outside and Pergamene inside. In this instance all the building materials are Athenian: limestone for the walls, Hymettian and Pentelic marble for the superstructure. The other major difference was the row of shops behind the colonnades on each story, twenty-one to a floor. With forty-two shops under a single roof, the stoa of Attalos begins to look like an early shopping mall, and we are invited to consider once again how little has changed since antiquity except the technology.

Other dynasts took an interest in Athens as well; Antiochos IV of Syria (175–164),

168. The reconstructed Stoa of Attalos in the Agora, 159–138 B.C.

known for his megalomania, worked on the abandoned temple of Olympian Zeus, a god with whom he felt a distinct affinity. An earlier temple had been left unfinished since the days of Peisistratos:

> For at Athens the architects Kallaischros, Antistates, Antimachides, and Porinos laid the foundations for Peisistratos when he was building a temple for Jupiter Olympius; but after his death, because a republican regime intervened, they abandoned the task they had begun. So it was that about two hundred years later (after Alexander the Great), when King Antiochos had promised to meet the expense of the work, a Roman citizen, Cossutius, with great ingenuity and supreme technical skill splendidly designed the great size of the cella, the dipteral arrangement of columns around it, and the symmetrical disposition of the epistyles and other decorative features. The building is known for its grandeur not only among the masses but also among experts. (Vitruvius 7 *praef.* 15)

The temple of Olympian Zeus envisioned by Antiochos was indeed a magnificent building. It measured just over 110 meters long and more than 43 meters wide, about the size of an American football field, including the end zones (see fig. 247). Of Pentelic marble with Corinthian columns set in a dipteral arrangement (three rows of columns on the ends and two rows down the long sides), it had eight columns across the front and twenty down the long sides: a forest of columns, 104 in all. Ancient authors suggest that the cella was to be open to the sky. The scale and plan made the Olympieion the match of the other giant temples of the Greek world, the Ionic ones at Samos, Ephesos, and Didyma near Miletos, and the Doric ones at Selinous and Akragas. The building in its Hellenistic phase was never

Left 169. The interior of the reconstructed Stoa of Attalos.

Right 170. A cross-section model of the Stoa of Attalos, showing colonnades, rooms, and roofing system.

171. The southeast corner of the temple of Olympieion Zeus, laid out and partially built by Antiochos IV of Syria (175–164 B.C.), finished under Hadrian in the 2nd century A.D.

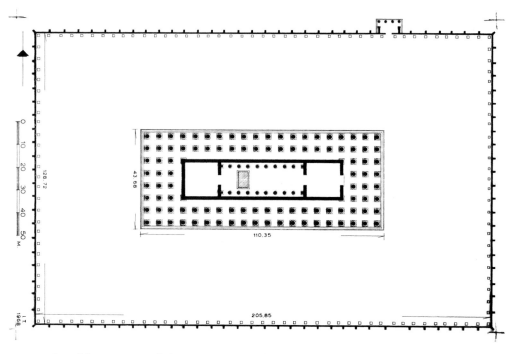

172. Plan of the sanctuary of Olympieion Zeus as finished by Hadrian, ca. A.D. 124–132. Note the dipteral plan, with two rows of columns all around (three rows on the ends).

fully completed, though careful analysis has confirmed Vitruvius' information that at least parts of the structure were raised to architrave level. Presumably abandoned at the death of Antiochos in 164, the temple was only finished some three hundred years later, under the Roman emperor Hadrian.

In contrast to the Olympieion, one of the most interesting monuments of Hellenistic Athens is also the smallest: the so-called Tower of the Winds or the Horologion (timepiece) of Andronikos:

173

> Some have held that there are four winds. . . . But those who have inquired more diligently lay down that there are eight: especially indeed Andronikos of Kyrrhos, who also for an example built at Athens an octagonal tower, and on the sides of the octagon had representations of the winds carved facing their currents. Above the tower he caused to be made a marble upright, and on that he placed a bronze Triton holding a rod in his right hand. He arranged it so it was driven around by the wind and always faced the current of air, with the rod as an indicator above the correct representation of the wind. (Vitruvius 1.6.4)

173. View of the Tower of the Winds, or Horologion, of Andronikos from the southeast, mid-2nd century B.C.

Varro, in the *Res Rusticae* (3.5.17), describes a building in Italy in terms of its similarity to the tower in Athens:

Inside, under the dome, the morning star by day and the evening star by night move round the lower part of the hemisphere in such a way as to indicate the hour. In the middle of the same hemisphere, which has a spindle in the center, is painted the cycle of the eight winds, like the Horologion at Athens made by the Kyrrhestian, and projecting from the spindle a pointer which moves so as to touch whatever wind is blowing at that time, so that anyone inside can tell.

The Athenian building survives virtually intact, lying east of the Roman marketplace. It is an octagonal tower, about 14 meters high, made of Pentelic marble. The roof, of wedge-shaped marble slabs, is original; the bronze Triton described by Vitruvius is long gone. There are two entrances into the building, at the northwest and northeast, each approached through a porch of two columns, pieces of which survive. In addition, there are the remains of a truncated circular chamber, also original, attached to the south side and rising two-thirds of the way up the wall.

At the top of each wall, as described by Vitruvius, are sculpted representations of the winds, shown as winged male figures flying toward the viewer's right. Inscriptions, now 174 barely legible, identify the eight winds: Boreas (north), Skiron (northwest), Zephyros (west), Lips (southwest), Notos (south), Euros (southeast), Apeliotes (east), and Kaikias (northeast). The figures are planned as a program; each wind carries an attribute appropriate to the weather that can be expected from that quarter. The northerly winds carry basins of rain or hailstones, the southerly ones flowers or the poop of a ship to indicate fair sailing. In addition, the southerly winds have bare feet and wear light mantles, while their northern counterparts wear boots and heavy cloaks.

174. Detail of the Tower of the Winds: (from left to right) Skiron (northwest wind), Zephyros (west wind), and Lips (southwest wind).

As the term *horologion* implies, the building served as a time-piece as well as a weather vane. Below the sculpted wind on each face are incised the radiating lines of a sundial. Unlike today, the ancient Greeks used temporal hours in their time-keeping, dividing each day into twelve equal periods of sunlight. This meant shorter hours in winter and longer hours in summer. The curving lines at each end of the radiating ones on the horologion therefore represent the summer and winter solstices and thus the longest and shortest days of the year. Whenever the sun was shining, it was possible to tell the time from several faces of the tower. Andronikos, the architect of the Tower of the Winds, is also known to have designed a handsome and sophisticated sundial, which was found on the island of Tenos (*IG* XII[5] 891).

Inside, the tower was intended to house a water clock. The circular chamber outside presumably held two superimposed tanks of water. Time was measured by letting water from the upper tank flow into the lower. An axle could be suspended over the water, and a chain wrapped around it, with a float on one end and the other end counterweighted. As the water rose, the axle would turn, providing the motion necessary to power the clock, by means of other chains attached to the axle, or toothed wheels, serving as gears. The actual clock would have been inside the tower, taking the form of a large disk which would rotate slowly, showing the passing hours, days, and phases of the moon. The clock itself was undoubtedly metal, and all traces of it have disappeared except for some cuttings in the marble floor. The interpretation suggested here derives from Vitruvius, who describes numerous sophisticated water-driven devices designed by Greeks in the Hellenistic period. In addition, a bronze astrolabe found in a shipwreck off the island of Antikythera, though fragmentary, has several interlocking gears, proving that the Greeks were capable of complex machinery at this time.

The date of the Tower of the Winds has been a matter of some controversy. For years it was dated to the middle of the first century B.C. Recent work, however, suggests that it should be dated about a century earlier, to around 150–125. This seems more probable given the history of Athens, which did not prosper in the first century. In addition, the water clock in the old Agora went out of use in the mid-second century B.C.; perhaps it was no longer deemed necessary with the construction of the new public clock. Finally, the architecture looks Hellenistic. We still await a detailed analysis of the sculpture, now heavily weathered.

There is also a question of who paid for the tower, since despite its small size, the tower is an elegant and costly building: marble throughout, with handsome architectural details inside and large sculpted slabs outside. In the search for a possible donor, several factors point to the Ptolemies of Egypt. Most important, perhaps, is the fact that virtually all the advances in timekeeping described by Vitruvius were developed in Alexandria. In addition, a longstanding friendly relationship existed between Athens and the Ptolemies. Third, the gymnasium given by Ptolemy is said by Pausanias to have been in the immediate vicinity. And, finally, the great lighthouse (*pharos*) of Alexandria, one of the seven wonders of the ancient world, was in part octagonal and also decorated with Tritons.

In later times the tower may have been used as an early Christian baptistery. During

175. The ruins of the South Square of the Agora, looking west along the Middle Stoa, mid-2nd century B.C.

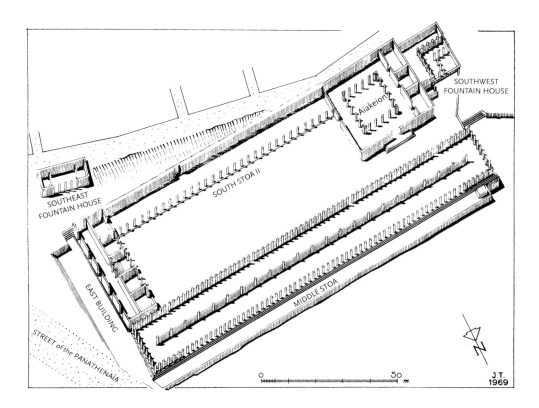

176. The South Square of the Agora, mid-2nd century B.C.

the Turkish period it was certainly used as an annex to the nearby mosque, and early European travelers describe and depict dervishes performing their whirling dances in the building.

    Other improvements were made in the Agora during the second century B.C., though
we cannot associate a specific donor with the changes. In addition to the Stoa of Attalos,
175   two more stoas were built in the Agora. The so-called Middle Stoa was built running east-
west across the square, dividing it into two areas of unequal size, the northern being the
larger. This marks a radical change in the use of the public space, highlighted by the fact
that one of the early boundary stones of the Agora was buried in place deep within the foundations. At just under 150 meters in length, the Middle Stoa is the longest in the Agora,
though shorter than the Stoa of Eumenes (about 167 meters). The stoa is of the Doric order,
with colonnades facing both north and south, and a central line of columns; there are no interior walls, though many of the column drums are dressed in such a way as to suggest that
a thin parapet ran between some of the columns. The building is generally modest—the
columns and superstructure are limestone, the roof is terra-cotta. Pottery from beneath the

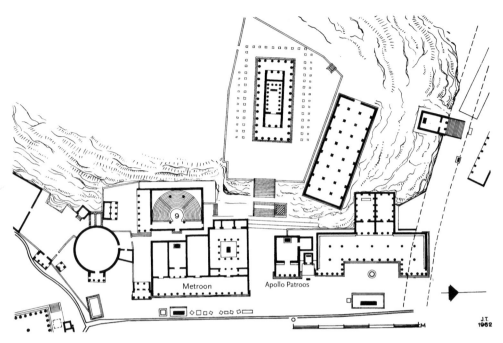

177. Plan of the west side of the Agora in the 2nd century B.C.

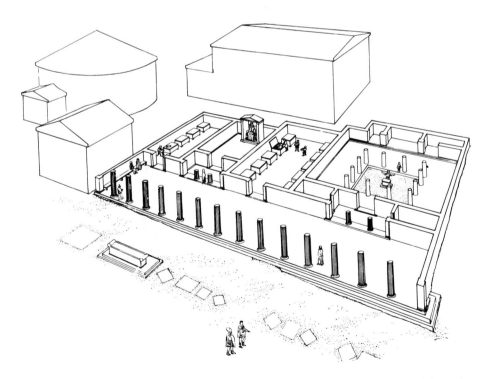

178. Cutaway view of the Metroon, the sanctuary of the Mother of the Gods (Meter) and the archive building of the city, mid-2nd century B.C.

floors suggests a date of around 180 for the start of its construction, though it may have taken a generation to complete.

South Stoa II, a simple, single Doric colonnade with a small fountain in the back wall, was built along the south side of the Agora, replacing the old fifth-century South Stoa I. It was built after the completion of the Middle Stoa, around the middle of the second century, and was connected to it on the east end by a small structure, known as the East Building. This had a long hall with a marble-chip floor, into which were set marble slabs with cuttings designed to hold wooden tables or similar furniture. The result is a complex known as the South Square, which was set off from the rest of the Agora. In all probability it served the commercial needs of the city.

176

Another building dated to the mid-second century was built along the west side of the Agora, on the ruins of the old Bouleuterion. This was the Metroon, which served both as a sanctuary of the Mother of the Gods and as the archive building of the city. Four rooms were set side by side, the northernmost a peristyle court open to the sky. An Ionic colonnade of Pentelic marble ran in front of the rooms, uniting them architecturally.

177, 178

With the colonnaded facade of the Metroon and the addition of new stoas, the old Agora began to look a little less haphazard and more like the great peristyle courts of the Hellenistic agoras of Asia Minor, as at Magnesia, Miletos, Ephesos, and Priene.

6

Roman Athens

Rome had been drawn into the internal conflicts between Greece and the successors of Alexander as early as the late third century B.C. Twice, in 197 and 168 B.C., the Romans had squashed a rising tide of Macedonian conquest. Finally, in 146 B.C., the Roman general Mummius smashed the power of the Achaian league and leveled the city of Corinth. Thereafter, Greece was ruled as if it were a Roman province. Archaeologically, there is nothing to mark that date in Athens: the Athenians did not suddenly start building with baked bricks, speaking Latin, or wearing togas. It seems clear that the many aspects of Romanization were part of a gradual process rather than a single moment in time. A far more useful date, archaeologically speaking, is 86 B.C., the year the Roman general Sulla took Athens after a long and bitter siege.

Athens had sided with King Mithradates of Pontos in his revolt against Rome. This was the first of four phenomenally poor political decisions the Athenians took vis-à-vis Rome in the course of the first century B.C. Later in the century Athens favored Pompey over Caesar, Cassius and Brutus over Antony and Octavian, and, finally, Antony and Cleopatra over Octavian (Augustus). Any other Greek city would have sunk without a trace as a result of such choices, but Athens survived. What saved it were the philosophical and cultural traditions, which the less-refined Romans greatly admired. The Roman enthusiasm for the city in this period is expressed by Cicero, who in 59 B.C. wrote that Athens was

> where men think that humanity, learning, religion, grain, rights, and laws were born and whence they were spread through all the earth.

Almost all the important figures of the end of the Roman republic and the beginning of the empire spent time in Greece, particularly in Athens. Many came as generals, since three crucial battles of the civil wars were fought on Greek soil: Pharsalos in 48 B.C. (Caesar against Pompey), Philippi in 44 B.C. (Antony and Octavian against Brutus and Cassius), and Actium in 31 B.C. (Octavian against Antony and Cleopatra). Others, men of letters, were drawn to Athens by the intellectual and educational opportunities: Cicero, Horace, and Varro are perhaps the best known.

Although the first century B.C. must have been a rather grim time, especially as the new emperor Augustus did not at first favor Athens, we find Roman Athens eventually continuing the patterns of the Hellenistic city. Large, impressive monuments continued to be built, only now wealthy individuals or Roman emperors paid the bills instead of Hellenistic dynasts. Fittingly enough, the monuments accurately reflect the educational and cultural role of Athens in the Roman world: odeia, libraries, gymnasia, and lecture halls predominate.

As noted, the transition can best be dated with Sulla's siege of Athens in 86 B.C. To take the city, Sulla breached the city wall at the northwest, not far from the Agora. His catapults, with a range of about 400 meters, may have done some damage to the monuments, but much of the city lay outside the direct line of fire. A few stone catapult balls have been recovered in the excavations of the Kerameikos, near where Sulla entered. Once the city was taken, it was plundered, and many people were killed, but there is no clear evidence of the deliberate or systematic destruction of buildings as occurred in Peiraieus, where the arsenal of Philon and probably the ship sheds were burned. Plutarch gives the most vivid account of the fall of Athens and the decision not to sack the city:

> Sulla himself, after he had thrown down and leveled the wall between the Peiraieus and Sacred Gates, led his army into the city at midnight. The sight of him was made terrible by blasts of many trumpets and bugles, and by the cries and yells of the troops, now let loose by him for plunder and slaughter, and by their rushing through the narrow streets with drawn swords. There was therefore no counting of the slain, but their numbers to this day are determined only by the area covered by their blood. Leaving aside those who were killed in the rest of the city, the blood that was shed in the agora covered all the Kerameikos inside the Dipylon Gate; indeed, many say that it flowed through the gate and flooded the suburb. But although many were slain this way, still more killed themselves out of pity for their native city, which they thought was going to be destroyed. This conviction made many of the best give up out of despair and fear, since they expected no humanity or moderation from Sulla. However,

partly at the urging of the exiles Meidias and Kalliphon, who threw themselves at his feet in supplication, and partly because all the Roman senators in his entourage interceded for the city, and being himself sated with vengeance by this time, after some words in praise of the ancient Athenians, [Sulla] said that he forgave a few for the sake of the many, the living for the sake of the dead. (*Sulla* 14.3–6)

In Athens, one venerable building was destroyed, but by the Athenians themselves. When it became clear that a final stand would have to be made on the Acropolis, Aristion, the leader of the pro-Mithradates faction, had the Athenians burn the old Odeion of Perikles (see figs. 114, 242) to prevent the huge roof timbers from falling into Sulla's hands and being used for siege machines:

A few ran feebly to the Acropolis; Aristion fled with them, after burning the Odeion, so that Sulla might not have timber ready to hand for an assault on the Acropolis. (Appian, *Mithradatic Wars* 38)

The partially excavated remains of the Odeion, consisting of parts of the northwest and northeast corners and the southernmost row of columns, therefore presumably represent a rebuilding. We learn that the building was restored for the Athenians within a generation by the king of Cappadocia, Ariobarzanes II (63–51 B.C.), from both Vitruvius (5.9.1) and the following inscription on a statue base:

Those appointed by him for the construction of the Odeion, Gaius and Marcus Stallios, sons of Gaius, and Menalippos, [set up the statue of] their benefactor King Ariobarzanes Philopator, son of King Ariobarzanes Philoromaios and Queen Athenais. (*IG* II² 3426)

At about the same time, the Roman governor of Cilicia, Claudius Appius Pulcher, dedicated a handsome propylon (gateway) for the sanctuary of Demeter and Kore at Eleusis. This is the first of many gifts to the sanctuary which give clear evidence of Roman enthusiasm for this particular cult. The building was made of Pentelic marble and presented an interesting combination of architectural orders, in a period when total consistency was not required. The columns have elaborately carved Corinthian capitals from which spring 179 the foreparts of griffins. The frieze, which ran above the three-fascia architrave, was Doric, with Eleusinian motifs carved both on the metopes and triglyphs: sheaves of wheat, a *cista mystica* (basket for hidden sacred offerings), rosettes, and bulls' heads. The architrave car-

179. Mixed Doric and Ionic entablature from the inner propylon at Eleusis, with Eleusinian motifs carved on the frieze and the dedicatory inscription in Latin on the architrave below, ca. 50 B.C. (Cf. fig. 255, "C")

ries the dedicatory inscription, in both Latin and Greek, defining the building as a gateway and giving the name of Appius (*CIL* III 547). This is one of the few instances of the use of Latin in Attica or Athens, a city which remained resistant to any language but Greek. Only a handful of the hundreds of inscriptions from Roman Athens are in Latin, in marked contrast to cities with a stronger colonial presence such as Corinth, Dion, or Philippi.

On the other side of the large doorway to the shrine, facing in toward the Telesterion, were two colossal caryatid columns: heavily draped female figures, each with a ritual basket (*cista*) on her head and a gorgoneion on her breast. One of the figures was carried off in the nineteenth century to the Fitzwilliam Museum in Cambridge, over the strong protests of the local inhabitants of the village; the other is on display in the small museum at Eleusis. The propylon is referred to in Cicero's correspondence to his friend Atticus (6.1) in 50 B.C.:

> There is one thing I wish you to consider. I hear that Appius is putting up a propylon at Eleusis. Shall I look a fool if I do so at the Academy? I dare say you may think so; if so, say so plainly. I am very fond of the city of Athens. I should like it to have some memorial of myself.

The propylon at Eleusis was finished after Claudius' death by his two nephews, in 48 B.C., making it one of the few buildings erected in the middle of the first century in Athens or Attica, as well as one of the earliest Roman benefactions. Its unusual architectural and sculptural program place it among the most interesting monuments of the Roman period.

The sea battle of Actium in 31 B.C. marked the defeat of Mark Antony and Cleopatra and the rise of Octavian (later Augustus) to the position of emperor. Antony had made

180

Athens one of his headquarters, and according to Plutarch the city was the scene of several unfavorable portents before the fatal battle:

> In Patras, while Antony was staying there, the Herakleion was destroyed by lightning; and at Athens the Dionysos in the gigantomachy was dislodged by the winds and carried down into the theater. Now, Antony associated himself with Herakles in lineage, and with Dionysos in his mode of life, as I have said, and he was called the New Dionysos. The same storm fell upon the colossal figures of Eumenes and Attalos at Athens, on which the name of Antony had been inscribed, and prostrated them, alone out of many. (*Antony* 60)

Not long after the Battle of Actium a small building was built on the Acropolis, known only from the dedicatory inscription carved on its architrave:

> The people to the goddess Roma and Caesar Augustus. Pammenes, the son of Zenon, of Marathon, being hoplite general and priest of the goddess Roma and Augustus Savior on the Acropolis, when Megiste, daughter of Asklepiades, of Halai, was priestess of Athena Polias. In the archonship of Areos, son of Dorion of Paiania. (*IG* II² 3173)

Octavian took the title of Augustus in 27 B.C., and it is assumed that the dedication dates to soon thereafter. Numerous fragments of the building have been found, which allow for the restoration of a small round structure with nine Ionic columns. In one of the earliest instances of classicizing in Athens, the columns are precise copies of those used on the east porch of the Erechtheion, with elaborately carved floral motifs at the top of the shafts. Details beyond that are unclear. The building has been restored as a monopteros, a circle of columns, measuring about 8.6 meters in diameter, and is usually assigned to a set of square foundations lying due east of the Parthenon. The monopteros is often referred to as a temple of Roma and Augustus, but this is open to question. The structure is surprisingly small for a temple, and the inscription does not say that it was one. It could equally well have

180. Caryatid with mystic basket from the inner propylon at Eleusis, ca. 50 B.C.

181. Dedicatory inscription on the architrave of the monopteros (circle of columns) east of the
Parthenon, late 1st century B.C.

been the frame for an altar of the cult of Roma and Augustus. Round altars are not uncom-
mon, and the imperial cult did not always require a temple. The people of Miletos, for instance, dedicated an altar to Augustus in the courtyard of their bouleuterion (council chamber). If the position near the Parthenon is accepted, this suggestion becomes more likely:
the square foundations are on an axis with the temple and lie to the east, just where one
might expect to find an altar. Worship of the imperial family as gods was a common feature
of life in the Greek east, where the tradition of ruler worship goes back at least to the early
Hellenistic period. It was no great difficulty to shift one's religious focus from a Hellenistic
king to a Roman emperor, simply a matter of practicality. In Asia Minor, especially, one
finds temples dedicated to virtually all the Roman emperors. In mainland Greece this
fawning on the new order was perhaps a bit more restrained, but nonetheless evident and
necessary.

    At about the same time, the imperial family made a significant gift to the Athenians
in the form of a huge concert hall, or odeion, in the middle of the Agora. It was built by
Agrippa, Augustus' son-in-law and general, who visited Athens in the years around 15 B.C.
182 An odeion was intended primarily for musical events and was usually a roofed building,
unlike most Greek theaters. The Odeion of Agrippa was large, measuring 51.4 by 43.2 meters, rising several stories in height, and having an internal span of some 25 meters. Its size
is noteworthy because, in its prominent location just north of the Middle Stoa, it completely

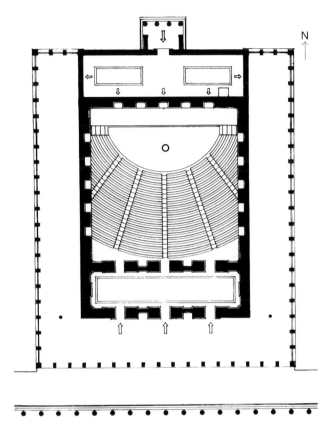

182. Plan of the Odeion of Agrippa, first phase, late 1st century B.C.

N ↑

dominated the Agora. The integrity of the old square was lost forever, and several of its traditional functions must have been transferred elsewhere or had long ceased to be needed.

The building was lavish, with a marble-paved orchestra and a raised stage decorated with sculpted herms; the stone seating could accommodate about a thousand people. 183 Outside, the building was decorated with monumental columns and pilasters of Pentelic marble in the Corinthian order. In return for this gift, Agrippa was honored by the Athenians, though in a somewhat economical fashion: the huge Hellenistic statue base which dominates the entrance to the Acropolis, originally occupied by the kings of Pergamon and later by Antony and Cleopatra, was simply reused for Agrippa (see fig. 167). A new statue went up, and a new inscription was carved over the old one:

The people set up Marcus Agrippa, son of Lucius, three times consul, as their own benefactor. (*IG* II² 4122)

Completing the rearrangement of the old Agora square was a temple to Ares, introduced just to the north of the odeion. A peripteral Doric temple of Pentelic marble, almost identical in many ways to the nearby Hephaisteion, it, too, dates to the fifth century B.C. Masons' marks of the Roman period and pottery from around its foundations, however, indicate that the building was dismantled and re-erected in the Agora early in Roman times. As 184 noted, it seems probable that the temple was built originally in the deme of Pallene and was

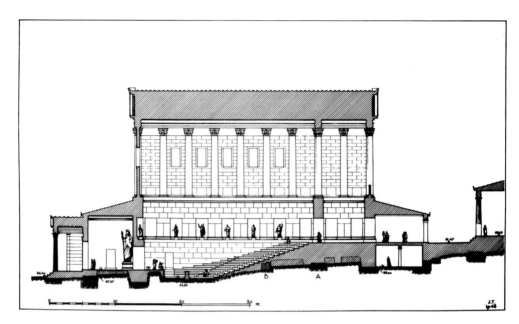

183. Cross-section of the Odeion of Agrippa, looking east.

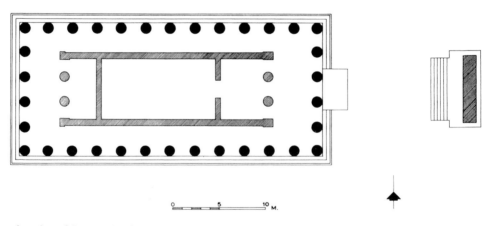

184. Plan of the temple of Ares, 5th century B.C., rebuilt in the Agora in the late 1st century B.C.

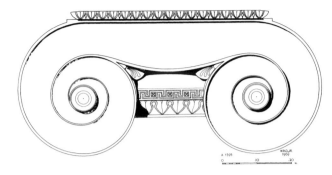

185. Ionic capital originally from the temple of Athena at Sounion, 5th century B.C., reused in the Agora in the 1st century A.D.

186. Ionic capital of the 5th century B.C., reused in the Agora in the early Roman period; note the traces of the original paint.

dedicated to Athena; it also looks as if its marble sima (gutter) was taken from a similar temple, that of Poseidon at Sounion. The identification of the temple as the one dedicated to Ares, god of war, is based on Pausanias' tour of the Agora. An inscription honors the adopted son of Augustus, Gaius Caesar, as "the new Ares," raising the possibility that the temple was re-erected to serve the needs of the imperial cult.

The temple of Ares is the most prominent and perhaps the earliest of a group of "wandering temples," Classical buildings collected from various sanctuaries in Attica, disassembled, and re-erected in central Athens in the first century B.C. and first century A.D. In other instances, only portions of the buildings have been transferred, leaving enough on the original site to allow a definite association. From Sounion, for instance, the marble sima from the temple of Poseidon was brought in and used to adorn the temple of Ares, and several of the Ionic columns of the temple of Athena (see figs. 104, 105) were also brought to Athens and reused in the Agora in the first century A.D. In addition, four 185 columns from the Classical building at Thorikos (see figs. 109, 110) were dismantled, carefully marked, and reassembled in Athens. In a third use, the drums of these four columns were employed as building blocks in the post-Herulian wall (see fig. 218), built along the east side of the Agora in A.D. 276–282.

In other instances, we can recognize reused material but remain ignorant of the original source in Attica. Two sets of handsome Ionic columns, still bearing traces of their painted decoration, fall into this category, as does a fine marble altar, tentatively assigned to 186 Zeus Agoraios, which in its second use stood east of the Metroon in the Agora. Many of the

Attic demes and their sanctuaries must have been virtually deserted by the early Roman period, and rather than waste these lovely examples of outstanding Classical architecture, the
Athenians or Romans recycled them in the form of new temples for downtown Athens.
The need for so many "new" temples may well have been to provide appropriate cult centers for the successive emperors of the new Roman empire.

Also dated to the first century B.C. is the construction of a new marketplace, or Agora,
some 100 meters east of the old one. The northern half still lies buried under the Fethiye
Camii (Mosque of the Conqueror, 1457) and the Church of the Taxiarchs, but the southern
half has been cleared sufficiently to allow a probable restoration of the plan. It takes the
form of a large peristyle court with Ionic colonnades of unfluted marble columns. The
eastern side had a row of shops behind the colonnade, and there was a fountain along
the south side. The building had two entrances, an Ionic propylon on the east side and a
187   classicizing Doric propylon on the west, facing back toward the old Greek Agora. This west-

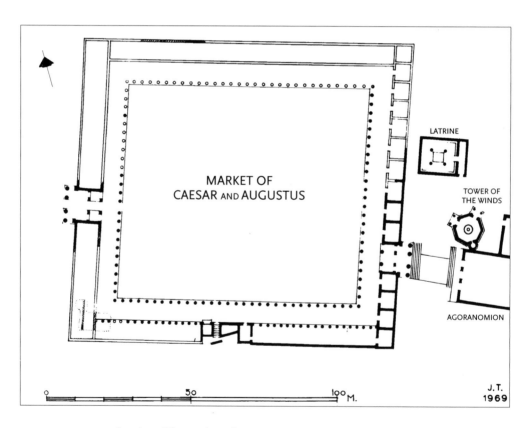

187. Plan of the market of Caesar and Augustus, 1st century B.C.

188. The gate of Athena Archegetis, western entrance into the Roman Agora, late 1st century B.C. The architrave of the classicizing Doric propylon carries the dedicatory inscription.

ern gateway carries the dedicatory inscription telling us that the building was paid for with money provided by Caesar and Augustus and was dedicated to Athena Archegetis (Leader) in the archonship of Nikias (11–9 B.C.).   188

Apparently it served as the principal market area of Athens, taking over that commercial function from the old Agora. When Pausanias   189 uses the term "agora" it seems likely that he is referring to this complex, which was in use as such during his visit; when he refers to the old Greek Agora the term he uses is "Kerameikos." The Roman Agora survived, with modifications, for centuries. In the second century A.D. Hadrian's edict on the price of oil was inscribed on the anta of the western gateway. Later still, the court was paved in reused marble slabs, some of them carrying copies of imperial letters written to the Athenians by Marcus Aurelius late in the second century.

Compared with this flurry of building activity reflecting the new Roman imperial interest in the city during the reign of Augustus, the first century A.D. was appreciably less active. Some of the itinerant temples were probably moved in during the century, and work was done in the Asklepieion (*IG* II² 1046, 3174, 4464), but there are few signs of building activity other than maintenance or repairs. A passing mention in an inscription to "work on the ascent" seems to refer to a monumental marble stairway built up to the Propylaia in the mid-first century A.D. (*IG* II² 2292). In addition, the old temple of Nemesis at Rhamnous

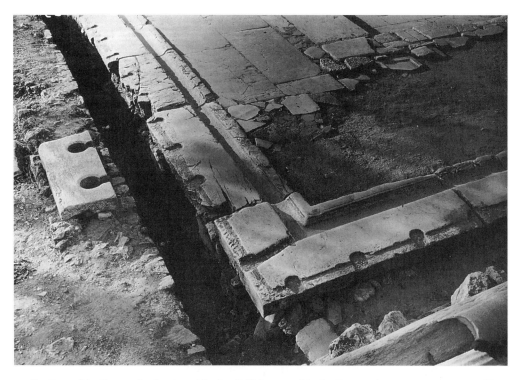

189. Part of the Roman latrine (seat block at left) just outside the Roman Agora; 1st century A.D.(?).

was extensively refurbished. Several of the cornice and frieze blocks from the east end are clearly of Roman workmanship. After it was repaired, the temple was rededicated to the wife of Augustus, Livia, in 45/6, three years after she was declared a goddess. An inscribed epistyle block of marble indicates that work was done on the scene-building of the theater of Dionysos (*IG* II² 3182) during the reign of Nero after 66, and Nero himself was honored with a large inscription of bronze letters, probably gilded, attached to the eastern epistyle of the Parthenon (see fig. 71).

A less edifying addition to the theater was the introduction of Roman blood sports: gladiatorial contests and wild beast hunts. Such displays were drawing crowds and criticism in Athens as early as the first century A.D.:

He [Apollonius] also corrected the following abuse at Athens. The Athenians ran in crowds to the theater beneath the Acropolis to witness human slaughter, and the passion for such sports was stronger there than it is in Corinth today; for they would buy for large sums adulterers and fornicators and burglars and cut-purses and kidnappers and such rabble, and then they would take them and arm them and set them to fight one another. (Philostratus, *Life of Apollonius* 22)

And:

But as matters now stand, there is no practice current in Athens which would not cause any man to feel ashamed. For instance, in regard to the gladiatorial shows the Athenians have so zealously emulated the Corinthians or, rather, have so surpassed them and all others in their mad infatuation that whereas the Corinthians watch these combats outside the city in a glen, a place that is able to hold a crowd but otherwise is dirty and such that no one would even bury a free-born citizen there, the Athenians look on this fine spectacle in their theater under the very walls of the Acropolis, in the place where they bring their Dionysos into the orchestra and stand him up, so that often a fighter is slaughtered among the very seats in which the hierophant and other priests must sit. (Dio Chrysostom 31.121)

A waist-high parapet of marble was added at some date, and there are cuttings on the theater seats, perhaps for the attachment of ropes to anchor netting or protective screens (see fig. 140).

To the first century A.D. can be dated the visit to Athens of the apostle Paul. His remarks in Acts (17:22–34) are addressed to the Council of the Areopagos, the conservative body responsible for the maintenance of ancestral laws. The court takes its name from the rocky outcrop northwest of the Acropolis where it originally sat. By as early as the fourth century B.C., however, the council is known to have convened in a variety of places, so we are uncertain as to exactly where Paul spoke in Athens. He had only limited success in this most pagan city, though one of his converts, Dionysios, was a member of the Areopagos court and in later times became the patron saint of Athens.

Statues of various members of the imperial family dressed as initiates or priests indicate a continuing Roman interest in the cult of Demeter and Kore at Eleusis. In addition, the philosophical schools flourished throughout the first century. Two of the students in Athens at this time were Plutarch and a descendant of Themistokles, still benefiting from his ancestor's prominence hundreds of years later:

Three cities, as most writers say, were given him [Themistokles] for bread, wine, and meat, namely, Magnesia, Lampsakos, and Myus. . . . For the lineal descendants of Themistokles there were also certain privileges maintained in

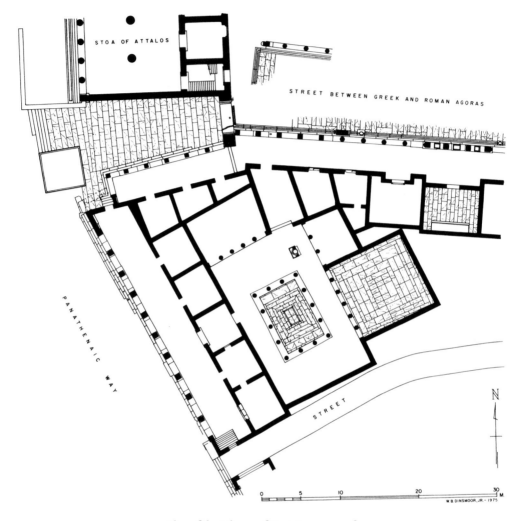

190. Plan of the Library of Pantainos, A.D. 98–102.

Magnesia down to my time, and the revenues of these were enjoyed by a
Themistokles of Athens, who was my intimate and friend in the school of Am-
monios the philosopher. (Plutarch, *Themistokles* 29–30)

In contrast to the relatively modest additions to the city in the first century, the second
century represents a high point for Athens, in terms of stability, wealth, and prestige, accompanied by numerous buildings funded by both private individuals and Roman emper-

191. Dedicatory inscription on the door lintel of the Library of Pantainos.

ors. The century began in the reign of Trajan with the construction of a building by a local Athenian, Titus Flavius Pantainos. His building, identified as a library, stood facing onto the Panathenaic Way, just south of the Stoa of Attalos. It consisted of three colonnades with shops behind, wrapped around a central courtyard and a single large square room paved in marble. The dedicatory inscription, carved on the lintel which spanned the main doorway, is worth quoting in full:

190

191

> To Athena Polias and to the Emperor Caesar Augustus Nerva Trajan Germanicus and to the city of the Athenians, the priest of the wisdom-loving [philosophical] Muses, Titus Flavius Pantainos, the son of Flavius Menander the diadoch [head of a school], gave the outer stoas, the peristyle, the library with the books, and all the furnishings within them, from his own resources, together with his children Flavius Menander and Flavia Secundilla. (Agora I 848)

Here is an inscription which epitomizes the cultural and educational role of Athens in the Roman world: a man who describes himself as the priest of the philosophical Muses and the son of the head of a school, dedicating a library. The date is around 98–102. Trajan is designated only as Germanicus; by the end of his reign in 117 he had added Dacicus (102) and Parthicus (115) to his name. The precise description of the parts of the building and the fact that the

192. The rules of the Library of Pantainos, inscribed on a herm shaft.

inscription runs up onto the moldings of the lintel block perhaps suggest that Pantainos made additions to a preexisting building. If so, perhaps it was the philosophical school of his father, Flavius Menander. The library rules were inscribed on a marble herm shaft

192   found nearby and sound remarkably familiar:

> No book is to be taken out since we have sworn an oath. The library is to be open from the first hour until the sixth. (Agora I 2729)

The next monument of note to go up during Trajanic times is among the most con-

193   spicuous in the city: that of Philopappos, which crowns the Mouseion Hill, the high point of the ridge west of the Acropolis (see fig. 148).

> The Mouseion is a hill within the an-
> cient circuit of the city, opposite the
> Acropolis, where they say that Mou-
> saios sang and, dying of old age, was
> buried. Afterward a monument was
> built here to a Syrian man. (Pausa-
> nias 1.25.8)

The monument is, in fact, the grave of Philopappos, one of the very few allowed within the city. For generations, since a purification of the city in Archaic times, the Athenians had buried their dead out- side the walls. The prohibition was in ef- fect into Roman times, as we learn in a letter to Cicero from Servius Sulpicius written on May 31, 45 B.C., concerning the death in Athens of their friend Marcellus:

> I could not prevail on the Athenians
> to make a grant of any burial ground
> within the city, as they alleged that

193. The funerary monument of Philopappos,
A.D. 114–116. (Cf. fig. 148)

they were prevented from doing so by their religious regulations; and we
must admit it was a concession they had never yet made to anybody. They did
allow us to do what was the next best thing, to bury him in the precinct of any
gymnasium we chose. We selected a spot near the most famous gymnasium
in the whole world, that of the Academy, and it was there we cremated the
body and after that arranged that the Athenians should put out tenders for the
erection on the spot of a marble monument in his honor. (Cicero, *Ad Fam.*
4.12.3)

Caius Julius Antiochos Philopappos was a distinguished man, consul at Rome during
Trajan's reign and a descendant of the kings of Commagene. He became an Athenian citizen, and we assume that he was a great benefactor of the city although we know of no specific deeds or works of his which merit the distinction he was accorded. His tomb features
a handsome curved marble facade decorated with inscriptions and sculpture, which stands
several stories high, facing the Acropolis. The lower part consists of a carved frieze showing Philopappos in a consular procession in a chariot, accompanied by assorted dignitaries.
Three niches above held statues of Philopappos and his royal antecedents, Kings Antiochos IV of Commagene and Seleukos Nikator, founder of the Seleucid dynasty. An inscription in Latin on one of the pilasters between the niches records Philopappos' career:

Caius Julius Antiochus Philopappos, son of Caius, of the Fabian tribe, consul,
and Arval brother, admitted to the praetorian rank by the Emperor Caesar Nerva
Trajan Optimus Augustus Germanicus Dacicus. (*IG* II² 3451 A–E)

The imperial titles used here to refer to Trajan allow us to date the inscription and
Philopappos' death to between 114 and 116. Behind the facade there was once a rectangular
burial chamber, presumably containing a sarcophagus, now long gone. The marble blocks
of the burial chamber were reused in the Frankish bell tower in the southwest corner of the
Parthenon.

Following the death of Trajan, Hadrian came to the throne in Rome. A philhellene,
he was especially fond of Athens and visited the city no fewer than three times during his
reign. Hadrian's official portrait in Greece carries a powerful image of a triumphant
Athena, patron of Athens, being crowned by victories while standing on the back of the wolf
of Rome. Hadrian made the city a center for his worship among Greek cities, and the Athe-   194
nians responded enthusiastically. No fewer than ninety-four altars dedicated to him have
survived in Athens. After describing the Olympieion, Pausanias gives a partial list of his   195
benefactions (1.18.9):

194. Statue of the Emperor Hadrian, A.D. 117–138; the cuirass shows Athena being crowned by Nikai and supported by the wolf of Rome.

195. Altar from Athens dedicated to Hadrian as savior and founder.

Hadrian also built for the Athenians a temple of Hera and Panhellenian Zeus [the Panhellenion], and a sanctuary to all the gods [the Pantheon]. But most splendid of all are a hundred columns, walls, and colonnades all made of Phrygian marble. Here too is a building adorned with a gilded roof and alabaster, and also with statues and paintings; books are stored in it. There is also a gymnasium named after Hadrian; it too has a hundred columns from the quarries of Libya.

The Olympieion is perhaps the single most imposing monument undertaken by Hadrian in Athens. He managed, resuming a project started more than three hundred years earlier, to finish the great Corinthian dipteral temple begun by Antiochos IV of Syria (see figs. 171, 172, 247) and, having finished it, installed a cult statue of Zeus:

It was Hadrian, the Roman emperor, who dedicated the temple and images of
Olympian Zeus. The image is worth seeing. It surpasses in size all other images
except the colossi at Rhodes and Rome. It is made of ivory and gold, and, considering the size, the workmanship is good. (Pausanias 1.18.6)

The temple was enclosed in a marble-paved precinct full of statues of Hadrian, set up by the
various Greek cities, and Hadrian himself carries the title "Olympios." The sanctuary was
presumably dedicated during Hadrian's final visit to Athens in 131/2.

Northwest of the enclosure is an associated monument, the so-called Arch of Hadrian. A single large arch spans the road which leads back toward the east end of the Acrop-   196
olis. It is decorated with Corinthian pilasters and columns, and supports an attic of more
columns and pilasters which form three bays, the central one topped by a pediment. The
form of the arch is noteworthy, for it is far less deep from front to back than most comparable Roman arches. Two simple inscriptions are carved on the architrave immediately above

the arch. On the west side, facing
the Acropolis, the text reads,
"This is Athens, the former [or
old] city of Theseus." The text
on the east side, facing the
Olympieion, reads, "This is the
city of Hadrian and not of Theseus." The arch thus seems to
serve as a sort of boundary stone,
either physical or temporal, between old and new Athens. The
laconic texts have caused some
difficulties for those trying to assess who gave the arch and why it
was placed where it is. If the Athenians had built it, we would expect a fuller dedication to the emperor, using all his proper titles.
Or Hadrian himself may have

196. Arch of Hadrian, east side, ca.
A.D. 132. (Cf. fig. 247)

built it, perhaps to define the limits of an area of Athens which is said in the *Historia Augustae* (20.4–6) to have been named for him:

> Though he cared nothing for inscriptions on his public works, he gave the name of Hadrianopolis to many cities, as, for example, even to Carthage and a section of Athens; and he also gave his name to aqueducts without number.

197 The other large building given to Athens was the Library of Hadrian, which has been partially excavated. Pausanias describes the elaborate building with its hundred columns, adding, almost in passing, that books are stored in it. Other sources refer more directly to the building as a library. It is a large complex, lying just north of the Roman Agora and taking the form of a huge peristyle court, measuring about 90 by 125 meters; in plan and design it somewhat resembles the great imperial fora of Rome, one of which also contained a library. Hadrian's library had a single entrance at the west, through a projecting propylon with four Corinthian columns of veined marble imported from Asia Minor. The entire western wall was of Pentelic marble, whereas all the other walls were of poros limestone. The western wall is further adorned with a series of fourteen projecting Corinthian columns, the capitals and bases of Pentelic marble and the large monolithic shafts of green-198 veined marble from Karystos, in southern Euboia. The northern half of this western facade survives virtually intact, and traces of the southern half have been excavated.

Inside the building, the columns of Phrygian stone have disappeared, but enough survives of the stylobate to determine that there were indeed a hundred of them, thirty on the long sides, twenty-two on the short. Behind the north and south colonnades the wall is broken by three large niches, the central one rectangular and the other two apsidal. All the rooms are confined to the eastern end, where the original walls stand up to three stories high in places. In the middle was the largest room, apparently designed to carry the wooden shelves or cabinets which would have housed

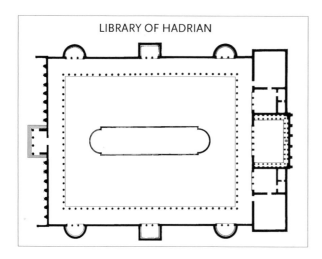

LIBRARY OF HADRIAN

197. Plan of the Library of Hadrian, ca. A.D. 132.

198. The north half of the west facade of the Library of Hadrian from the northwest. The Corinthian columns along the wall have shafts of Carystian marble from southern Euboea; the fluted column at the extreme right, from the propylon, is made of marble from Asia Minor.

the scrolls of the library collection. Smaller rooms on either side may have served for administration. The two corner rooms were probably lecture halls; they are partially paved in marble with foundations for banked rows of seats. Within the open-air courtyard there was a long, shallow reflecting pool, curved at either end. Only a small portion of the building was actually given over to books. The colonnades and the court with its pool presumably provided a space for reading and peripatetic philosophical discussion.

Other buildings of Hadrianic date have been uncovered throughout Athens. The foundations of a large templelike building found under the modern houses of Plaka, east of the Roman Agora, can almost certainly be identified with the Panhellenion referred to by Pausanias. And in the old Greek Agora, a basilica of Roman type was erected in Hadrianic times at the northeast corner of the square. Only its southern half has been cleared, enough to show that it had marble floors and piers decorated with sculpted figures. Basilicas, usually enclosed three-aisled halls, were the Roman equivalent of the Greek stoas: multifunctional public buildings. Early on they served as markets, but by the imperial period they were often used for administration and as tribunals for magistrates and other judicial bodies.

Another benefaction, not mentioned by Pausanias, was a huge new aqueduct, begun by Hadrian and finished by his successor, Antoninus Pius, in 140. Water was brought from springs on the lower slopes of Mount Parnes, more than 20 kilometers away. For the most part it was carried underground in a tunnel measuring about 0.7 by 1.6 meters, reached by manholes at frequent intervals. Two sets of supporting piers for the arches of aqueducts which cross a shallow ravine in the modern suburb of Nea Ionia have often been associated with the Hadrianic line. The initial terminus of the aqueduct was a huge reservoir halfway up the southwestern slopes of Lykabettos, to the northeast and outside the walls of ancient Athens. This reservoir, measuring about 26 by 9 by 2 meters deep, remained in use into the twentieth century and gives its name to the modern square: Dexameni (Reservoir). The

199. Left half of the dedicatory inscription of the Hadrianic aqueduct, finished by Antoninus Pius in A.D. 140. Nineteenth-century watercolor showing its reuse in an eighteenth-century wall; the block now lies in the National Gardens.

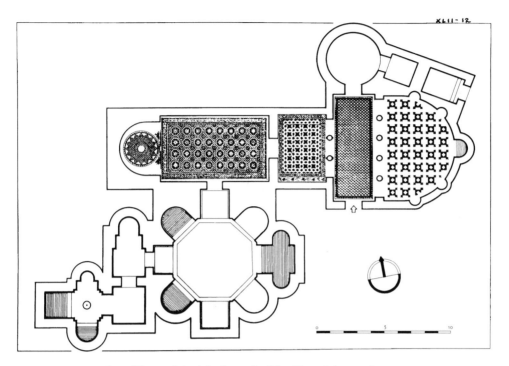

200. Plan of the Hadrianic bath north of the Olympieion, 2nd century A.D.

reservoir was fitted with a handsome columnar facade, indicating that it probably served as a *nymphaion,* or monumental fountain house. Four Ionic columns carried an entablature, with an arcuated (curved) architrave over the central bay. Early drawings show that this facade stood intact into the fifteenth century; eighteenth-century drawings show only the left half in place, and that was dismantled in 1778. The architrave, part of which survives in the National Gardens, carried a dedicatory inscription in Latin:

199

> The Emp[eror] T[itus] Ael[ius] Hadrian Antoninus Aug[ustus] Pius Con[sul] III, Trib[unician] Po[wer] II P[ater] P[atriae] completed and dedicated the aqueduct to New Athens begun by his father, the divine Hadrian. (*CIL* III, 549)

A large lead pipe carried the water from the reservoir into the lower city, where it would have been widely distributed. One plausible terminus was a large nymphaion at the southeast corner of the Agora. Though in a ruinous state, the foundations suggest that this was a large hemicycle, facing north, looking down the Panathenaic Way. The building would have been two stories high, decorated with niches and statues, with water flowing into a

large semicircular basin below. A possible parallel would be the nymphaion built at
Olympia by Herodes Atticus.

The great need for the new water would have been to supply the baths which sprang
up all over the city throughout the Roman period. In all, more than two dozen such establishments have been located, many built or in use during the second century. These were
discovered in rescue excavations and have since been reburied, but a fine example can be
seen just north of the Olympieion. It has all the standard features: an entrance hall, changing rooms, and successive bathing areas with cold, warm, and hot pools. Several of the
rooms were heated with a hypocaust system, a raised floor which allowed hot air from
nearby furnaces to circulate underneath in a manner not unlike central heating. The rooms
are various shapes and sizes, lavishly decorated with marble columns and floors of either
mosaic or *opus sectile* (slabs of different colored marbles set in patterns). Many of the walls
have niches which would have carried marble sculpture. Such rich, elegant baths were a
common feature of Roman life, in many ways a defining element of Roman civilization all
over the Mediterranean and Europe, just as the gymnasium was essential to the Greek way

201. Theater of Dionysos, Hadrianic frieze of the scene-building, with scenes from the life of Dionysos,
2nd century A.D.

202. Theater of Dionysos, Silenoi from the scene-building.

of life. The Greeks and the Athenians had public baths, of course, some going back to the fifth century B.C., but they were far more modest in construction and seem not to have fulfilled the same social role as the Roman versions.

The theater of Dionysos was not neglected either. A raised stage was added to accommodate Roman tastes, its facade decorated with reliefs showing events in the career of Dionysos. Large figures of woolly Silenoi, the companions of Dionysos, were added to the decorations of the scene-building itself.

201, 202

203. Hadrianic bridge over the
Kephisos River at Eleusis, ca. A.D.
125. (Cf. fig. 124)

In addition to Athens,
Hadrian and his successors
paid particular attention to the
sanctuary at Eleusis, which was
extensively improved and ag-
grandized throughout the century. A feature of several of the
new buildings was the deliberate copying or adaptation of a
monument already standing in
Athens.

The earliest structure we
can date with any probability
to the second century is a bridge built by Hadrian to carry the Sacred Way (see fig. 124)
over the Eleusinian Kephisos River, which flowed only a kilometer or so east of the sanctuary and at times could be a raging torrent. We have references to flooding as early as the
fourth century B.C., and inscriptions and a poem indicate that the river had been bridged
in 320–319 B.C. by one Xenokles:

> Go, go, then, initiates, to the temple of Demeter, fearing not the winter floods.
> So safe a bridge has Xenokles, son of Xeinis, thrown across this broad river.
> (*Anth. Pal.* 9.147)

Hadrian himself was initiated into the mysteries in A.D. 125 and, according to Eusebius,
built a bridge at that time. It survives in good condition. Fifty meters long and 5 meters
wide, it is built of well-cut limestone blocks, with four arches spanning the course of the
river, which has silted up completely in modern times.

Once the Sacred Way reached the sanctuary at Eleusis, the visitor was led into a magnificent outer courtyard, rich in marble. Because the mysteries were so secret, this is as far
as Pausanias goes with his description (1.38.6–7):

The Eleusinians have a temple of Triptolemos, and another of Artemis Propylaia and of Poseidon Patroos, and a well called Kallichoron [of the fair dances], where the Eleusinian women first danced and sang in honor of the goddess. They say that the Rarian plain was the first to be sown and the first to bear crops, and therefore it is their custom to take the sacrificial barley and to make cakes for the sacrifices out of its produce. Here is shown what is called the threshing floor of Triptolemos and the altar. But my dream forbade me to describe what is within the wall of the sanctuary; and surely it is clear that the uninitiated may not lawfully hear of that from the sight of which they are excluded.

The forecourt was an irregularly shaped area, measuring as much as 70 meters across in places and paved with thick limestone slabs (see fig. 255). Near the middle of the court, and some 20 meters outside the gateway into the sanctuary, was a small marble Doric temple usually identified as that of Artemis Propylaia, set on a low podium. Several 204 of the architectural elements survive and indicate that the temple was tetrastyle amphiprostyle. Built in the second century A.D., it features the Doric order and the amphiprostyle plan so favored in the fifth century B.C., suggesting that we have here deliberate

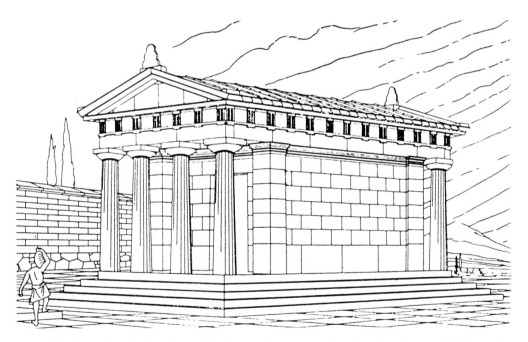

204. Temple of Artemis Propylaia at Eleusis, seen from the northeast, 2nd century A.D. (Cf. fig. 255)

205. Kallichoron well at Eleusis, seen from the south, with the steps of the greater propylon at left, 2nd century A.D.

classicizing, even if a known Classical predecessor has not been recognized. It is reminiscent of the probable ground plan of another Artemis temple, the one at Brauron.

Other monuments lined the forecourt of the sanctuary. To the southeast was an ornate fountain done in the Corinthian order with an elaborately carved entablature. Round depressions worn deep into the steps indicate the position of eight spouts which delivered water from a central basin. The supply aqueduct can still be traced in parts across the plain, though less easily than in the nineteenth century. It brought water from springs at the ancient deme of Phyle on Mount Parnes, about 15 kilometers to the northeast.

The Sacred Way enters the forecourt from the northeast. Two other roads enter the area as well, from the northwest and the southeast. At the juncture, each of these secondary streets was spanned by a large marble arch which was almost an exact replica of the Arch of Hadrian near the Olympieion at Athens. The arches carried identical inscriptions, different from the Athenian prototype: "The Panhellenes to the two goddesses and to the emperor." Numerous statue bases found in the area honor the family of Hadrian's successor, Antoninus Pius, and it may be that the arches were dedicated either during his reign or possibly in that of his successor, Marcus Aurelius.

Just to the left of the main gateway, outside the sanctuary wall, the paving of the Roman forecourt breaks, and within a sunken area can be seen an early stone-lined well set in a small enclosure. This is almost certainly the Kallichoron well mentioned by Pausanias (1.38.6) as the place where the daughters of King Keleus found Demeter grieving for her lost daughter, Persephone.

Next to the well is the centerpiece of the Roman forecourt, the greater propylon. The whole platform is preserved, along with a great deal of the superstructure. These remains indicate that the propylon is a wonderfully close replica of the central hall of the fifth-century Propylaia of the Acropolis in Athens (see figs. 76, 77, 255). A facade of six Doric

206. Gable of the greater propylon of Eleusis, with an imperial portrait, 2nd century A.D.

columns gives access through an Ionic hall to five doorways which lead through a portico of six more Doric columns into the sanctuary. So close is the copy that the interior Ionic column bases are cut as though set on a final resting surface, while the floor is elsewhere raised a centimeter or so, in imitation of the protective surfaces which were never cut away in the unfinished Classical Propylaia. And the doorway with the most footwear on the threshold is in both instances the one all the way to the left.

There are one or two modifications. The propylon at Eleusis is built on nearly level ground; the only stairs, therefore, are those on the facade, and there are none inside leading up to the doors as in the Athenian prototype. And the Eleusis gateway had a huge sculpted bust set in a shield (*imago clipeata*) carved in both pediments. One is well preserved, though the figure—certainly a Roman emperor of the second century A.D.—cannot be identified with certainty. Hadrian (117–138, initiated in 125), Antoninus Pius (138–161), and Marcus Aurelius (161–180, initiated 176) are all candidates. Fragments of a dedicatory inscription on the architrave are too slight to allow a reading. The steps and thresholds of the greater propylon are sufficiently well preserved to allow certainty that no wheeled traffic entered the sanctuary through this gateway. In contrast, there are what seem to be deep and well-used ruts running through the earlier inner propylon of Claudius Appius Pulcher, and there must have been a major shift in the traffic patterns of the sanctuary between the mid-first and mid-second centuries.

Within the sanctuary another building generally dated to the second century stands on the right just before the Telesterion, at the top of a long flight of stairs. Its paltry remains

207. Small pedimental figures from Temple F at Eleusis, 2nd century A.D. (Cf. fig. 255, "D.") Compare the figures at left with those on the west end of the Parthenon (fig. 13).

have been restored with a *distyle-in-antis* (two columns between the antae) plan. Of interest is the pedimental sculpture associated with the temple. Several of the figures are one-third-scale copies of figures in the west pediment of the Parthenon, making the prosaically 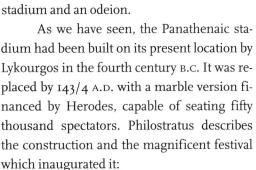 207 named Temple F a further example of the extensive classicizing found in so many of the buildings of Roman Eleusis.

The great Telesterion had a Roman phase as well (see fig. 256). Built into the foundations for one of the interior supports in the northeast part of the building is an inscribed base from the late first century A.D., providing a *terminus post quem* for a major reconstruction of at least part of the building well on in the Roman period. Marcus Aurelius is often credited with this rebuilding, and the occasion which is thought to have necessitated the repairs is a raid on Greece by the Costobocs during his reign.

Athens was blessed throughout the second century not only with the attention of three successive Roman emperors, Hadrian, Antoninus Pius, and Marcus Aurelius, but also by a local benefactor, Herodes Atticus of Marathon, who was both wealthy and generous. The 208 source of the family fortune was a huge treasure discovered by his father in a house he owned near the theater. Herodes himself was a prominent Roman citizen and philosopher, who served for a time as the tutor of future emperors. He is known to have made lavish dedications throughout Greece: the stadium at Delphi, a nymphaion at Olympia, and, probably, a refurbishment of the Peirene fountain at Corinth. Two large monuments in his native Athens are specifically attributed to him: the stadium and an odeion.

As we have seen, the Panathenaic stadium had been built on its present location by Lykourgos in the fourth century B.C. It was replaced by 143/4 A.D. with a marble version financed by Herodes, capable of seating fifty thousand spectators. Philostratus describes 209 the construction and the magnificent festival which inaugurated it:

When he [Herodes] was offered the crowning honor of the Panathenaic festival, he made this announcement: "I shall welcome you, Athenians, and those Greeks who attend and those athletes

208. Portrait of the Athenian philosopher and philanthropist Herodes Atticus, 2nd century A.D.

209. Reconstruction of the Panathenaic stadium built by Herodes Atticus around A.D. 144 and rebuilt for the first modern Olympic Games, of 1896.

who compete, in a stadium of pure white marble." In accordance with this promise he completed within four years the stadium on the other side of the Ilissos, and thus constructed a monument that is beyond all other marvels, for there is no theater that can rival it. Moreover, I have been told the following facts concerning this Panathenaic festival. The robe of Athena that was hung on the ship was more beautiful than any painting, with folds that swelled before the breeze; and the ship, as it took its course, was not hauled by animals but slid forward by means of underground machinery. Setting sail at the Kerameikos with a thousand rowers, it arrived at the Eleusinion, and after circling it, passed by the Pelasgikon: and thus escorted came by the Pythion to where it is now moored. The other side of the stadium is occupied by a temple of Tyche [Fortune], with an ivory statue of her as mistress of all. (*Vit. Soph.* 550)

On the hill west of the stadium lie the heavy concrete remains of a podium temple and a few blocks of marble, presumably the foundations of the temple of Tyche. Opposite them, on the hill northeast of the stadium, are the remains of a long conglomerate foundation of the right dimensions for a ship shed to house the Panathenaic ship.

Like Philostratus, Pausanias was also impressed by the stadium (1.19.6):

Wonderful to see, though not so impressive to hear of, is a stadium of white marble. One may best get an idea of its size as follows. It is a hill rising above the Ilissos, of a crescent shape in its upper part and extending thence in a double straight line to the bank of the river. It was built by the Athenian Herodes, and the greater part of the Pentelic quarries was used up in its construction.

The stadium was joined to the rest of Athens by a three-arched bridge which spanned the Ilissos River. This bridge survived until 1778, at which time it was torn down to provide   210 building material for a wall around Athens. Excavated in 1869–1870, the stadium itself was completely rebuilt to serve as the venue for the first modern Olympic Games in 1896. Little of the original structure remains in situ, though the reconstruction is remarkably faithful. Double herms from the running track are preserved, along with fragments of marble thrones decorated with owls.

    The second monument built by Herodes for the Athenians was the huge Odeion, or music hall, on the south slopes of the Acropolis. Pausanias describes it only when he is in   211 Patras in the Peloponnese, and he tells us why (7.20.6):

210. Nineteenth-century view of the bridge built in the second century over the Ilissos River.

211. View of the Odeion of Herodes Atticus from the west, ca. A.D. 160, before modern restoration.

The Odeion [of Patras] is the grandest in Greece, except for the one at Athens, which excels it in both size and style. The latter was erected by the Athenian Herodes in memory of his dead wife. In my book on Attica, this music hall is not mentioned because my description of Athens was finished before Herodes began to build it.

Philostratus also comments on the building and its dedication:

Herodes also dedicated to the Athenians the theater in memory of Regilla, and he made its roof of cedar wood, though this wood is considered costly even for making statues. These two monuments then are at Athens, and they are such as exist nowhere else in the Roman Empire. (*Vit. Soph.* 551)

Herodes' wife, Regilla, died around 160, so the Odeion must date to between then and the 170s, when Pausanias finished his book and Herodes died.

The building features a marble auditorium in the form of a half-circle, with a seating capacity of around five thousand people. It had a raised stage and a three-story scene-building, of which numerous arches survive. The building would have been decorated inside with marble revetment, columns, and sculptures. The entrance hall to the south was floored with mosaics of mixed geometric and curvilinear designs. The radius of the auditorium is 38 meters, and it must have been a great achievement to span it in antiquity, for there are no traces of any interior supports. Not only are odeia usually roofed buildings, but Philostratus makes specific mention of the cedar used in the roof of this building. Furthermore, the early excavations uncovered ash, carbonized beams, and roof tiles on the floor of the orchestra, presumably remnants of the roof from the burning of the building by the Herulians in 267.

The need for the Odeion of Herodes perhaps sheds light on the history of the old Odeion of Agrippa in the Agora, for it is hard to see why two such buildings would be necessary. As it turns out, the excavations of the Odeion of Agrippa suggest that its roof, with a span of about 25 meters, collapsed in the middle of the second century. The building was rebuilt, but the span of the roof was drastically decreased, and the capacity of the auditorium shrank to about five hundred people. The building seems thereafter to have been used primarily as a lecture hall, often for philosophical discourses. Herodes himself seems to have used it in this way:

They assembled in the theater in the Kerameikos which is called Agrippeion; and as the day went on and Herodes delayed the Athenians became restive,

212. Giant from the facade of the rebuilt Odeion
of Agrippa, mid-2nd century A.D.

thinking that the lecture was being
canceled. So it became necessary for
Alexander to come forward to give
his discourse before Herodes arrived. (Philostratus, *Vit. Soph.* 2.5.4)

With the collapse and subsequent reuse of
the Odeion of Agrippa for lectures, there
would have been a need for the new
Odeion of Herodes. The restoration of the
Odeion of Agrippa included an elaborate
new facade, which was decorated with
huge piers in the form of colossal figures
of giants (with snaky tails) and tritons
(with fishy tails). Their torsos and some of
the heads are copies of the figures of Poseidon and Hephaistos in the Parthenon
pediments; it appears that artists had access to the pediments, allowing them to
make drawings or casts at this time. Note
also that the small-scale copies of Parthenon pedimental figures used in Temple F at Eleusis date to this same period.

Herodes served as archon at Athens and as consul at Rome and clearly spent time in
and owned properties in several places. We have no fewer than two hundred inscriptions
pertaining to his career or family. Not all his duties were onerous: he served as the president of the Iobacchoi, a religious association in honor of Bacchos, god of wine. Their club-
house has been excavated in the valley west of the Acropolis; it is a large rectangular hall
measuring about 10 by 20 meters, with two smaller rooms adjoining. In its ruins was also
found a column which carries a long inscription (*IG* II² 1368) preserving the minutes of the
meeting at which Herodes was elected president. The rules of the club are recorded and
make it clear that the proper worship of Bacchos required the membership to consume
large quantities of wine with some frequency. The regulations governing behavior at club
gatherings are accordingly reminiscent of those applying to a college fraternity:

213. Rules of the Iobaccheion, presided over by Herodes Atticus, ca. A.D. 170.

No Iobacchos who has not paid his contributions for the monthly and annual meetings shall enter the gathering until the priests have decided either that he must pay or that he may be admitted. If anyone starts a fight or is found acting disorderly or occupying the seat of any other member or using insulting or abusive language to anyone, the person so abused or insulted shall produce two of the Iobacchoi to state upon oath that they heard him insulted or abused, and he who was guilty of the insult or abuse shall pay to the society 25 light drachmas.

One of Herodes' private estates, in Kynouria, south of Argos, has recently been excavated and has produced a villa of extraordinary wealth in terms of mosaics, architecture, and sculptural adornment. In Attica, Herodes is associated in particular with two demes: Kephisia and Marathon. In Kephisia, parts of a villa have been found together with inscriptions referring to Herodes, along with a burial chamber with four marble sarcophagi which seem to have been used by his friends or family. These remains are only a small part of the luxurious estate he maintained in the garden suburb of Kephisia; the Roman Aulus Gellius paints an evocative picture of the rich lifestyle enjoyed there in the second century:

While we were students at Athens, Herodes Atticus, a man of consular rank and true Greek eloquence, often invited me to his country houses near that city, in company with the honorable Servilianus and several other of our countrymen who had withdrawn from Rome to Greece in quest of culture. And there at that time, while we were with him at the villa called Kephisia, both in the heat of the summer and under the burning autumnal sun, we protected ourselves

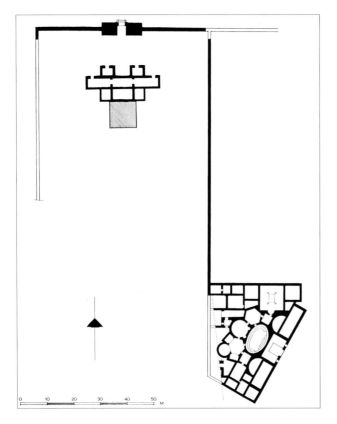

214. Bath and temple of the Egyptian gods at Herodes' estate at Marathon, 2nd century A.D. (Cf. fig. 47)

against the trying temperature by the shade of its spacious groves, its long, soft promenades, the cool location of the house, its elegant baths with their abundance of sparkling water, and the charm of the villa as a whole, which was everywhere melodious with splashing waters and tuneful birds. (*Attic Nights* 1.2.1–2)

Several monuments are also associated with Herodes in his home deme of Marathon. Part of what seems to be his estate has been excavated on the seashore at the south end of the plain. The remains include a large bathing establishment with a handsome

214 oval pool in the center. Nearby is a shrine of the Egyptian gods (Isis, Sarapis, and Anoubis), who were popular in Greece throughout the Hellenistic and Roman periods. The foundations of a small podium temple survive, along with the enclosure wall and gate-

215 way. Two large Egyptian-style striding figures were found, together with a lintel block decorated with a representation of a cobra. Portraits of Herodes and the imperial family of Rome were found in the same area some two hundred years ago and are now in the Louvre.

Other remains have been found farther inland on the plain. On a low ridge at the end of the Avlon Valley, there is a long rubble wall enclosing a barren area with no view of the sea: not prime real estate. Pottery and tiles litter the area, which was entered through a marble gateway. The gate takes the form of an arch, and inscriptions on either side inform us

216 that this is the "Gate of Immortal Harmony" and that everything on one side belongs to Herodes and on the other to his wife, Regilla. The piers of the arch carry poems recording

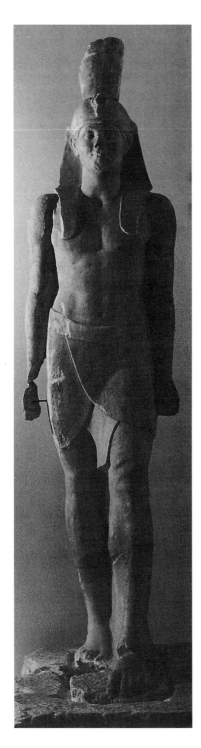

Herodes' sorrow at the death of Regilla, and the gateway was once flanked by two marble statues of seated figures, presumably Herodes and Regilla.

Finally, at the deme of Oinoe, also part of the plain of Marathon, there is an enigmatic marble building which may well have been the work of Herodes. Only partially excavated, it is some sort of hydraulic establishment, drawing water from a nearby spring. Large square piers and shallow rectangular basins or dining couches form a series of bays which are separated from the center of the building by thin parapets. The whole installation is made of marble and carefully built. It was probably the work of Herodes, though we have no inscriptions or portraits to make the association certain.

Around 178, according to Philostratus, Herodes

> died at the age of about seventy-six, of a wasting sickness. Though he expired at Marathon and had left instructions to his freedmen to bury him there, the Athenians carried him away by the hands of the ephebes and took him to the city; and every age went out to meet the bier with tears and cries, as would sons bereft of a good father. They buried him in the Panathenaic stadium. (*Vit. Soph.* 565–566)

Thus when Pausanias visited Athens, he described a city at the height of its urban development, full of famous old monuments next to magnificent recent additions reflecting the city's role as the cultural and educational center of the Mediterranean. Adorned with handsome public buildings and filled

215. Egyptianizing statue from Herodes' estate at Marathon.

216. Fragment from the arch of the
Gate of Immortal Harmony, leading
into Regilla's estate at Marathon, 2nd
century A.D.

with philosophers and sophists
enjoying imperial favor, Athens
in the second century experi-
enced a period of well-being and
success unrivaled since the days
of Perikles.

7

Late Roman Athens

As the Roman Empire began its decline late in the second century A.D., Athens suffered as well. Barbarian raids in Greece are attested to as early as the second century after Christ, with an attack by the Costobocs mentioned by Pausanias (10.34.5) and in inscriptions (*IG* II² 3411 and 3639). Other invaders were in northern Greece by the 250s, and there is a reference to repairs of the old circuit wall of the city during the reign of Valerian. Athens itself was first devastated during a raid by the Herulians in 267. Coming out of the Black Sea and terrorizing Ionia and the Aegean islands, the Herulians completely destroyed the lower city of Athens before they were eventually driven off by two thousand Athenians under the command of the archon Herennios Dexippos. Dexippos himself wrote an account of the invasion.

The archaeological evidence for the destruction is impressive. The extent of the damage can be seen most clearly in the Agora, where many buildings were affected. The Odeion of Agrippa, for instance, is first referred to in the excavation notebooks as "the burnt building" from the heavy deposit of burned debris which covered the monument as a result of the Herulian sack. The area of the Dipylon, the Metroon, the Stoa of Attalos, the Middle Stoa, the temple of Ares, the Library of Hadrian, the Stoa of Eumenes, and numerous private houses all show clear signs of the devastation. Less clear is the degree of damage to the northwest part of the Agora and the great temples on the Acropolis.

The destruction completely altered the character of the city. The old, extensive Themistoklean circuit wall, appropriate when Athens was the most powerful city-state of Greece in the fifth century B.C., made little sense when it was a small provincial university

223

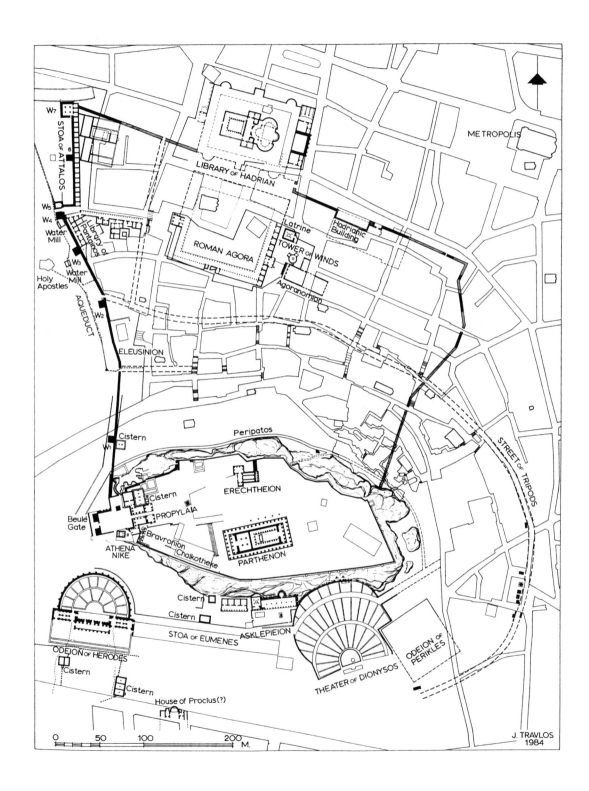

W7

STOA of ATTALOS

LIBRARY of HADRIAN

METROPOLIS

W5

W4

Water
Mill

Library of
Pantainos

W3

Water
Mill

Holy
Apostles

AQUEDUCT

W2

ELEUSINION

Latrine

Hadrianic
Building

ROMAN AGORA

TOWER of WINDS

Agoranomion

Cistern

W1

Peripatos

ERECHTHEION

Cistern

Beulé
Gate

PROPYLAIA

Bravronion

ATHENA
NIKE

Chalkotheke

PARTHENON

Cistern

Cistern

STOA of EUMENES

ASKLEPIEION

ODEION of HERODES

Cistern

Cistern

House of Proclus(?)

STREET of TRIPODS

ODEION of
PERIKLES

THEATER of DIONYSOS

0   50   100   200   M.

J. TRAVLOS
1984

218. The post-Herulian wall where it passes along the east side of the Agora, with numerous reused architectural blocks, including (extreme left) column drums from the "stoa" at Thorikos, ca. A.D. 282.

town in the third century A.D., unable to maintain or garrison it. Within some fifteen to twenty years after the Herulian invasion, the Athenians had laid out a new circuit on a much more modest scale. The new wall started just outside the old Propylaia, where a sec- 217 ond gate was built, protected by two flanking towers. It then followed the east side of the Panathenaic Way down into the Agora, using the western stoa of the ruined Library of Pantainos and the door-wall of the Stoa of Attalos for its line. At the north end of the Stoa of Attalos it turned due east, incorporating the south wall of the Library of Hadrian. The library enclosure projected beyond the northern line of the wall, perhaps as a separate fort. East of the library the wall takes a jog to the south.

It has long been argued that the wall continued south, to hook up with the eastern end of the Acropolis, but it now seems far more probable that it swung around the east end of the Acropolis to enclose the area of the south slopes as well. The old Greek Agora was clearly outside the circuit and no longer the center of town. The shattered remains of its buildings were in fact reused as building material. Where the wall passes through the Agora, it is composed almost entirely of architectural blocks, and the new gate of the Acropolis is built in large part of the Doric elements of the choregic monument of Nikias. The 218, 219

Opposite 217. Late Roman Athens, with the 3rd century A.D. wall as it runs north of the Acropolis.

219. Post-Herulian gate to the Acropolis (late 3rd century A.D.), with the reused Doric entablature of the Nikias monument (320/19 B.C.).

wall is constructed of two good faces of masonry with rubble thrown in between; coins embedded in the mortar indicate that construction was begun in the reign of Probus (276–282) and suggest some delay in refortifying the city after 267.

An inscription records that some sections of the wall were paid for by private contributions:

As Amphion raised the walls of Thebes with the music of his kithara, so now do I, Illyrios, follower of the sweet-voiced Muse, build the walls of my home city. (*IG* II² 5199)

Much of the archaeological evidence for the late Roman city lies unexplored to the east, hidden under the modern buildings of Plaka, and we have only indirect evidence from such peripheral areas as the old Greek Agora and the Kerameikos. The literary sources indicate one important fact for the economy of the city: the philosophical and rhetorical schools continued to flourish and to draw scholars and students from all over the Mediterranean. The city's relative prosperity and reputation are referred to in a passage written around 359:

Corinth is very active in commerce and has an outstanding structure of an amphitheater. Athens has the centers of higher learning and ancient historical monuments and something worthy of special mention, the Acropolis, where by means of so many standing statues it is wonderful to see a so-called war of

220. Plan of a philosophical school(?) on the slopes of the Areopagos, 4th to 6th century A.D.

the ancients. (*Expositio totius mundi et gentium,* 52)

This picture is borne out by the evidence of numerous substantial villas built on the north slopes of the Areopagos and on the south slopes of the Acropolis. These are large, well-appointed establishments, with marble peristyles, private baths, mosaic floors, and collections of earlier sculpture. One might

220, 221

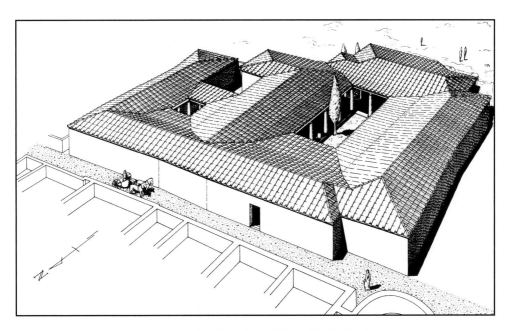

221. Reconstruction of the philosophical school.

guess at the outset that these rich houses were the homes of the philosophers, sophists, and
222   other teachers, who were the aristocracy and the wealthy men of Roman Athens. As early as
the second century they were charging fees for their courses and using their houses as private schools. Eunapius describes the house of the sophist Julian of Cappadocia early in the
fourth century:

> The author himself saw Julian's house at Athens; poor and humble as it was,
> nevertheless from it breathed the fragrance of Hermes and the Muses, so
> closely did it resemble a holy temple. This house he had bequeathed to Pro-
> haeresius. There too were erected statues of the pupils whom he had most ad-
> mired; and he had a theater of polished marble made after the model of a public
> theater but smaller and of a size suitable to a house. For in those days, so bitter

222. Philosophical school, with arches and apsidal pool, 4th to 6th century A.D.

223. Youthful Herakles discarded down a well in the philosophical school in the first half of the 6th century A.D.

was the feud at Athens between the citizens and the young students—as if the city after those wars of hers was festering within her walls the peril of discord—that none of the Sophists ventured to go down into the city and discourse in public, but they confined their utterances to their private lecture theaters and there discoursed to their students. (Eunapius, *Lives* 483)

Eunapius refers to an important feature of the schools at Athens: they were pagan institutions. Established in the old gymnasia, their adherents worshiped Herakles, Hermes, the Nymphs, and the Muses. Even the official advent of Christianity under Constantine in 325 seems to have had minimal impact on the city. Athens remained pagan until the end of antiquity.

223

In addition to the large houses of the fourth century, several Athenian baths show signs of construction or renovation, and there is good evidence that the Attic lamp industry was flourishing, particularly in the area of the Kerameikos. Many of these lamps were exported all over Greece and farther afield, from Spain to South Russia; in Attica they begin to appear in large numbers in the mountain caves of Pan, especially at Vari and on Mount Parnes. These are the first of literally hundreds of lamps to be deposited in the two caves during the fifth and sixth centuries. No convincing explanation has been put forth for this intense interest in Pan or his caves after years of relative neglect. Elsewhere in Attica there is little evidence of significant activity in the fourth century.

The theater of Dionysos also continued to be used in this period. The last substantial stage, decorated with the reused sculpted frieze blocks of the second century A.D. (see fig. 201), carries a late dedicatory inscription:

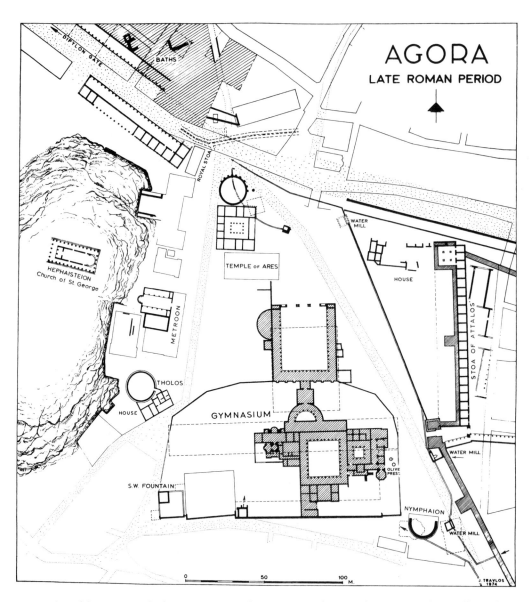

AGORA

LATE ROMAN PERIOD

DIPYLON GATE

BATHS

ROYAL STOA

WATER MILL

HEPHAISTEION
Church of St George

TEMPLE of ARES

HOUSE

METROON

STOA OF ATALOS

THOLOS

HOUSE

GYMNASIUM

WATER MILL

OLIVE PRESS

S.W. FOUNTAIN

NYMPHAION

WATER MILL

0   50   100 M.

J. TRAVLOS
1974

224. Plan of the Agora in the late Roman period, ca. 450 A.D., showing the post-Herulian wall at right
and the palace(?) in the center.

For you, lover of the sacred rites, this beautiful *bema* [speakers' platform, stage] has been built by Phaidros, son of Zoilos, archon of life-giving Athens. (*IG* II² 5021)

The next danger to threaten the city came with Alaric and his Visigoths in 396. The literary sources give two versions of his attack. Zosimus tells us that Athena and Achilles appeared and so frightened Alaric that he made peace and withdrew, leaving Athens and Attica unharmed. Claudian, Saint Jerome, and Philostorgius suggest, on the other hand, that the city was taken. Not enough work has been done within the circuit of the post-Herulian wall to allow us to assess the effect of Alaric's visit. Outside the walls, however, in the area of the old Agora and the Kerameikos, there are distinct signs of his unfriendly presence. Several of the Agora buildings on the west side which survived the Herulians in 267 (Tholos, Stoa of Zeus, Apollo Patroos) now show signs of damage. The bishop Synesios vis-

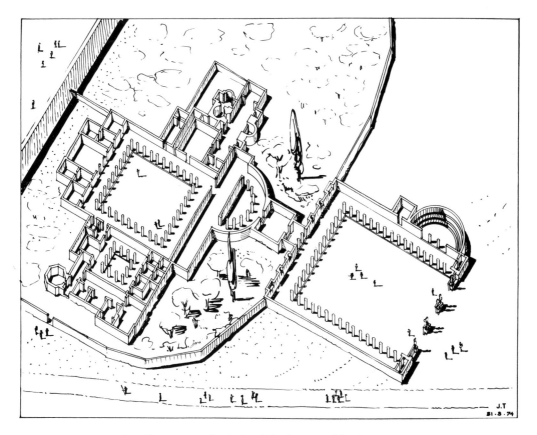

225. Late Roman complex (palace?) in the area of the Agora, ca. A.D. 420.

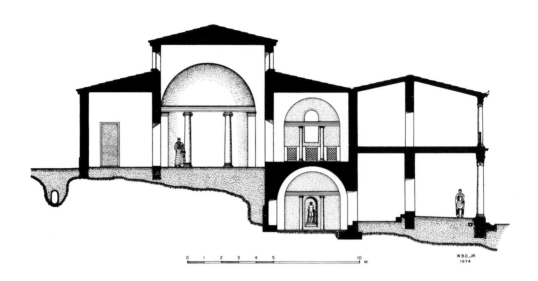

226. Late Roman building over the Library of Pantainos, early 5th century A.D.

ited Athens soon afterward, between 395 and 399, and was not impressed with what he saw: the Painted Stoa bereft of paintings and the philosophers of the city replaced by bee-keepers. The Areopagos houses, on the other hand, continued to be occupied into the fifth and sixth centuries, with no clear evidence of ill effects from Alaric's visit. In Attica, the final destruction of Eleusis is usually attributed to Alaric.

224   A revival of sorts can be dated to the first half of the fifth century. In the old Agora the Hellenistic Metroon was partially refurbished and the third room from the south provided with a mosaic floor. The most impressive new construction was a huge complex covering 225 the old Odeion of Agrippa and most of the South Square. Its entrance was at the north, where several of the old second-century giants and tritons (see fig. 212) were re-erected on new high pedestals built of reused material. Behind them was a vast complex of court-yards, rooms, octagonal and apsidal chambers, and a small bath. The date from pottery and finds seems to be the first quarter of the fifth century. Its identification and function are uncertain; it has the appearance of an elaborate villa, and perhaps served as an official residence.

     Just to the north a large square building of some 25 meters a side was built at about the same time; it had a group of rooms set around a central courtyard. Another large complex, also dated to the early fifth century, incorporated the old northern stoa of the Library 226 of Pantainos. It had two stories, with niches set in the walls, a small courtyard, and a small bathing complex; again, no evidence has been recovered to shed clear light on either the function or identification of the building.

One of the individuals responsible for Athens in the early fifth century, and perhaps for some of the renewal we have been noting, was Herculius, prefect of Illyria in 408–412. For whatever reason, he was honored with statues, one on the Acropolis dedicated by the Sophist Apronianos (*IG* II² 4225) and a second erected near the west door of the Library of Hadrian and dedicated by a certain Plutarch, who may have been one of the most prominent philosophers or Sophists of the city. This same Plutarch, a pagan, was himself honored for paying on three occasions the costs of the Panathenaic ship, still making its voyage to the Acropolis well into the fifth century.

Within the confines of the old library we find the first substantive architectural evidence of Christian activity, dated to the fifth century, closely following yet another attempt to shut down the pagan sanctuaries, this time by Theodosius II in 435. This is a large building with four apses, all but the eastern apse set off by colonnades to form an ambulatory. To the west, a broad hallway gives access to the structure through three doors. The simple   227

227. Tetraconch (5th century A.D.) in the courtyard of the Library of Hadrian, with colonnade of later church (7th century A.D.).

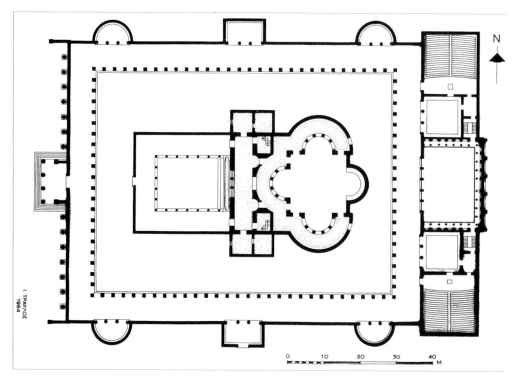

228. Tetraconch in the Library of
Hadrian.

apse at the east and the presence
of a narthex and atrium at the
west now make it almost certain
that we have here a church, the
earliest yet known from Athens.
The date is based on the style of

229. Roman relief of Artemis,
disfigured by Christians in the 6th
century A.D., found in the pagan
philosophical school occupied by
Christians after 529. (Cf. figs. 220–
222)

the mosaic floors, which decorate the ambulatory and some of the western rooms. Though dwarfed by its setting in the court of the old library, the "Tetraconch," as it is sometimes called, is a large building, measuring about 40 meters on a side, with the centralized plan often favored for churches of this period.   228

The other common form of early Christian church, the long, three-aisled basilica, makes its appearance slightly later in the fifth century. The first was built in southeast Athens along the banks of the Ilissos River, where the remains can still be seen today. Several other basilicas came to be built in the same general area thereafter. The conversion of pagan temples to Christian use seems to be a late phenomenon in Athens, for the most part dating to the sixth and seventh centuries. With the gradual rise of Christianity, numerous fifth-century basilicas are also to be found throughout the countryside in Attica, often near the old deme sites: Brauron (Philaidai), Porto Raphti (Steireia), and Eleusis.

A single sentence in Procopius (*Bell. [Vand]* 3.5.23) suggests that Greece was the victim of a Vandal incursion in the fifth century. A layer of ash and debris found along the west side of the Agora seems to confirm this reference, as does a hoard of almost five hundred

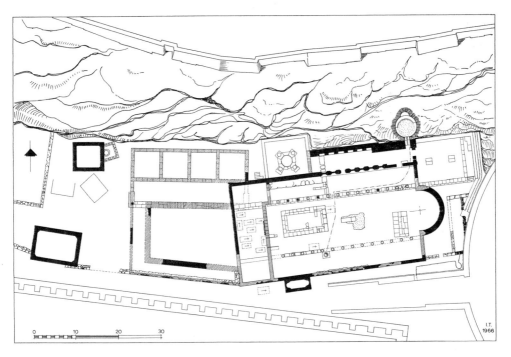

230. Plan of the early Christian basilica built over the remains of the Asklepieion, 6th century A.D.
(Cf. fig. 149)

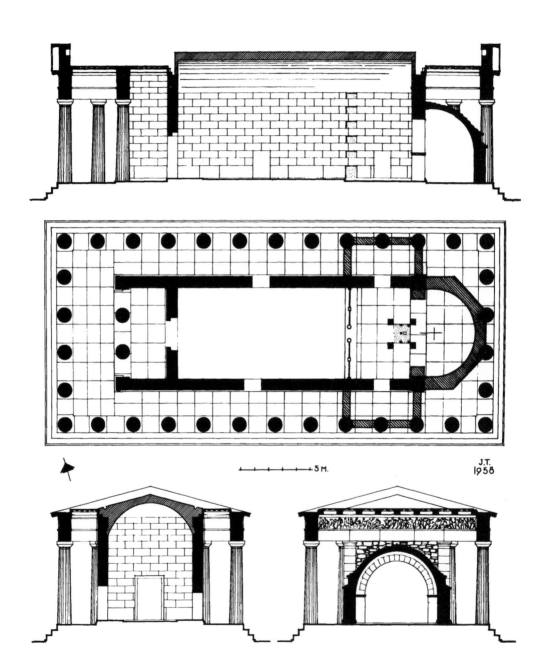

231. Plan of the Hephaisteion as converted into a Christian church in the 7th century.

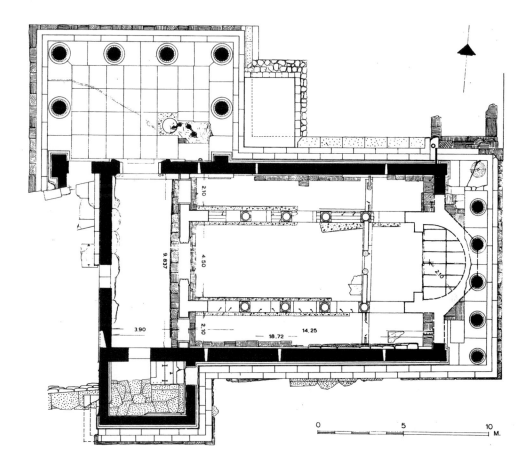

232. The Erechtheion, as converted into a Christian basilica, 7th century.

bronze coins, the latest dating to the reign of Leo I (457–474). Also during the second half of the fifth century the great bronze statue of Athena Promachos, which had been a land-mark on the Acropolis for centuries, was removed to Constantinople. It stood thereafter in the Forum of Constantine until it was torn to pieces by drunken rioters in 1203.

The reign of the Christian emperor Justinian in Constantinople (527–565) in many ways marks the end of ancient Athens. The old pagan schools of the city finally proved too popular for their own good, more than five hundred years after the birth of Christ. In 529 Justinian issued a decree forbidding any pagan to teach philosophy in Athens. This, more than any barbarian incursion, was the death knell of the city. With the closing of the schools after more than nine hundred years, Athens began a decline into insignificance.

In at least one instance we may be able to see Christians at work as a result of this decree. In one of the large houses on the Areopagos, probably used as a private philosophical school, several sculptures were mutilated and a fine mosaic floor panel, presumably carrying some offensively pagan scene, was torn up and replaced with marble slabs. Other

229

sculptures were thrown down two wells in the house. The final occupants were apparently Christians, who furnished the house with lamps decorated with crosses and a sigma table, used for reenactments of the Last Supper. Soon after, the old temples and sanctuaries were probably converted to Christian use. The Parthenon was converted late in the reign of Justinian, and a basilica was built on the ruins of the popular shrine of Asklepios at about the

230

same time. The Hephaisteion and Erechtheion were not converted until perhaps the sev-

231, 232

enth century. In the case of both the Parthenon and the Hephaisteion we can see the hands of Christians at work mutilating the sculpted metopes which stayed in place on the building. Pieces of the temple and statue at Rhamnous are so thoroughly beaten into tiny fragments that here, too, we should probably recognize the work of zealots.

The physical decline of the city was hastened by another invasion, by the Slavs, in 582–583. All the fifth-century buildings in the old Agora, including the large houses on the slopes of the Areopagos, go out of use, buried under a thick layer of debris which was not touched until the excavations began in the twentieth century. The Tetraconch in the Library of Hadrian was destroyed and replaced in the seventh century by a basilica made up of a pitiful and ill-suited array of reused material. The emperor Constans II spent the winter of 662–663 in Athens, a sojourn which must have required some modest revival of the city. Thereafter Athens enters a period of extreme decline which lasted for several centuries, until the emergence of a new town with numerous small churches in the eleventh and twelfth centuries (see fig. 233).

Epilogue

The later history of Athens is of interest not only on its own terms but also because of its impact on the antiquities of the city. As we have seen, the plunder of early monuments for later building projects dates back to ancient times; in Athens the process began as early as the Persian Wars. The barbarian incursions of late antiquity also had a devastating impact on many Athenian monuments, starting with the Herulians in 267 A.D. and continu-

233. The church of the Holy Apostles, ca. 1000, undergoing restoration in the 1950s.

234. The Acropolis in the Frankish period, with additional fortifications, the Propylaia turned into a
palace, and the Parthenon used as a cathedral, 13th to 15th centuries.

ing with the Visigoths in 395, the Vandals in the second half of the fifth century, and the
Slavs in 582–583. The shift from paganism to Christianity, though slow and late in Athens,
also had a profound effect on the sanctuaries and temples, including the Parthenon, the
Erechtheion, and the Hephaisteion, all of which were remodeled.

After two centuries of virtual abandonment, the area of the old Agora revived in the
tenth century, and by the eleventh was a crowded urban neighborhood, with houses shar-
ing party walls and little evidence of open land. Numerous small churches, like the Holy
233   Apostles in the Agora, were built in the lower city to serve the needs of a substantial population. From this time on, large blocks for building could be found simply by digging a bit,
far easier than quarrying new ones, and many Athenian monuments were stripped for this
type of recycling throughout the Middle Ages. Several of the Byzantine churches of Athens,
built between 1000 and 1200, reused ancient material liberally. The Little Metropolis
church, next to the cathedral, is an excellent example, full of ancient sculptures and reused
architectural blocks. In Attica, the church at Daphni (see fig. 124) was built on the ruins of
an old sanctuary of Apollo; its name comes from his sacred tree, the laurel (*daphne*).

The varied fortunes of medieval Athens also played a large role in the fate of individual monuments. In 1204 the Franks besieged Athens and took it from the Byzantines dur-

ing the Fourth Crusade. Burgundian knights controlled Athens from 1204 to 1311, and   234
Daphni was used as a Cistercian monastery, while the Parthenon was rededicated to the
Virgin Mary as a Catholic church. Also during this time, the Klepsydra spring was heavily
fortified, as was the area of the Propylaia. Several dozen large towers can be seen dotting   235
the landscape of Attica; they were apparently a preferred means of managing the countryside in Frankish times. From 1311 to 1385 Athens was under the control of the Catalans, who
were responsible for building a palace and a church of Saint Bartholomew in the ruins of
the Propylaia, as well as for refortifying several of the old border forts of Attica, especially
Panakton. From 1385 to 1456 Athens was governed by a Florentine family, the Acciajuoli.
They are responsible for the huge tower at the west end of the Acropolis, which dominated
the citadel until it was dismantled in 1875. The Propylaia served as the palace of the Acciajuoli, and the Acropolis remained heavily fortified.

Following the fall of Constantinople in 1453, the Turks took Athens, in 1456. Soon afterward the Mosque of the Conqueror (Fethiye Camii) was built over the ruins of the Ro-

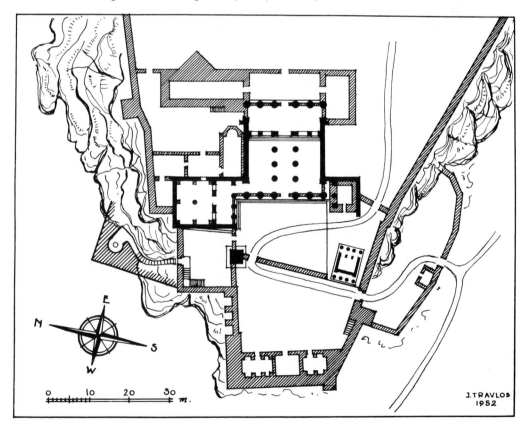

235. Plan of the Propylaia after it was rebuilt as a Frankish palace.

man Agora and an early Christian basilica. The nearby Tower of the Winds became a center for dervishes. Christian churches continued alongside Islamic monuments. In 1669 a
Cistercian monastery was founded, incorporating in its fabric the old Lysikrates monu-
236   ment. Turkish rule was interrupted briefly by a devastating attack and occupation by the
Venetians in 1687–1688. The Nike temple was dismantled to provide material for additional fortifications on the Acropolis. During the siege, the Venetians bombarded the
citadel from the hills to the west. The Parthenon shows the effects of hundreds of artillery
hits, one of which pierced the roof, ignited the powder stored within, and blew up the building, which had remained largely intact until then. Taken as trophies by the Venetians were
three marble lions that stand in front of the arsenal in Venice today, including one from the
Peiraieus which gave its name to the medieval harbor, Porto Leone.

The second period of Turkish domination corresponds to the period of decline for
the Ottoman Empire. Edward Dodwell's description in 1819 of the reuse of a column of the
Olympieion in 1759 gives a vivid picture of the fate of many of the antiquities of the city:

> The single column which stood towards the western extremity of the temple, was
> thrown down many years ago, by the orders of a Voivode of Athens, for the sake of
> the materials, which were employed in constructing the great mosque in the bazar
> [*sic*]. It was undermined and blown down by gunpowder; but such was its mas-
> sive strength, that the fourth explosion took place before it fell. The Pasha of Egri-
> pos inflicted upon the Voivode a fine of seventeen purses (8,500 Turkish piastres)
> for having destroyed those venerable remains. (Had the laudable practice of fin-
> ing dilapidators continued to the present time, the Athenian temples would have
> been saved from their destruction.) The Athenians relate, that, after this column

was thrown down,
the three nearest to
it were heard at
night to lament the
loss of their sister!
and that these noc-
turnal lamentations
did not cease to ter-

236. The Lysikrates
monument, used as a library
in the Capuchin monastery,
17th century. (Cf. fig. 141)

237. The Acropolis in 1801–1805, with the Propylaia in the foreground.

rify the inhabitants, till the sacrilegious Voivode, who had been appointed governor of Zetoun, was destroyed by poison. (*Tour Through Greece*, I, p. 390)

In 1778 the Turkish governor, Hadzi Ali Haseki, built a new wall around the lower city (see fig. 199), sacrificing several ancient monuments with its construction, including the facade of the Hadrianic-Antonine aqueduct on Lykabettos Hill, and, probably, the Roman bridge (see fig. 210) over the Ilissos River in front of the stadium. Hadrian's Arch was incorporated in its entirety as a gate in the new circuit. The headquarters of the chief Ottoman official, the voivode, was built into the southwest corner of the Library of Hadrian. The Acropolis itself was intensively occupied in the eighteenth century. Drawings and paintings by early travelers show the citadel covered with small private houses, with the Parthenon and Propylaia looming above them. Mosques continued to be built. A small mosque constructed within the blown-out ruins of the Parthenon in the years around 1700 was only dismantled in 1842 when part of it collapsed. Lord Elgin arrived in Athens in the early 1800s and, after negotiations with the authorities in Constantinople, removed many of the better-preserved sculptures from the Acropolis and from the Parthenon itself. The legality of his actions and the question of the eventual return of the marbles to Greece remain hotly debated issues.

237, 238

The Greek War of Independence did considerable damage to Athens. Two sieges in particular were devastating, in 1821–1822, when the Turks were driven out of the Acropolis, and in 1826–1827, when they retook the citadel. During these operations much of the lower city was destroyed, including several ancient monuments, such as the choregic monuments of both Thrasyllos and Lysikrates. The most famous European philhellene, Lord Byron, stayed in Athens for six months; his name appears carved on the temple of Poseidon at Sounion. Byron died of a fever at Mesolonghi in northwest Greece; other Europeans died in Athens fighting for Greek independence. The Hephaisteion, used as a Protestant cemetery since 1799, was the burial ground of several foreign philhellenes, whose memorial inscriptions can still be made out on the interior walls.

With the establishment of Athens as the capital of the Greek state in 1833 the deliberate destruction of the monuments of the ancient city ceased, after more than 1,500 years. Since then, happily, efforts have gone into recovery and restoration, in an attempt to preserve the antiquities from the modern hordes—better-intentioned but no less dangerous—who come to see and appreciate the monuments of ancient Athens. The Archaeological Society was founded in 1837, and the Archaeological Service of the Ministry of Culture carries out more than a hundred salvage excavations a year in Athens and Attica. It also oversees the restoration of the many monuments which serve to remind us of Athens' long and glorious past.

238. Model of the Parthenon after the explosion of 1687, with the addition of the 17th-century mosque, removed ca. 1840.

SITE SUMMARIES

Athens

The archaeology of Athens encompasses more than a century of excavation and scholarship. Beyond the study of standing monuments, there have been systematic excavations of many other areas for decades. In addition, the rapid development of the modern city has required hundreds of rescue digs, carried out by the Archaeological Service under restraints of time, money, and logistics. Included here is a general bibliography of the archaeology of Athens, which will lead the reader to the thousands of specialized studies available; this is followed by a brief account, discussion, separate bibliography, and notes about some of the principal areas of ancient Athens (asterisks indicate especially significant items in the bibliography). In addition to the published works cited here, a huge file of material on the monuments and history of the exploration of Athens has been compiled by J. Binder at the American School of Classical Studies, and an unpublished collection of ancient testimonia on the buildings of the lower city compiled by R. E. Wycherley is stored in the Stoa of Attalos. The results of the recent excavations throughout Athens for the construction of the new Metro, amounting to some 70,000 square meters, have been preliminarily published in a handsome exhibition catalogue: N. Stampolides and L. Parlama (eds.), Ἡ Πόλη κάτω ἀπό τήν Πόλη (Athens, 2000).

BIBLIOGRAPHY

Ἀρχεῖον τῶν Μνημείων τῶν Ἀθηνῶν καὶ Ἀττικῆς, 2 vols. Athens, 1992–1993.
*Binder, J. The Monuments and Sites of Athens: A Sourcebook. Forthcoming.
Biris, K. Αἱ Ἀθῆναι ἀπο τοῦ 19ου εἰς τὸν 20ον αἰῶνα. Athens, 1966.

Castren, P. (ed.) *Post-Herulian Athens: Aspects of Life and Culture in Athens, A.D. 267–529.* Helsinki, 1994.

Frazer, J. G. *Pausanias' Description of Greece.* London, 1913. Book I, with commentary.

Goette, H. R. *Athen-Attika-Megaris.* Cologne, 1993.

Harrison, J. *Primitive Athens as Described by Thucydides.* Cambridge, 1906.

Hill, I. T. *The Ancient City of Athens.* Cambridge, 1953.

*Judeich, W. *Topographie von Athen,* 2d ed. Munich, 1931.

Laborde, L. E. S. J., Compte de. *Athènes aux XVe, XVIe et XVIIe siècles.* Paris, 1854.

Malouchou-Tufano, Ph. *Ἡ Ἀναστήλωση τῶν Ἀρχαίων Μνημείων στή Νεώτερην Ἑλλάδα (1834–1839).* Athens, 1998.

Mountjoy, P. *Mycenaean Athens.* Göteborg, 1995.

Papageorgiou-Venetas, A. *Athens: The Ancient Heritage and the Historic Cityscape in a Modern Metropolis.* Athens, 1994. See especially pp. 269–321.

TAPA (Ministry of Culture), *Τό Ἔργο τοῦ Ὑπουργείου Πολιτισμοῦ στόν Τομέα τῆς Πολιτικῆς Κληρονομιᾶς.* 3 vols. Athens, vol. 1: 1997; vol. 2; 1998; vol. 3; 1999.

*Travlos J. *Bildlexikon zur Topographie des Antiken Attika.* Tübingen, Germany, 1988. See pp. 26–33 for an updated bibliography of Athenian archaeology to 1985.

*Travlos, J. *Pictorial Dictionary of Athens.* London, 1971.

Travlos, J. *Πολεοδομική Ἐξέλιξις τῶν Ἀθηνῶν.* Athens, 1960.

Wycherley, R. E. *The Stones of Athens.* Princeton, N.J., 1978.

ACROPOLIS

DESCRIPTION, HISTORY, AND SIGNIFICANCE

239, 240, 241   The Acropolis was the citadel of Athens, used as a place of refuge in hard times and as the principal sanctuary of the city in Greek and Roman times (see figs. 2, 14, 52). A spine of hard limestone, it rises steeply out of the surrounding plain to a height of about 150 meters above sea level, and the only easy approach is from the west. The fortunes of Athens over the centuries can often be read in the degree of accessibility to the Acropolis: broad ramps and large gateways built in times of peace, additional walls, winding paths, bastions, towers, and small doorways in times of trouble. The area on top, fortified from the Bronze Age to the nineteenth century, measures about 110 meters north to south by 250 meters east to

Opposite, top 239. Model of the Acropolis from the northwest.
Opposite, bottom 240. Aerial view of the Acropolis from the west.

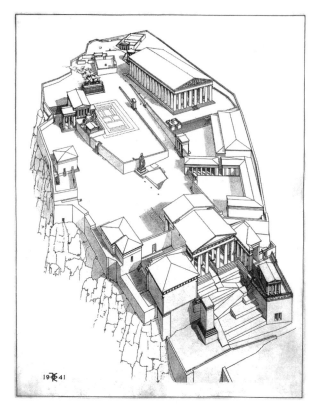

241. Drawing of the restored Acropolis from the northwest.

west. Here in the Late Bronze Age would have stood a palace, comparable to the ones known from Mycenae, Tiryns, and Pylos.

In the historical period the Acropolis was given over to the cult of Athena. Large Doric temples were built in her honor in the sixth century B.C., along with dozens of marble votive statues and several small Doric buildings of limestone (see figs. 25–29, 40, 41). All these were swept away when the Persians burned the Acropolis in 480/79 B.C. Even the shattered fragments were respected, however, having been dedicated to the goddess, and when the Athenians cleaned up the area, they carefully buried much of this Archaic material, thereby preserving it (see figs. 42, 43, 52–54). In general, though broken, the Archaic material is in better shape than the Classical, which suffered all the ill effects of prolonged exposure and gradual disintegration. Much of the early material, buried and left undisturbed less than a century after it was made, still preserves some of the original painted decoration.

In the fifth century the Acropolis became the focal point of the great Periklean rebuilding program to replace the temples destroyed by the Persians (see figs. 76, 80). Under the general direction of Pheidias, an army of architects, sculptors, masons, painters, and artisans built the Parthenon, the Propylaia, the temple of Athena Nike, and the Erechtheion in the second half of the fifth century. These crowning achievements of Greek architecture are what one still sees today, in some cases after several programs of restoration. A few lesser monuments and sanctuaries no longer survive above the lowest courses. In the southwest corner there was a sanctuary of Artemis Brauronia, and just east of that the Chalkotheke, a large storeroom for bronze dedications and weapons. Dozens of statues were dedicated out in the open, many of which survived to the Roman period and are described in detail by Pausanias.

BIBLIOGRAPHY

General

Brouskari, M. *The Acropolis Museum*. Athens, 1974.

Brouskari, M. *The Monuments of the Acropolis*. Athens, 1997.

Bundgaard, J. *The Excavations of the Athenian Acropolis, 1882–1890: The Original Drawings*. Copenhagen, 1974.

Bundgaard, J. *Parthenon and the Mycenaean City on the Heights*. Copenhagen, 1976.

Buschor, E. *Die Tondacher der Akropolis*. 2 vols. Berlin, 1929–1933.

Economakis, R. (ed.) *Acropolis Restoration: The SSAM Interventions*. London, 1994.

Graef, B., and E. Langlotz. *Die antiken Vasen von der Akropolis zu Athens*. Berlin, 1925–1933.

Harris, D. *The Treasures of the Parthenon and Erechtheion*. Oxford, 1995.

Heberdey, R. *Altattische Porosskulptur*. Vienna, 1919.

Hurwit, J. *The Athenian Acropolis*. Cambridge, 1998.

Iakovides, S. *Ἡ Μυκηναϊκή Ἀκρόπολις τῶν Ἀθηνῶν*. Athens, 1962.

Jahn, O., and A. Michaelis. *Arx Athenarum a Pausania Descripta*. Bonn, 1901.

Kavvadias, P., and G. Kawerau. *Die Ausgrabung der Akropolis*. Athens, 1907.

Knell, H. *Perikleische Baukunst*. Darmstadt, Germany, 1979.

Payne, H. *Archaic Marble Sculpture from the Acropolis*. London, 1936.

Raubitschek, A. E. *Dedications from the Athenian Akropolis*. Cambridge, 1949.

Rhodes, R. *Architecture and Meaning on the Athenian Acropolis*. Cambridge, 1995.

Schneider, L., and C. Hocker. *Die Akropolis von Athen*. Cologne, 1990.

Schrader, H. (ed.) *Die archaischen Marmorbildwerke der Akropolis*. Frankfurt, 1939.

Wiegand, T. *Die archaische Poros-Architektur der Akropolis zu Athen*. Leipzig, 1904.

Notes

For the Chalkotheke, see L. LaFollette, "The Chalkotheke on the Athenian Acropolis," *Hesperia* 55 (1986), pp. 75–87. For the Temple of Roma and Augustus, see W. Binder, *Der Roma-Augustus Monopteros auf der Akropolis in Athen und sein Typologischer Ort* (Stuttgart, 1969). For the Athena Promachos by Pheidias, see B. Pick, "Die Promachos des Pheidias und die Kerameikos-Lampen," *Ath. Mitt.* (1931), pp. 59–74, E. Harrison, "Preparations for Marathon, the Niobid Painter, and Herodotus," *Art Bulletin* (1972), pp. 390–402, and the building accounts for nine years in *IG* I³ 435.

Parthenon

Brommer, F. *Die Parthenon-Skulpturen: Metopen, Fries, Giebel, Kultbild.* Mainz, 1979.

Korres. M., et al. *Μελέτη Ἀποκαταστάσεως τοῦ Παρθενῶνος.* 5 vols. Athens, 1983–1994. See especially vol. 1, pp. 171–197, for a bibliography.

Orlandos, A. K. *Ἡ Ἀρχιτεκτονική τοῦ Παρθενῶνος.* 3 vols. Athens, 1977–1978.

Tournikiotis, P. (ed.) *The Parthenon and Its Impact on Modern Times.* Athens, 1994.

Notes

All aspects of the sculptural program of the Parthenon continue to generate a huge bibliography. For recent work and an overview since Brommer, see I. Jenkins, *The Parthenon Frieze* (British Museum, 1994). In particular, a recent suggestion has been made that the central scene of the east frieze is not related to the Panathenaia but shows the preparations for the sacrifice of the daughter of Erechtheus (J. Connelly, "Parthenon and Parthenoi: A Mythological Interpretation of the Parthenon Frieze," *AJA* 100 [1996], pp. 53–80), answered by Jenkins (*The Parthenon Frieze*) and by E. Harrison ("The Web of History: A Conservative Reading of the Parthenon Frieze," in *Worshipping Athena,* ed. J. Neils [Madison, Wis., 1996], pp. 198–214). The work on the restoration of the Acropolis monuments has led to several important joins and observations on the Parthenon sculpture by A. Mantis. Other recent works on the sculpture include: B. Nagy, "Athenian Officials on the Parthenon Frieze," *AJA* 96 (1992), pp. 55–69, M. C. Root, "The Parthenon Frieze and the Apadana Reliefs at Persepolis," *AJA* 89 (1985), pp. 102–122, K. Schwab, "Parthenon East Metope XI: Herakles and the Gigantomachy," *AJA* 100 (1996), pp. 81–90, and K. Schwab, "The Parthenon Metopes and Greek Vase Painting" (Ph.D. diss., New York University, 1988). For the inscription honoring Nero in 61/2, see A. Spawforth, "Symbol of Unity? The Persian Wars Tradition in the Empire," in *Greek Historiography,* ed. S. Hornblower (Oxford, 1994), pp. 233–237.

Propylaia

Bundgaard, J. A. *Mnesicles, a Greek Architect at Work.* Copenhagen, 1957.

DeWaele, J. *The Propylaia of the Akropolis in Athens.* Amsterdam, 1990.

Dinsmoor, W. B., Jr. *The Propylaia to the Athenian Acropolis.* Vol. 1: *The Predecessors.* Princeton, N.J., 1980.

Eiteljorg II, H. *The Entrance to the Athenian Acropolis Before Mnesicles.* Boston, 1995.

Tanoulas, T., et al. *Μελέτη Ἀποκαταστάσεως τῶν Προπυλαίων.* Athens, 1994.

Notes

The arrangement and function of the Pinakotheke has continued to draw the attention of scholars. J. A. Bundgaard (*Mnesicles,* above) saw the arrangement as a reflection of earlier structures; J. Travlos (*Pictorial Dictionary of Athens* [London, 1971], p. 482 and figs. 614, 618, and 619) and P. Hellstrom ("The Asymmetry of the Pinacotheca—Once More," *Op. Ath.* 11 [1975], pp. 87–92) have argued that the room served as a dining room. W. B. Dinsmoor, Jr. ("The Asymmetry of the Pinakotheke—For the Last Time?" *Hesperia Suppl.* 20 [Princeton, N.J., 1982], pp. 18–33), has more plausibly explained the unusual form as being the result of the design and the use of modules in planning the building. For important work on the Medieval entrance to the Acropolis and the resultant use and modifications of the Propylaia, see T. Tanoulas, *Τά Προπύλαια τῆς Ἀθηναϊκῆς Ἀκροπόλεως κατά τόν Μεσαίωνα,* 2 vols. (Athens, 1997; English summary in vol. 2, pp. 283–313; English translations of captions of figures and drawings are available free of charge from J. Binder, 54 Souidias St., Athens 10676, Greece).

Temple of Athena Nike

Brouskari, M. *Τό Θωράκιο τοῦ Ναοῦ τῆς Ἀθηνᾶς Νίκης.* Athens, 1999.

Carpenter, R. *The Sculpture of the Nike Temple Parapet.* Cambridge, 1929.

Mark, I. S. *The Sanctuary of Athena Nike in Athens. Hesperia Suppl. 26.* Princeton, N.J., 1993.

Ziro, D. *Μελέτη Ἀποκαταστάσεως τοῦ ναοῦ τῆς Ἀθηνᾶς Νίκης.* 2 vols. Athens, 1994.

Erechtheion

Herington, C. J. *Athena Parthenos and Athena Polias.* Manchester, U.K., 1955.

Papanikolaou, A., "The Restoration of the Erechtheion." In R. Economakis (ed.) *Acropolis Restoration: The CCAM Interventions.* London, 1994. Pp. 136–149.

Paton, J. M., et al. *The Erechtheum.* Cambridge, 1927.

Notes

"Erechtheion" is a modern name; in antiquity the building was known as the "old temple," "the temple in which there is the old statue," or the "temple of Athena Polias." K. Jeppesen has argued that there were two separate buildings, one dedicated to Erechtheus, one to Athena Polias. See K. Jeppesen, *The Theory of the Alternate Erechtheion* (Arhus, Denmark, 1987), and N. Robertson, "Athena's Shrines and Festivals," in *Worshipping*

242. Model of the Acropolis from the southwest, with the buildings on the south slopes below. From left to right: The Odeion of Herodes Atticus, the Stoa of Eumenes, the Asklepieion (behind), the theater of Dionysos, and the Odeion of Perikles.

Athena, ed. J. Neils (Madison, Wis., 1996), pp. 27–77. For remarks on the interior arrangement see O. Palagia ("A Nike for Kallimachos' Lamp?" *AJA* 88 [1984], pp. 515–521). For the form of the early cult statue, see J. Kroll, "The Ancient Image of Athena Polias," in *Hesperia Suppl. 20* (Princeton, N.J., 1982), pp. 65–76.

ACROPOLIS SLOPES

DESCRIPTION, HISTORY, AND SIGNIFICANCE

The lower slope of the Acropolis was ringed in antiquity by an ancient path known as the peripatos. Above this walkway the terrain was covered with sanctuaries virtually all the way around. The sanctuaries on the north slope are generally less substantial architecturally than those on the south, often confined to the shallow caves or to small open-air areas in front of scarps into which niches have been carved. Here worshipers honored Pan and the Nymphs (see fig. 112), Apollo Hypo Makrais (in the Roman period; see fig. 113), Aphrodite and Eros, Aglauros, and other unidentified deities. A portion of the northwest slopes, and perhaps the whole area, was enclosed by an early (pre–fifth century B.C.) circuit wall known as the Pelargikon. Within its circuit the Klepsydra spring (see fig. 68) offered an important source of water from late Neolithic times until the nineteenth century.

More substantial sanctuaries claimed the sunny, welcoming south slopes (see fig. 114). 242 Here was the sanctuary of Dionysos, with its temples, stoa, odeion, and huge theater (see figs. 138–40), home to the great plays of early Western drama. Further west was the Asklepieion (see fig. 149), the Athenian sanctuary of the primary healing deity of Greece, with its temple, altar, and dormitory, along with hundreds of votives dedicated by suppliants whom the god had healed. An inscription (*IG* II² 4994) indicates that Hermes, Aphrodite, Pan, the Nymphs, and Isis were all worshiped on the terrace to the west. Below was the long stoa built by King Eumenes of Pergamon in the second century B.C. to provide shelter for the thousands attending the theater (see figs. 165, 166). Further west were several more small sanctuaries, to Themis, Isis, and others, including one to Nymphe, who was closely associated with the ritual of marriage. Among these stood the lavish Odeion (see fig. 211), or concert hall, given by the local philanthropist Herodes Atticus in about A.D. 160. In late Roman times the southwest slope below the Odeion of Herodes was covered with large private houses.

EXCAVATIONS

The slopes of the Acropolis have been excavated many times by various institutions. The Klepsydra fountain and other monuments on the north slope were excavated by the American School of Classical Studies in a series of campaigns during the 1930s. The sanctuary of Dionysos and the theater were first excavated by the Greek Archaeological Society in 1838, with further work carried out for most of the nineteenth century. The society also excavated the sanctuary of Asklepios, in 1876–1877. Finally, the society cleared the Odeion of Herodes in 1848–1858, while much of the rest of the south slope was excavated by the Archaeological Service between 1955 and 1959. The Odeion of Perikles remains largely unexcavated.

BIBLIOGRAPHY

North Slope

Broneer, O. "Excavations on the North Slope of the Acropolis." *Hesperia* 6 (1937), pp. 161–263.

Broneer, O. "Excavations on the Slopes of the Acropolis." *AJA* 44 (1940), pp. 252–256.

Broneer, O. "A Mycenean Fountain on the Athenian Acropolis." *Hesperia* 6 (1937), pp. 161–263.

Parsons, A. "Klepsydra and the Paved Court of the Pythion." *Hesperia* (1943), pp. 191–267.

South Slope

*Korres, M. *Arch. Delt.* 35 (1980), B, pp. 9–21.
Papathanasopoulos, Th. *Μνημεῖα τῆς Νότιας Πλευρᾶς τῆς Ἀκρόπολης.* Athens, 1993.
Papathanasopoulos, Th. *Το Ὠδεῖο τοῦ Περίκλη.* Rhethymnon, 1999.
Walker, S. "A Sanctuary of Isis on the South Slope of the Athenian Acropolis." *BSA* 74 (1979), pp. 243–279.

Aglaurion

Dontas, G. "The True Aglaurion." *Hesperia* 53 (1983), pp. 48–63.

Asklepieion

Aleshire, S. *The Athenian Asklepieion.* Amsterdam, 1989.

Odeion of Herodes Atticus

Tobin, J. *Herodes Atticus and the City of Athens.* Amsterdam, 1997. Pp. 185–194.

Odeion of Perikles

Kotsidu, H. *Die musischen Agone der Panathenäen in archaischer und klassischer Zeit.* Munich, 1991.
Robkin, A. "The Odeion of Perikles." Ph.D. diss., Univeristy of Washington, 1975.

Theater of Dionysos

Dörpfeld, W., and E. Reisch. *Das griechische Theater.* Athens, 1896.
Pickard-Cambridge, A. W. *The Theater of Dionysus in Athens.* Oxford, 1946.
Polacco, L. *Il teatro di Dioniso Eleuterio ad Atene.* Rome, 1990.
Townsend, R. "The Fourth-Century Skene of the Theater of Dionysos at Athens." *Hesperia* 55 (1986), pp. 421–438.

Notes

The various uses of the Odeion of Perikles are described in the following ancient sources: cavalry (Xenophon *Hell.* 2.4.8–10, 24); law court (Aristophanes *Wasps* 1107–1111, Demosthenes *Against Neaira,* 52, 54); grain (Demosthenes *Against Phormio* 37); philosophers (Diogenes Laertius 7.183–185, Plutarch *Moral.* 605.14 and 1033 D–E); and musical contests (Plutarch *Perikles* 13.9–11).

AGORA

DESCRIPTION, HISTORY, AND SIGNIFICANCE

The Agora was a large open square on sloping ground northwest of the Acropolis (see fig. 4). It was designed as the civic center of the town, and was reserved for gather- 243 ings of citizens for a variety of purposes: elections, processions, open-air markets, os-tracisms, athletic events, and dramatic performances. Around its sides were set most of the public buildings of the city (see fig. 30). These included the Bouleuterion (senate 244, 245 building), the Metroon (archives), the magistrates' offices, the law courts, and the mint. Stoas—long, shady, colonnaded buildings—and fountain houses provided shelter and refreshment for the throngs who met here on a daily basis. Statues and other memorials reminded the Athenians of former military triumphs and the achievements of their pre-decessors.

The Agora was laid out in its present location sometime in the sixth century B.C. (see figs. 44, 59, 66), replacing an older civic center which lies several hundred meters to the east, still awaiting excavation. Thereafter, its development reflects the history of Athens, showing signs of expansion in the fifth century (see fig. 121) and in the latter part of the fourth century (see fig. 150), revival in the second century (see fig. 177), and a cultural flo-rescence in Roman times. Military interventions by the Persians in 480/79, the Romans under Sulla in 86, the Herulians in A.D. 267, Alaric in 395/6, the Vandals in the 470s, and the Slavs in 582/3 have all left their marks on the area.

The Agora receives special attention as the center of ancient Athens and thus the place where Athenian democracy was first developed and practiced. Buildings represent-ing all three branches of government—executive, legislative, and judiciary—have come to light, along with numerous small objects used in the day-to-day running of the city: ballots, allotment machines, archives, water clocks, tokens for payments, and sets of official weights and measures. Of particular interest are the thousands of inscriptions (more than 7,500), which record a variety of information not available from other sources.

EXCAVATIONS

Parts of the Agora area were never completely buried: the Hephaisteion (Theseion), the statues of the giants and tritons of the Odeion of Agrippa, and the ruins of the Stoa of

243. Model of the Agora and Acropolis, seen from the northwest.

Attalos. These were explored in the nineteenth century by the Greek Archaeological Society and the German Archaeological Institute. The extension of the Athens-Peiraieus railway in 1891 created a broad trench through the area, though it did surprisingly little damage. Full-scale excavations were undertaken by the American School of Classical Studies starting in 1931, a project which has continued for seven decades. Four hundred modern houses have been removed in order to excavate the site. All the finds, together with the records of their recovery, are housed in the reconstructed Stoa of Attalos (1953–1956), which serves as the site museum.

BIBLIOGRAPHY

Camp, J. *The Athenian Agora*. London, 1986.

Camp, J. *The Athenian Agora Guide*. 4th ed. Athens, 1990.

Thompson, H. A., and R. E. Wycherley. *The Athenian Agora*. Vol. 14: *The Agora of Athens*. Princeton, N.J., 1972.

Wycherley, R. E. *The Athenian Agora*. Vol 3: *The Literary and Epigraphical Testimonia*. Reprint. Princeton, N.J., 1973.

Notes

For the rich Iron Age grave of a woman, see E. Smithson, "The Tomb of a Rich Athenian Lady, ca. 850 B.C.," *Hesperia* 37 (1968), pp. 77–116, and N. Coldstream, "The Rich

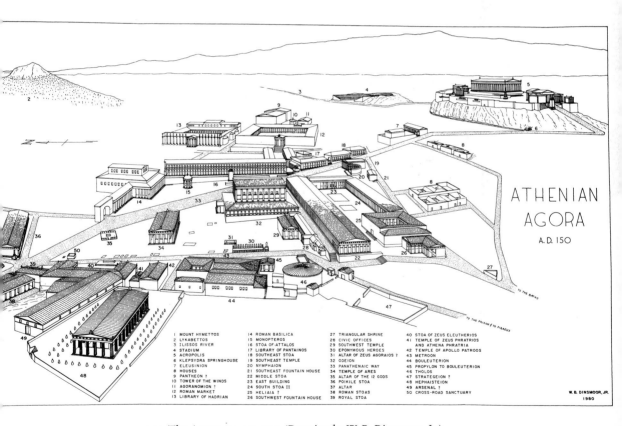

1 MOUNT HYMETTOS	14 ROMAN BASILICA	27 TRIANGULAR SHRINE	40 STOA OF ZEUS ELEUTHERIOS
2 LYKABETTOS	15 MONOPTEROS	28 CIVIC OFFICES	41 TEMPLE OF ZEUS PHRATRIOS
3 ILISSOS RIVER	16 STOA OF ATTALOS	29 SOUTHWEST TEMPLE	AND ATHENA PHRATRIA
4 STADIUM	17 LIBRARY OF PANTAINOS	30 EPONYMOUS HEROES	42 TEMPLE OF APOLLO PATROOS
5 ACROPOLIS	18 SOUTHEAST STOA	31 ALTAR OF ZEUS AGORAIOS ?	43 METROON
6 KLEPSYDRA SPRINGHOUSE	19 SOUTHEAST TEMPLE	32 ODEION	44 BOULEUTERION
7 ELEUSINION	20 NYMPHAION	33 PANATHENAIC WAY	45 PROPYLON TO BOULEUTERION
8 HOUSES	21 SOUTHEAST FOUNTAIN HOUSE	34 TEMPLE OF ARES	46 THOLOS
9 PANTHEON ?	22 MIDDLE STOA	35 ALTAR OF THE 12 GODS	47 STRATEGEION ?
10 TOWER OF THE WINDS	23 EAST BUILDING	36 POIKILE STOA	48 HEPHAISTEION
11 AGORANOMION ?	24 SOUTH STOA II	37 ALTAR	49 ARSENAL ?
12 ROMAN MARKET	25 HELIAIA ?	38 ROMAN STOAS	50 CROSS-ROAD SANCTUARY
13 LIBRARY OF HADRIAN	26 SOUTHWEST FOUNTAIN HOUSE	39 ROYAL STOA	

ATHENIAN AGORA A.D. 150

W. B. DINSMOOR, JR. 1980

244. The Agora, ca. A.D. 150. (Drawing by W. B. Dinsmoor, Jr.)

Athenian Lady of the Areiopagos and Her Contemporaries," *Hesperia* 64 (1995), pp. 391–403. For the ratio of eighth- to seventh-century graves, see J. Camp, "A Drought in the Late Eighth Century B.C.," *Hesperia* 48 (1979), pp. 397–411. The date of the layout of the Classical Agora has been the subject of considerable scholarship recently. Suggestions range from the time of Solon (Thompson and Wycherley, *Agora,* vol. 14, pp. 25–26), through Peisistratos and his sons (T. L. Shear, Jr., "Tyrants and Buildings in the Archaic Athens," in *Athens Comes of Age* [Princeton, N.J., 1978], pp. 1–19, and J. Camp, "Before Democracy: The Alkmaionidai and Peisistratidai," in *The Archaeology of Athens and Attica under the Democracy,* ed. W. Coulson et al. [Exeter, U.K., 1994], pp. 7–12), or Kleisthenes and the new democracy (T. L. Shear, Jr., "Ἰσονομου τ᾿ Ἀθηνᾶς ἐποιησάτην: The Agora and Democracy," in *The Archaeology of Athens and Attica under the Democracy,* ed. Coulson et al., pp. 225–248, and Shear, "The Persian Destruction of Athens: Evidence from Agora Deposits," *Hesperia* 62 [1993], pp. 383–482) to post-Persian (E. Francis and M. Vickers, "The Agora Revisited: Athenian Chronology c. 500–450 B.C." *BSA* 83 [1988], pp. 143–167, H. A. Thompson, "Athens Faces Adversity," *Hesperia* 50 [1981], pp. 345–346, Thompson, "The Pnyx in Models, " in *Hesperia Suppl. 20* [Princeton, N.J., 1982], pp. 136–137, and Thompson, *Πρακτικά τοῦ XII Διεθνοῦς Συνεδρίου Κλασικῆς Ἀρχαιολογίας* [Athens, 1988], pp. 198–204). For the identification and date of the Metroon-Bouleuterion complex, see also S. Miller in *Studies in the Ancient Greek Polis,* ed. K. Raaflaub and M. H. Hansen (Stuttgart, 1995), pp. 133–156, with a reply by T. L. Shear, Jr., on pp. 157–190.

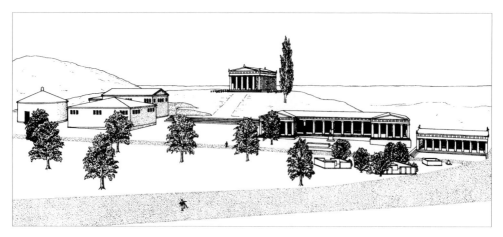

245. Public buildings on the west side of the Agora. From left to right: the Tholos, the Old Bouleuterion (Metroon), the New Bouleuterion, the Hephaisteion, the Stoa of Zeus Eleutherios, and the Royal Stoa.

Other buildings have been the subject of controversy as to identification or date:

A. Matthaiou has argued in a lecture (1997) that the Stoa Poikile is better identified as the Stoa of the Herms.

The building long identified as the Heliaia law court is now better understood as the Aiakeion, a sanctuary of the Aeginetan hero Aiakos (Herodotos 5.89). See R. Stroud, *The Athenian Grain-Tax Law of 374/3 B.C. Hesperia Suppl. 29* (Princeton, N.J., 1998).

The Leokoreion, sanctuary of the daughters of Leos, who were sacrificed to save the city during a plague, has been identified by some with a crossroads enclosure found east of the Royal Stoa. See H. A. Thompson, "Some Hero Shrines in Early Athens," in *Athens Comes of Age* (Princeton, N.J., 1978), pp. 101–102.

The identification of the Hephaisteion has been challenged by E. B. Harrison in "Alkmenes' Sculptures for the Hephaisteion," *AJA* 81 (1977), pp. 137 ff., 265ff., and 411ff., esp. pp. 421–426.

C. Hedrick, in "The Temple and Cult of Apollo Patroos in Athens," *AJA* 92 (1988), pp. 185–210, denies the existence of a temple and cult statue of Apollo Patroos in the sixth century B.C.

The date of the surviving remains of the Altar of the Twelve Gods has been lowered to the fifth century by L. Gadbery, "The Sanctuary of the Twelve Gods in the Athenian Agora: A Revised View," *Hesperia* 61 (1992), pp. 447–489.

The identification of the temple of Ares as originally belonging to Athena from Pallene has been made by M. Korres in *ΗΟΡΟΣ* 10–12 (1992–1998), pp. 83–104.

The Altar of Aphrodite Ourania has been identified at the northwest corner of the Agora, but a large marble treasury (*thesauros*) inscribed with her name was found several hundred meters away, in Plaka. See C. Tsakos in *ΗΟΡΟΣ* 8–9 (1990–1991), pp. 17–27, and Kazamiakis, in *ΗΟΡΟΣ* 8–9 (1990–1991), pp. 29–44. See also M. Osanna, "Il problema topografico del Santuario di Afrodite Urania ad Atene," *ASAtene* 66–67 n.s., 50–51 (1988–1989), pp. 73–95. Rome, 1993.

KERAMEIKOS

DESCRIPTION, HISTORY, AND SIGNIFICANCE

Kerameikos is an ancient term meaning the "potters' quarter." In antiquity it was an extensive area defined by boundary stones (found in situ), stretching at least from the northwest corner of the classical Agora to well outside the city walls, more than half a kilo-

246   meter away. In the Roman period the term referred to a still larger area; both Pausanias and
Philostratus use the term *Kerameikos* to refer to buildings in the area we now know as the
Agora of Classical times. In modern times, the term has been used to describe the area under excavation by the German Archaeological Institute, where three of the boundary stones
are found.

The excavations have uncovered one of the longer, better preserved sections of city
wall (figs. 136, 137), as well as the principal burial ground of ancient Athens. The section of
wall, which can be traced for about 175 meters, shows varied masonry styles, indicating up
to six distinct building phases as the wall base was raised over time. Only the lower part was
originally made of stone; higher up, mudbrick was used. The earliest phase is that laid out
by Themistokles just after the Persian destruction of 480/79 B.C., while the latest phase
may date to the time of Justinian in the sixth century A.D. Intermediate phases probably

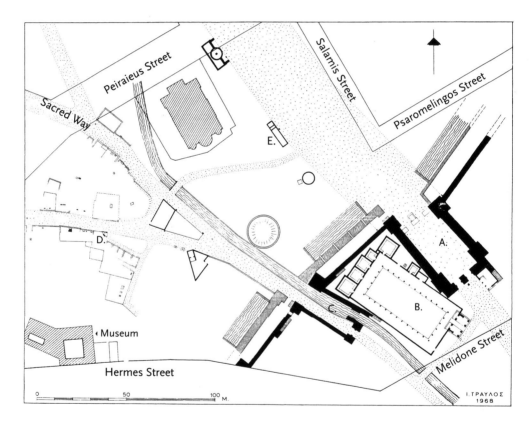

246. The Kerameikos excavations of the German Archaeological Institute: (A) Dipylon Gate;
(B) Pompeion; (C) Sacred Gate and Eridanos River; (D) Dexileos Monument; (E) Tomb of
the Lakedaimonians.

represent the rebuilding under Konon in the 390s B.C. and Athenian preparations for war with the Macedonians late in the fourth century B.C.

Two important gates of the city have also been excavated here (see fig. 137). The larger, to the northeast, is the Dipylon, the main gate of Athens, which opens out onto a broad street leading to the Academy, about a kilometer and a half outside the city wall. To the southwest is the so-called Sacred Gate, which carried the road followed by the great procession which made its way to Eleusis at the time of the celebration of the mysteries. The Eridanos River also exits the city through the Sacred Gate. Squeezed in between the two gates, just inside the walls, is the Pompeion (see fig. 132), used as the starting point of the Panathenaic procession (*pompe*), which made its way up to the Acropolis.

Long before the wall or gates were built, the banks of the Eridanos were used by the early Athenians as a burial ground, and hundreds of graves dating from around 1200 to 600 B.C. have been carefully excavated in the area. Burial continued after the wall was built but only outside the circuit, along the lines of the roads. Hundreds more graves, now marked with stelai, reliefs, sculpted animals, or marble vases, were built in the Classical period, followed by much simpler grave markers in the Hellenistic period (see figs. 133, 158–161). The burials continue into Roman times. Despite the area's name, there is little evidence of potteries, though the lamp-making industry was well-established in the area in the late Roman period.

Somewhere in the immediate vicinity of the Kerameikos, perhaps just to the northwest, was the most important burial ground of ancient Athens, the Demosion Sema. This was where individuals of note and those who had died in battle were buried at state expense, a great honor in antiquity. Thucydides (2.34) describes the ritual, in which the cremated remains of the fallen were buried by tribe, and a huge crowd assembled to hear a funeral oration delivered over the grave by a leading citizen. He also records the most famous oration preserved from antiquity, the funeral oration of Perikles in the first year of the Peloponnesian War (431/30). Casualty lists were inscribed over the graves and several dozen of these have been recovered; sculpted reliefs were also erected.

Ironically, the one *polyandreion* (multiple grave) we have for fallen war dead in Athens is the grave of the Lakedaimonians who died in 403, which is set up along the south side of the street leading from the Dipylon (see figs. 129, 130).

EXCAVATIONS

A huge deposit of alluvium, up to 8 meters deep, covered the area of the Kerameikos excavations in the nineteenth century. Chance digging for sand exposed the first grave stelai in the 1860s. Systematic excavations were carried out by the Greek Archaeological Society from 1870 until 1913. Since then the work has been carried on by the German Archaeological Institute. A small museum was built on the site in 1937.

Excavations for the Metro just northwest of the area excavated by the German Institute have brought to light several multiple graves from the second half of the fifth century B.C. The date and the number of skeletons found piled on top of one another has led to the plausible suggestion that these represent burials of those who died as a result of the plague in 430–426, during the Peloponnesian War.

A claim has been made in public lectures and in the press that several graves of the Demosion Sema were excavated in 1997 at 35 Salamina Street: see *Τό Ἔργο τοῦ Ὑπουργείου Πολιτισμοῦ στόν Τομέα τῆς Πολιτιστικῆς Κληρονομιᾶς* (Athens, 1997), pp. 68–69. Farther out on the road to the Academy the family burial plot of Lykourgos has apparently been uncovered; see A. Matthaiou, *ΗΟΡΟΣ* 5 (1987), pp. 31–44.

BIBLIOGRAPHY

Kerameikos, Ergebnisse der Ausgrabungen, I–XIV. Berlin and Munich: Deutsches Archäologisches Institut. Final reports by various scholars on the German excavations.

Clairmont, C. W. *Classical Attic Tombstones.* 8 vols. Kilchberg, Switzerland, 1993–1995.

Conze, A. *Die attischen Grabreliefs.* 4 vols. Berlin, 1893–1922.

Knigge, U. *The Athenian Kerameikos: History, Monuments, Excavations.* Athens, 1991.

Stampolides, N., and L. Parlama (eds.) *Ἡ Πόλη κάτω ἀπό τήν Πόλη,* Athens, 2000. See especially pp. 271–273 for plague burials.

MOUSEION HILL, PNYX, AREOPAGOS
DESCRIPTION, HISTORY, AND SIGNIFICANCE

The ridge which runs to the west of the Acropolis had several ancient monuments associated with it. Most prominent, on the northeastern side of the ridge, was the Pnyx (see figs. 127, 147, 148), the meeting place of the Athenian Assembly. All Athenian citizens were eligible to gather every ten days or so to vote on legislation prepared and proposed by the *boule* (senate of five hundred). The area seems first to have been used for meetings late in the sixth or early in the fifth century B.C., though almost nothing of the early phase remains. The massive curved retaining wall built to support the auditorium and the rock-cut speaker's platform are assigned to a third phase of construction, dated roughly 345–335 B.C. On top of the ridge are the beddings for two stoas which were laid out but never built.

To the south, the Mouseion Hill is the high point, site of a Macedonian fort in the third century B.C. and now crowned by the elaborate marble grave of Philopappos (see fig. 193), dated to the early second century A.D. In the hollow east of the ridge and west of the Acropolis, an extensive residential district has been cleared, with houses, streets, and small sanctuaries dating from Classical to Roman times.

Northwest of the Acropolis and south of the Agora the bare rock of the Areopagos (Hill of Ares) rises up (see fig. 1). Site of the first homicide trial—of the god Ares for killing Poseidon's son Halirrhothios—the hill was the seat of a venerable Athenian council of elders and supreme court. Originally the council had great constitutional powers, which were eroded away over the years with the rise of democracy. The council was made up of retired magistrates and tended to be very conservative; the best modern parallel might be the British House of Lords, once extremely powerful and now reduced to little more than a ceremonial role. In the historical period, the Council of the Areopagos still served as a homicide court. In later times, Saint Paul addressed it in its role as the guardian of traditional Athenian ways. The rock top has some quarried and worn surfaces, but there is little to indicate the presence of a council chamber or the nature of any other possible facilities.

EXCAVATIONS

The Areopagos and Philopappos Hill have always been visible. The hollow east of the Pnyx was excavated by the German Archaeological Institute in the 1890s, and the clearing of the Pnyx itself was a joint Greek-American excavation carried out in the 1930s.

BIBLIOGRAPHY

Areopagos

Wallace, R. *The Areopagos Council to 307 B.C.* Baltimore, 1989.

Philopappos

Kleiner, D. *The Monument of Philopappos.* Rome, 1983.

Pnyx

Forsén, B., and G. Stanton (eds.) *The Pnyx in the History of Athens*. Helsinki, 1996.

Kourouniotes, K., and H. Thompson. "The Pnyx in Athens." *Hesperia* 1 (1932), pp. 90–217.

West Slope of Acropolis

Dörpfeld, W. "Die Ausgrabungen am Westabhange der Akropolis II." *Ath. Mitt.* 20 (1895), pp. 161–206.

Korte, A. "Bezirk eines Heilgottes." *Ath. Mitt.* 18 (1893), pp. 231–256.

Notes

The dates, form, and function of the Pnyx in its three phases are still being debated: see the proceedings of the 1995 Finnish conference in Athens (above, under Forsén and Stanton). The stratigraphy of the third phase of the Pnyx is particularly vexing; the great retaining wall is surely Greek and probably dates to the fourth century B.C., but pottery found deep down behind it is demonstrably Roman: see S. Rotroff and J. Camp, "The Date of the Third Period of the Pnyx," *Hesperia* 65 (1996), pp. 263–294. On the Areopagos, M. Korres now restores a small fifth-century B.C. Ionic temple based on cuttings in the rock and architectural elements found in the Agora. An inscription (Agora I 6524) seems to indicate that there was at least one building there, and possibly two: a bouleuterion and a *synedrion* (council chamber), though no traces have been recognized: see B. D. Meritt, "Greek Inscriptions," *Hesperia* 21 (1952), pp. 355–359, and R. E. Wycherley, "Two Notes on Athenian Topography," *JHS* 75 (1955), pp. 117–121.

OLYMPIEION, SOUTHEAST ATHENS

DESCRIPTION, HISTORY, AND SIGNIFICANCE

The principal monument southeast of the Acropolis is the great precinct and temple dedicated to Olympian Zeus. The huge temple was laid out in the sixth century B.C. during the tyranny of the Peisistratids (see figs. 34, 171, 172). It was left unfinished for centuries until Antiochos IV of Syria started work on a marble dipteral temple of the Corinthian order in the early second century B.C. This too was abandoned and left unfinished for close to three hundred years, until Hadrian finally completed the project.

Southeast of the precinct, on land which slopes down to the Ilissos River, there are numerous traces of antiquity, all in a terrible state of preservation and of uncertain identity. The river itself was lined with sanctuaries and offered a cool retreat from the city, to judge from Plato's description of a visit by Sokrates and Phaidros (*Phaidros* 229–230). Across the river was the marble stadium built by Herodes Atticus in the second century A.D. (see fig. 209), as well as the little fifth-century B.C. Ionic temple assigned to Artemis Agrotera (see fig. 97). Farther downstream were the old Peisistratid fountain house, the Enneakrounos, and the gymnasium of Kynosarges.

Just north of the Olympieion is the area usually associated with the second great philosophical school of Athens, founded by Aristotle in 335 B.C. in an area known as the

247. Southeast Athens from the Acropolis. In the middle, Hadrian's Arch and the temple of Olympian Zeus, with the Panathenaic stadium at upper left and Mount Hymettos beyond.

Lyceum. It consisted of a grove sacred to Apollo Lykeios and a gymnasium. No certain architectural traces have been found in situ, but a cluster of inscriptions found in the area seems to give its general location. As recently as 1997 and 1998, herms with portraits of the philosopher Chrysippos and the comic poet Eupolis came to light in the area during construction around the parliament building. Some modest remains uncovered in 1996 several hundred meters farther east have been identified as the remains of the *palaistra* (wrestling ground) of the gymnasium, but as of 2000 the identification remains unsubstantiated.

EXCAVATIONS

The Olympieion was excavated in 1883–1884 by the British and in 1922 by the Germans. The area around it was explored by the Greek Archaeological Society in excavations from 1886 to 1907 and in the 1960s. The stadium was cleared and studied in 1869–1870 by the German architect E. Ziller before the reconstruction was undertaken.

BIBLIOGRAPHY

Southeast Area

Billot, M. F. "Le Cynosarges, Antiochos et les tanneurs: Questions topographie." *BCH* 116 (1992), pp. 119–156.
Billot, M. F. *Arch. Delt.* (1961–1962), and *Chron.* pp. 9–14.

Lyceum

Lynch, J. P. *Aristotle's School.* Berkeley, 1972.

Olympieion

Tolle-Kastenbein, R. *Das Olympieion in Athen.* Cologne, 1994.

Stadium

Gasparri, C. "Lo stadio Panatenaico." *ASAtene* 36–37 (1974–1975), pp. 313–392.
Tobin, J. "Some New Thoughts on Herodes Atticus's Tomb, His Stadium of 143/4, and Philostratus VS 2.550."*AJA* 97 (1993), pp. 81–89.

Notes

The little Ionic temple above the Ilissos (to Artemis Agrotera?) has been the subject of some controversy as to date: see M. M. Miles, "The Date of the Temple on the Ilissos River," *Hesperia* 49 (1980), pp. 309–325, and W. Childs, "In Defense of an Early Date for the Frieze of the Temple on the Ilissos." *Ath. Mitt.* 100 (1985), pp. 207–251.

ADDITIONAL SPECIALIZED AND RECENT ATHENIAN BIBLIOGRAPHY

General

Habicht, C. *Athens from Alexander to Antony.* Cambridge, Mass., 1997.
Hoff, M., and S. I. Rotroff (eds.) *The Romanization of Athens.* Exeter, U.K., 1997.

Long Walls

Conwell, D. "The Athenian Long Walls: Chronology, Topography, and Remains." Ph.D. diss., University of Pennsylvania, 1992.

Panathenaia

Habicht, C., and S. Tracy. "New and Old Panathenaic Victor Lists." *Hesperia* 60 (1991), pp. 187–236.
Neils, J. (ed.) *Goddess and Polis.* Hanover, U.K., 1992.
Neils, J. (ed.) *Worshipping Athena.* Madison, Wis., 1996.

Roman Agora

Hoff, M. "The Roman Agora at Athens." Ph.D. diss., Boston University, 1988.
Hoff, M. "The So-Called Agoranomion and the Imperial Cult in Julio-Claudian Athens." *AA* 109 (1994), pp. 93–117.

Ancient Nomenclature of Lykabettos and Tourkovouni

Biri, K. *Αἱ Τοπωνυμίαι τῆς Πόλεως καὶ τῶν Περιχώρων τῶν Ἀθηνῶν.* Athens, 1971. Pp. 13–15, 25–30, and 64–65.

Tower of the Winds

Kienast, H., "The Tower of the Winds in Athens: Hellenistic or Roman?" In *The Romanization of Athens,* ed. M. Hoff and S. I. Rotroff. Exeter, U.K., 1997.

Röttlander, R., et al., "Untersuchungen am Turm der Winde in Athen." *JÖAI* (1989), pp. 55 ff.

Von Freeden, J. *ΟΙΚΙΑ ΚΥΡΡΕΣΤΟΥ.* Rome, 1983.

Attica

Attica, the territory of ancient Athens, was divided in the historical period into 139 demes (see figs. 7, 39). Many of these demes were districts or neighborhoods within the city itself, but others were separate settlements scattered throughout the countryside. Each 248 had its own administration and civic organizations, and at the local level each passed decrees and built buildings independently. The demes also sent representatives for the administration of Athens as a whole. Proportional representation was an essential element of Athenian democracy; thus we can determine the relative size of each deme by the number of representatives it provided to the *boule* (senate) of five hundred. Acharnai, for instance, was the largest deme, sending twenty-two representatives every year, while other demes were so small that they would send only a single representative in rotation with other small settlements. Excavations at such deme sites as Thorikos, Rhamnous, and Aixone show that the demes were fully developed urban centers, with close-packed houses and streets, shops, and small sanctuaries all crowded together.

Considerable archaeological and historical research has been devoted in recent years to the demes and archaeology of Attica. The starting point for work on Attica is now J. Travlos' monumental study, *Bildlexikon zur Topographie des antiken Attika* (Tübingen, 1988). It includes summaries and numerous drawings and photographs of almost all the sites in Attica, together with a comprehensive bibliography up to the mid-1980s. Individual studies on the political organization and topography of the demes, the defenses of Attica, the cults, and other matters are listed below in a general bibliography, followed by summaries of individual sites or areas.

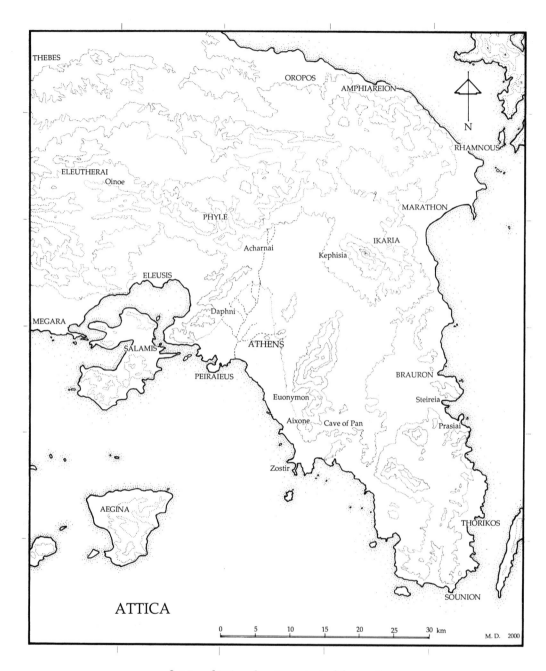

M. D.   2000

248. Map of Attica, showing principal deme sites.

BIBLIOGRAPHY

Topography and Political Organization

Barber, R. *A Guide to Rural Attika*. Np., 1999.

Eliot, C. W. J., *The Coastal Demes of Attika. Phoenix Suppl. 5*. Toronto, 1962.

Hanriot, C. *Topographie des demes*. Paris, 1853.

Haussoullier, B. *La Vie municipale en Attique*. Paris, 1884.

Lambert, S. *The Phratries of Attica*. Ann Arbor, Mich., 1993.

Osborne, R. G. *Demos: The Discovery of Classical Attika*. Cambridge, 1985.

Pantelidou-Gofa, M. *Ἡ Νεολιθική Ἀττική*. Athens, 1997.

Traill, J. *Demos and Trittys*. Toronto, 1986.

Traill, J. *The Political Organization of Attica. Hesperia Suppl. 14*. Princeton, N.J., 1975.

Von Schoeffer, V. "Demoi," *RE* 5.1 (1903), cols. 1–31.

Whitehead, D., *The Demes of Attica 508/7–ca. 250 B.C.* Princeton, N.J., 1986.

Cults

Deubner, L. *Attische Feste*. 2d ed. Berlin, 1966.

Solders, S. *Die ausserstadtischen Kulte und die Einigung Attikas*. Lund, Sweden, 1931.

Wickens, J. "The Archaeology and History of Cave Use in Attica." Ph.D. diss., Indiana University, 1986.

Defense

McCredie, J. *Fortified Military Camps in Attica, Hesperia Suppl. 11*. Princeton, N.J., 1966.

Munn, M. *The Defense of Attica*. Berkeley, 1993.

Ober, J. *Fortress Attika*. Leiden, Netherlands, 1985.

Quarries

Goette, H. "Die Steinbruche von Sounion." *Ath. Mitt.* 106 (1991), pp. 201 ff. (on Agrileza).

Korres, M. *From Pendeli to the Parthenon*. Athens, 1993.

Notes

In addition to the demes and sanctuaries, a number of individual farmsteads have come to light, also widely spread across the countryside. The owner of such a property would be enrolled as a citizen in a deme, but he was not required to actually reside in that deme. Only a few of these houses have been excavated, but many more have been recognized from their surface remains. They usually consist of the house itself, made up of several rooms grouped around an open courtyard; a well-built tower of several stories for security and storage; and a threshing floor nearby to process grain.

The house most extensively excavated and published on is situated below the cave at Vari: see J. E. Jones, L. H. Sackett, and A. J. Graham, "An Attic Country House Below the Cave of Pan at Vari," *BSA* 68 (1973), pp. 355–452. There has been considerable discussion recently over whether the Athenians in Attica lived in these isolated farmsteads or primarily in nucleated deme centers. Some thirty farms have now been located throughout Attica, a substantial number considering how many deme sites remain unrecognized. See R. Osborne, "'Is It a Farm?' The Definition of Agricultural Sites and Settlements in Ancient Greece," in *Classical Landscape with Figures* (London, 1987), and Osborne in *Agriculture in Ancient Greece,* ed. B. Wells (Stockholm, 1992), pp. 21–25. Also M. Langdon, "The Farm in Classical Attica," *CJ* 86 (1991), pp. 209–213, and J. Roy, "The Countryside in Classical Greek Drama, and Isolated Farms in Dramatic Landscapes," in *Human Landscapes in Classical Antiquity,* ed. G. Shipley and J. Salmon (London, 1996), pp. 98–118.

ACHARNAI

DESCRIPTION, HISTORY, AND SIGNIFICANCE

Acharnai was by far the largest deme of Attica. It sent twenty-two representatives annually to the boule, which suggests its population amounted to around 4 percent of the total citizen population of Athens. Thucydides (2.20) refers to the three thousand hoplites Acharnai provided for the army, and a count of preserved Athenian names indicates that the Acharnians were, in fact, the most numerous. Despite its large size, Acharnai has been almost invisible archaeologically, a problem for those who put faith in surface surveys alone. Thucydides locates it precisely 12 kilometers north of Athens. Two important inscriptions have come from the area, but little else. One inscription carries a version of the ephebic oath as well as a version of the oath which was taken by the Greeks before the Battle of Plataia in 479 B.C. The other inscription concerns the founding of an altar for Ares and Athena Areia, one of the few Athenian cult monuments for the god of war.

Acharnai was in the direct line of fire during the Peloponnesian War, and it was occupied and ravaged by the Spartans during their first invasion of Attica. They approached from the west by way of Eleusis, through the wide pass between Mount Aigaleos and Mount Parnes, later blocked in the fourth century by the so-called Dema wall. Aristophanes also emphasized the importance of Acharnai in this period, producing a play, *The Acharnians,* in 425 in which he poked fun at one of their main activities, making charcoal on nearby Mount Parnes (ll. 330–360).

A major Mycenaean site should be located just to the south (Menidhi; see fig. 7), where one of the four tholos tombs known in Attica was found.

EXCAVATIONS

A few scant traces of Acharnai have come to light in rescue excavations as the modern suburb of Menidi has developed. Among them, the tholos tomb was excavated by the German Archaeological Institute in 1879, and the Dema wall was surveyed by a British team in the 1960s.

BIBLIOGRAPHY

Inscriptions

Daux, G. "Deux steles d'Acharne." Χαριστήριον εἰς Ἀναστάσιος Κ. Ὀρλάνδος. Athens, 1964. Vol. 1, pp. 78–90.

Holleaux, M. "Séance du 13 juillet 1932." *CRAI* (1932), pp. 237–238.

Tod, M. *Greek Historical Inscriptions II.* Oxford, 1948. No. 204, pp. 303–307. (See also Lykourgos, *Against Leokrates,* 80 ff., and Diodoros Siculus 11.29.2 ff.)

Dema Wall

Jones, J. E., H. Sackett, and W. Eliot. "TO DEMA: A Survey of the Aigaleos-Parnes Wall." *BSA* 52 (1957), pp. 152–189.

Munn, M. *The Defense of Attica.* Berkeley, 1993.

Tholos

Benzi, M. *Ceramica Micenea in Attica.* Milan, 1975. Pp. 149–160.

Lolling, H., et al. *Das Kuppelgrab bei Menidhi.* DAI 1880.

Wolters, P. "Vasen aus Menidi." *JDAI* 13 (1898), pp. 13–28, and "Vasen aus Menidi II." *JDAI* 14 (1899), pp. 103–135.

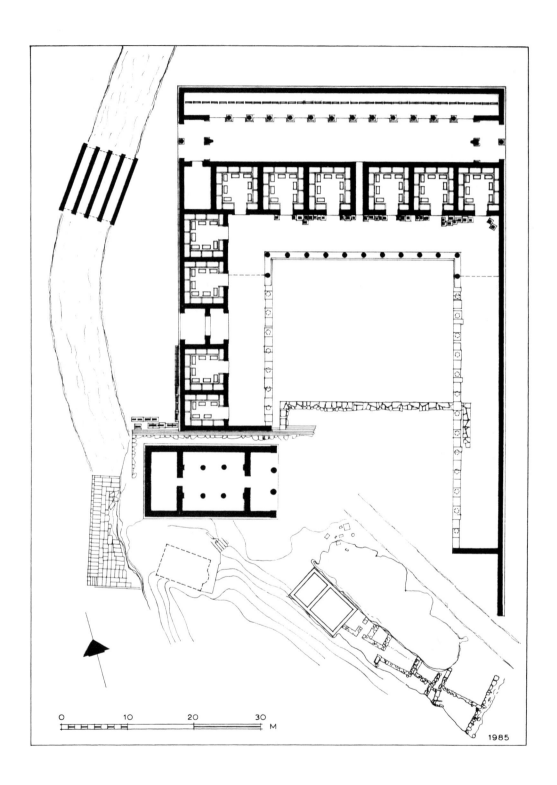

1985

O   10   20   30   M

250. Statue of a young girl or "bear" (*arktos*) from Brauron, 4th century B.C.

BRAURON

DESCRIPTION, HISTORY, AND

SIGNIFICANCE

The sanctuary of Artemis at Brauron (see fig. 118) lay near the sea on the east coast of Attica, in the territory of the deme of Philaidai, which lies about a kilometer and a half to the west. Brauron itself was said to have been one of the twelve cities of early Attica (see fig. 7). All phases of Bronze Age habitation have been found on the acropolis of Brauron, while Mycenaean chamber tombs have been excavated on the slopes to the east.

The sanctuary of Artemis seems to have been founded in the Geometric period, in the ninth or eighth century B.C., and numerous early votives were recovered from the sacred spring: pottery, jewelry, and objects of wood and ivory (see fig. 119).

The sanctuary was especially important to women; Artemis, as a virgin goddess, had to be appeased in matters of childbirth. The cult was an old one with primitive associations. Iphigeneia, in a version of the myth by Euripides, was said to have been its first priestess and to be buried there:

> Thou Iphigeneia on the hallowed heights
> Of Brauron on this goddess shall attend,
> Her priestess, dying shall there be interred,
> Graced with the honor of gorgeous robes

Opposite 249. The Sanctuary of Artemis at Brauron, 6th to 5th century B.C.

251. Votive krateriskoi from Brauron, showing girls running and dancing around an altar, 5th century B.C.

Of finest texture, in their houses left
By matrons who in childbed pangs expired.
(*Iphigenia in Tauros*, ll. 1462–1467)

Women who were successful in childbirth would offer a set of clothing to Artemis, and many inscriptions listing these offerings have been discovered at the sanctuary, along with numerous statues of young boys and girls dedicated by thankful parents. The clothing of those who died would be offered to Iphigenia. Between the ages of seven and ten, young Athenian girls were also expected to serve for a year as attendants in the sanctuary at Brauron, during which time they were said to be "playing the bear." According to assorted late traditions, this practice began as an act of appeasement to placate Artemis when the goddess, angered by the killing of a pet bear, sent a plague against Athens. Special ritual vases showing young girls running or dancing around an altar, found only at Brauron and at one or two other shrines to Artemis in Attica (Acropolis, Mounychia), have been recovered in large number.

The earliest architecture on the site is the temple, thought to date to the late sixth century B.C. It is represented by foundations and several limestone fragments of the Doric order: column shafts, frieze blocks, and an anta capital. More building was done in the fifth century, after the Persians had plundered and presumably destroyed the sanctuary in 480 (Pausanias 3.16.7–8). Most interesting is a stoa built in the 420s, during the Peloponnesian War, and never entirely finished. The stoa is an innovative building. On either end of the central colonnade, two wings projected. The architect clearly struggled with the problem of the spacing of columns vis-à-vis the Doric frieze where it turns an interior corner or reentrant angle.

The stoa was used to display numerous votives, in the form of reliefs and small marble statues, which stood within the colonnade. In addition, many people would pass through the colonnade to get to the rooms behind. Clearly, open visibility and ease of access were desired for the stoa (unlike a temple), so the columns were more widely spaced, not randomly but every three frieze units rather than every two, which had been the rule up to this point. With their characteristic raised borders and sockets for the legs of wooden couches, the rooms of the stoa may be identified with confidence as dining rooms.

North of the dining rooms was an elongated courtyard, attached to the stoa but entered independently through large doors at east and west. A row of square supports roofed the northern section, in which was set a long stone channel or groove divided into segments by stone barriers. This arrangement seems to be without parallel, and its function is a mystery. Perhaps the channel held boards on which the sets of dedicated clothing were displayed.

Also dated to the fifth century is a fine stone bridge spanning the stream flowing from the sacred spring. Large limestone slabs were set on a series of parallel walls built in the streambed. Heavy wheel ruts suggest that the main approach to the sanctuary was by land, over the bridge from the northwest. Numerous other buildings are attested to for the sanctuary but have not yet been found. An inscription lists several buildings in need of repair: a temple, a *parthenon, oikoi* (rooms), an *amphipoleion* (building for temple servants), stables, a gymnasium, and a *palaistra* (wrestling ground). It is not clear whether the gymnasium and the palaistra were for the girls or for Athenian men competing in some festival in honor of Artemis.

The site was abandoned in the third century B.C., perhaps as part of the general abandonment of Attica when the Macedonians controlled Athens. It was soon silted over by the Erasinos River, which flows through the Livadi Plain, and was left largely undisturbed thereafter. There are only slight indications of any Roman activity, in the second century A.D.: there is a brief mention in Pausanias, suggesting that he saw an old wooden statue there (1.33.1), and a relief of Polydeukion, Herodes Atticus' boyfriend, was found nearby. An early Christian basilica built some 1,000 meters to the west makes little use of ancient material, almost certainly an indication that the location of the old sanctuary had been forgotten.

EXCAVATIONS

Brauron was untouched until well into the twentieth century. Then excavations were carried out by J. Papademetriou for the Greek Archaeological Society from the late 1940s

until the early 1960s. No excavation has been done since, though the stoa was restored and
studied by Ch. Bouras in the mid-1960s. The rest of the architecture, as well as the rich collections of pottery, sculpture, and inscriptions from the site, await final study and publication. A large and growing bibliography primarily concerns the cult.

BIBLIOGRAPHY

Bouras, Ch. Ἡ Ἀναστήλωσις τῆς στοᾶς τῆς Βραυρῶνος. Athens, 1967.

Demand, N. *Birth, Death, and Motherhood in Classical Greece*. Baltimore, 1994.

Kontis, J. *Arch. Delt.* 22 (1967), A′, pp. 156–206.

Linders, T. *Studies in the Treasure Records of Artemis Brauronia Found in Athens*. Stockholm,
    1972.

Papademetriou, J. "The Sanctuary of Artemis at Brauron," *Scientific American*, June 1963,
    pp. 110–120.

Travlos, J. *Bildlexikon zur Topographie des antiken Attika*. Tübingen, 1988. Pp. 55–80 (with
    bibliography).

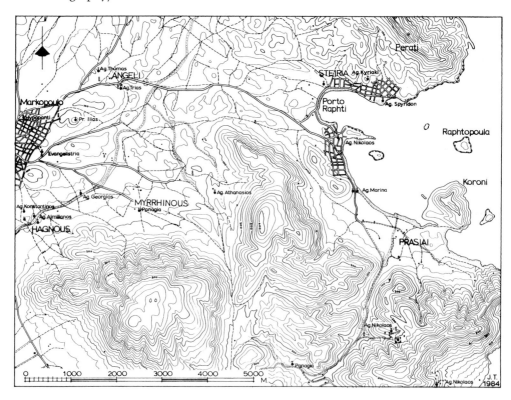

Notes

For a discussion of the complexities of the stoa, with its reentrant interior angles and the need for corner extension, see J. Coulton, *BSA* 62 (1967), pp. 132–146. For the characteristic off-center door of Greek dining rooms, see S. Miller, *The Prytaneion* (Berkeley, 1978), pp. 219–224, and N. Bookidis and R. Stroud, *The Sanctuary of Demeter and Kore: Topography and Architecture. Corinth 18, Part 3* (Princeton, N.J., 1997), pp. 393–421.

EAST COAST: STEIREIA, PRASIAI (PORTO RAPHTI, KORONI, PERATI)

DESCRIPTION, HISTORY, AND SIGNIFICANCE

Numerous antiquities cluster around the modern bay of Porto Raphti, between Brauron and Thorikos on the east coast of Attica. Two ancient demes shared the bay, Steireia on the north and Prasiai on the south. Early traditions concerning Steireia survive in Pausanias (10.35.5): when he visited the small Phocian town of Stiris not far from Delphi, he claimed that the inhabitants were Athenian, having migrated to Phocis from Steireia in the Bronze Age with Peteos during the reign of King Aigeus, Theseus' father. 252

The earliest remains are east of Steireia near modern Perati, where a complete cemetery with 279 Late Bronze Age tombs was excavated, though no trace of the associated settlement has been found (see fig. 7). The ancient road to Steireia is mentioned in one of the dialogues preserved in the Platonic corpus (*Hipparchos* 228–229). Steireia was also the source of good limestone, easily loaded on ships because the quarry lay near the sea, at the northeast end of the harbor. An inscription of the mid-fifth century (*IG* I³ 395) calls for Steireian stone to be quarried and transported to Eleusis.

The deme of Prasiai, on the south of the bay, was the departure point for sacred embassies to Apollo on the island of Delos. Traces of the local Apollo sanctuary have recently come to light with the discovery of part of an archaic kouros and its inscribed statue base, signed by the sculptor Pythis.

Just northeast of the deme site is the high rocky peninsula of Koroni (see fig. 162), which is covered with antiquities. Two rubble walls run along the ridges of the hill, and there is a separately fortified acropolis. Between the two walls, traces of many small structures can be made out, several of which have been excavated. From the material recovered

Opposite 252. Eastern Attica, showing the demes of Steireia, Prasiai, Myrrhinous, and Hagnous. Also shown is the area of Perati (late Mycenaean cemetery), Raphtopoula (monumental seated marble statue), Koroni (Ptolemaic fort), and the find-spot of Phrasikleia (near the Panaghia church at Myrrhinous).

it seems certain that the site was a fortified military camp, used by Ptolemaic troops from Egypt in their attempt to free Athens from Macedonian control during the Chremonidean War in the 260s B.C. Half the bronze coins found on the hill are of Ptolemy II, and many of the amphora stamps are better paralleled in Egypt than in Attica. The pottery from the site can therefore be used as a reliable fixed point for the chronology of Hellenistic ceramics.

253   At the entrance to the harbor lies a small, steep conical island. At the top is a large seated figure carved in Pentelic marble. It has been there for centuries, and its seated pose gives the bay its modern name, Porto Raphti (the Port of the Tailor). Although the statue is considerably weathered, enough survives to allow the probable identification of a male figure, dated to the second century A.D.; there is no good way of identifying the individual portrayed nor the reason his image was erected on the island.

EXCAVATIONS

The Perati Cemetery was first excavated by Staies and later, in the 1960s, by S. Iakovides for the Greek Archaeological Society. A selection of the finds is on display in the Brauron Museum. The fort at Koroni was excavated by members of the American School of Classical Studies in the 1960s under the direction of E. Vanderpool. The kouros from Prasiai was excavated by O. Kakovoyianni for the Attica Ephoreia of the Archaeological Service.

BIBLIOGRAPHY

Koroni

McCredie, J. R. *Fortified Military Camps in Attica. Hesperia Suppl. 11.* Princeton, N.J., 1966.
Vanderpool, E., et al. "A Ptolemaic Camp on the East Coast of Attica." *Hesperia* 31 (1962), pp. 26–61.
Vanderpool, E., et al. "Koroni: The Date of the Camp and the Pottery." *Hesperia* 33 (1964), pp. 69–75.

Perati

Iakovides, S. *The Excavations of the Nekropolis of Perati.* Berkeley, 1981.

Prasiai

Apostopoulou-Kakovoyianni, O. In *Archaische und Klassische Griechische Plastik,* ed. H. Kyrieleis. Mainz, 1986.

Notes

H. Lauter-Bufe has questioned the generally accepted interpretation of the remains at Koroni in "Die Festung auf Koroni und die Bucht von Raphti," *Marburger Winckelmann-Program* (1988), pp. 67–102. The sex of the large seated marble "tailor" at the head of the harbor has been disputed between S. Miller, who claimed it was a male figure ("The Colossus of Porto Raphti Reconsidered," *Hesperia* 41 [1972], pp. 192–197), and C. Vermeule, who opted for female ("The Colossus of Porto Raphti in Attica," *Hesperia* 31 [1962], pp. 62–81, and "The Colossus of Porto Raphti: A Roman Female Personification," *Hesperia* 45 [1976], pp. 67–76). The deep undercutting behind the calves seems to favor a male figure (women tended to wear long drapery and did not show their legs). Usually overlooked among early travelers who describe the figure is the Italian artist S. Pomardi, who reported the figure as male.

253. Nineteenth-century photograph of the seated statue at Porto Raphti, 2nd century A.D.

ELEUSIS

DESCRIPTION, HISTORY, AND SIGNIFICANCE

Eleusis lies on the shore of a large bay 21 kilometers west of Athens. It was an important deme site as well as the location of the sanctuary of Demeter. The mysteries celebrated here made Eleusis one of the most important cult places in all Greece. The deme occupied a long ridge at the edge of the Rarian or Thriasian Plain, and the sanctuary lay at the east end of the ridge. The site has been inhabited since at least the early Bronze Age, and all periods are represented thereafter (see

254, 255 fig. 21).

According to one source, the *marmor Parium* (Epoch 12, lines 23–24), Demeter arrived at Eleusis in 1409 B.C., searching for her daughter Persephone, who had been carried
off into the underworld by Ploutos. Demeter was treated well by the royal family of Eleusis
and eventually was recognized as a goddess. She taught the Eleusinians the secret of agriculture and ordered the king to build her a sanctuary under a projecting spur of rock. She
and Eleusis are thereafter inextricably linked with the fertility of the land. Her cult was unlike those of most Olympian gods; it featured secret nocturnal rites, watched only by the initiates. Because the penalty for revealing the mysteries was death, the secret was well kept;
even today we know little about the cult for certain.

Though there are Bronze Age remains under the sanctuary, the earliest certain evidence of cult activity dates to the late eighth century B.C., in the form of votive offerings and
piles of ash. Once established, the sanctuary stayed in use for more than a thousand years,
256 until it was destroyed by the Visigoths in A.D. 395 (see figs. 204–207). The focal point of the
257 sanctuary was the Telesterion, or hall of mysteries (see figs. 98, 99). This was a large hall
which grew steadily in size throughout the centuries, its roof supported by numerous interior columns. In all, some eight or nine distinct architectural phases can be made out, dating from the early sixth century B.C. until the second century A.D. Almost as much as
Athens itself, Eleusis was favored in Roman times, and several of the emperors are known
to have been initiated into the mysteries. Many of the monuments surviving on the site date
from the first century B.C. to the late second century A.D.

Eleusis was the westernmost Attic deme on the coast and thus something of an out-
post facing the Peloponnese, home of such long-standing enemies as the Megarians,
Corinthians, and Spartans (see fig. 146). The sanctuary itself was protected by a substantial
fortification wall, which had several building phases, starting in the sixth century B.C. under the Peisistratids (see fig. 37). The acropolis to the west was also walled, and Eleusis was
one of the principal garrison forts of Attica from at least as early as the fourth century B.C.

Eleusis was reached from Athens by the Sacred Way, lined with tombs and sanctuaries for much of its 21 kilometers (see fig. 124). The monuments were described by Polemon
in the second century B.C. in a long account (now lost) and by Pausanias in the second century A.D. Still preserved is the sanctuary of Aphrodite in the pass through Mount Aigaleos,
with inscribed rock-cut niches for votive offerings, several of which have been recovered
(see figs. 125, 126). Just outside Eleusis, the Sacred Way crossed the Eleusinian Kephisos
River via a bridge; an early fourth-century bridge has disappeared but was replaced by one
built by Hadrian in A.D. 125 (Eusebius, *Chron.* 2.166; see fig. 203).

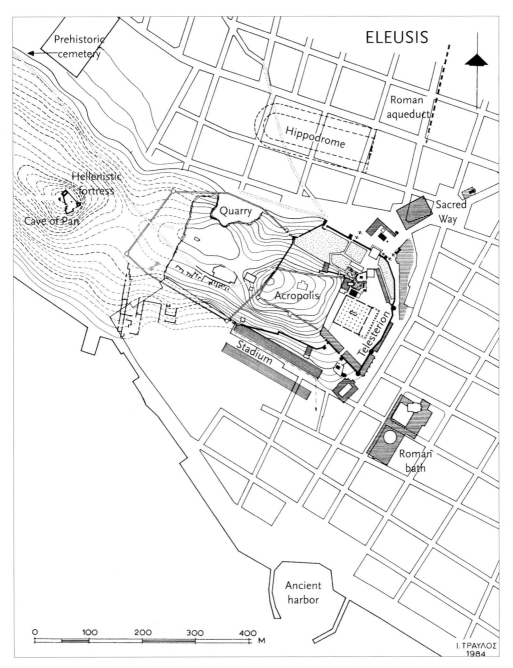

254. Eleusis, plan of deme site and sanctuary of Demeter.

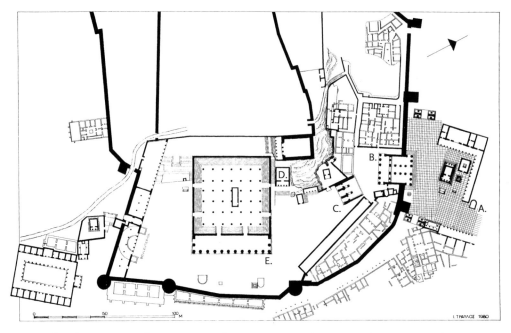

255. Eleusis, sanctuary of Demeter in 2nd century A.D.: (A) forecourt with the temple of Artemis
Propylaia and the Kallichoron well; (B) outer (greater) propylon (2nd century A.D.); (C) inner propylon
(1st century B.C.); (D) Temple F; (E) Telesterion.

EXCAVATION

Eleusis has been excavated by various scholars for the Archaeological Society almost
continuously from 1882 to the 1950s, including successively, D. Philios, A. Skias, K. Kourouniotis, A. Orlandos, J. Travlos, G. Mylonas, and M. Kosmopoulos.

BIBLIOGRAPHY

Clinton, K. "The Eleusinian Mysteries: Roman Initiates and Benefactors: Second Century
      B.C.–267 A.D.," *ANRW*, part 2, vol. 18.2 (1989), pp. 1499–1537.
Clinton, K. *Myth and Cult: The Iconography of the Eleusinian Mysteries*. Stockholm, 1992.
Mylonas, G. *Eleusis and the Eleusinian Mysteries*. Princeton, N.J., 1961.
*Travlos, J. *Bildlexikon zur Topographie des antiken Attika*. Tübingen, 1988. Pp. 91–164 (with
      bibliography through 1985).
Ziro, D. *Ἡ Κυρία Εἴσοδος τοῦ Ἱεροῦ τῆς Ἐλευσίνος*. Athens, 1991.

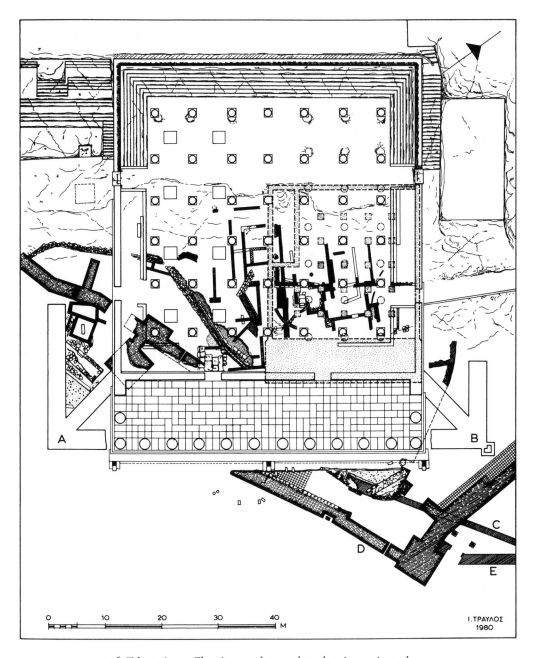

256. Telesterion at Eleusis, actual-state plan, showing various phases.

257. Archaic Telesterion and early fortification wall, 6th to 5th century B.C.
(Watercolor by Peter Connolly)

Notes

For the argument that the cult at Eleusis does not go as far back as the Mycenaean age, see P. Darque, "Les Vestiges myceniens découverts sous le Telesterion d'Eleusis," *BCH* 105 (1981), pp. 593–605. For the Homeric Hymn to Demeter, see J. H. Richardson, *The Homeric Hymn to Demeter* (Oxford, 1974), and H. Foley, *The Homeric Hymn to Demeter* (Princeton, N.J., 1993). For the view that there was no Kimonian phase to the Telesterion, see T. L. Shear, Jr., "The Demolished Temple at Eleusis," in *Hesperia. Suppl. 20* (Princeton,

N.J., 1982), pp. 128–140. For the financial administration of the sanctuary in the fifth century, see M. B. Cavanaugh, *Eleusis and Athens* (Atlanta, Ga., 1996). R. Townsend has argued that the Telesterion was rebuilt virtually from the ground up in the late second century A.D.: see "The Roman Rebuilding of Philo's Porch and the Telesterion at Eleusis," *Boreas* 10 (1987), pp. 97–106. For the Sacred Way see J. Travlos, *Bildlexikon zur Topographie des antiken Attika.* (Tübingen, 1988), pp. 177–190.

IKARIA

DESCRIPTION, HISTORY, AND SIGNIFICANCE

The site of the ancient deme of Ikaria lies on the wooded north slopes of Mount Pentele. The excavated area is often referred to as the deme center, though in fact all the buildings and most of the inscriptions concern the cults of Apollo and Dionysos. The worship of Dionysos and the origins of both winemaking and early theater were important on the site, and the memory of the god survives in the modern toponym for the area, Dionyso.

The site consists of several buildings and a theater. The theater dates to no later than   258
the early fourth century B.C. and, like the other deme theaters, has a rectilinear orchestra. Opposite the wall of the scene-building, and almost parallel to it, a straight line of foundations carried five limestone thrones, the *proedria,* or front-row seats of honor. Apparently the rest of the audience sat on the slopes of the hill behind. To the northwest of the theater is the largest building on the site, a temple of Pythian Apollo. It had a front porch, in which reliefs were found, a cella with a central hearth or altar, and, at some period, a small back chamber, perhaps an *adyton*—a secret room, common to many temples of Apollo. There were no columns. This is one of the most securely identified temples in Greece: on the threshold of the doorway is inscribed in large letters, "The Pythion of the Ikarians" (*IG* II² 4976). There are traces of other buildings and several large bases. Associated with one of these bases is the large late Archaic statue of a seated figure of Dionysos (see fig. 33), now in the National Museum, holding his wine cup (*kantharos*) in his right hand.

Numerous inscriptions and several reliefs were found as well. Many of these are choregic monuments, set up to celebrate victories in the dramatic contests. Almost all the pieces of the best-preserved example remain on the site. The structure takes the form of a small hemicycle of gray limestone blocks with a bench running around the inner face. These exedras, as they are called, are fairly common dedications, designed to carry statuary. Cuttings on the roof indicate that this one displayed some sort of monument, presumably the prize itself. An inscribed epistyle ran across the top, reading, "Hagnias, Xanthippos, and Xanthides, having been victorious, set this up" (*IG* II² 3098).

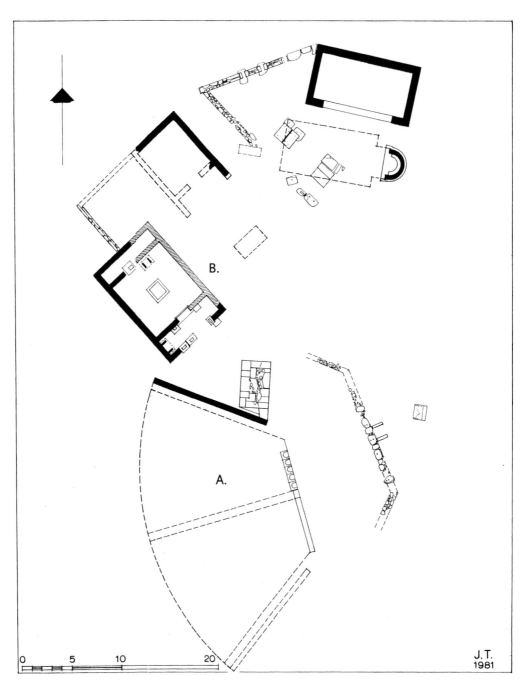

B.

A.

J.T.
1981

0   5   10   20

258. Ikaria, Sanctuary of Dionysos, 6th to 4th century B.C.: (A) Theater; (B) the Pythion.

Most of the evidence from the site suggests that it was active in the sixth to fourth centuries B.C.; it is not clear how much, if at all, it was used thereafter.

EXCAVATIONS

The site of Ikaria was investigated in 1888–1889 by the American School of Classical Studies under the direction of C. D. Buck. No excavation has been undertaken since, though some cleaning and restudy was carried out in 1981.

BIBLIOGRAPHY

Biers, W., and T. Boyd. "Ikarion in Attica, 1881–1981." *Hesperia* 51 (1982), pp. 1–18.

Buck, C. D. "Discoveries in the Attic Deme of Ikaria in 1888." *AJA* 5 (1889), pp. 5–33, 154–181, 304–319, 461–477.

Romano, I. "The Archaic Statue of Dionysos from Ikarion." *Hesperia* 51 (1982), pp. 398–409.

Travlos, J. *Bildlexikon zur Topographie des antiken Attika*. Tübingen, 1988. Pp. 85–87.

MARATHON

DESCRIPTION, HISTORY, AND SIGNIFICANCE

The Plain of Marathon lies on the sea to the northeast, cut off from the rest of Attica by Mount Pentele (see fig. 47). A large, level coastal plain, it attracted human habitation from early times and was occupied throughout antiquity. The earliest remains go back to the Middle Neolithic: pottery in the cave at Oinoe and a settlement under the modern town of Nea Makri. From the early Bronze Age the partially excavated cemetery at Tsepi has been excavated, as well as traces of a settlement by the sea at Plasi. Middle Helladic tumuli, enclosing individual burials, have been found at Vrana, next to the modern museum. The Mycenaean period is represented by a tholos tomb (see fig. 11), which had the skeletons of two horses formally laid out in the *dromos* (entrance corridor). Pottery and a gold cup were found inside the tomb in two burial pits. Architecturally, the tholos is of interest because of the elaboration of the entrance at the juncture of dromos and doorway. Also unusual is the fact that the tomb was set into level ground in the plain, with a sloping dromos; generally

259. Horses buried in the dromos of
the Mycenaean tholos tomb at
Marathon, 15th century B.C.
(Cf. fig. 11)

tholoi are cut into the slope of a hillside. All the Attic tholoi show individual characteristics which set them apart from the more familiar examples known in the Argolid.

The Geometric period is represented by numerous graves found along the ancient road which skirts the northeast slopes of Mount Agrieliki, southeast of the museum at Vrana. From early times the plain was occupied by four settlements which later became demes in the reorganization of 508/7: Marathon, Probalinthos, Oinoe, and Trikorynthos. Collectively they were known as the Marathonian Tetrapolis (four cities). Their political unity was weakened when they were assigned to two different tribes during the Kleisthenic reforms; Probalinthos was allocated to Pandionis and the other three to Aiantis. Their unity and corporate identity survived in cult activity, however. They worshiped Dionysos collectively, and long after it was incorporated into the Athenian state the Tetrapolis continued to send its own delegations to Apollo at Delphi which were distinct from those sent by Athens. The locations of Oinoe, Trikorynthos, and Probalinthos seem relatively secure; Marathon is harder to place with any certainty.

More than anything, Marathon is famed for the battle which took place on the plain in 490 B.C. between the Athenians with their Plataian allies and the Persians, a campaign described at length by Herodotos (6.96–120). The topography of the batttle has been the subject of intense scholarship, not least because it provides one of the best opportunities to test Herodotos' reliability as a historian. Various remains survive in the plain to guide our interpretation of his account.

When the Athenians arrived to confront the Persians, they encamped in a sanctuary of Herakles. Two fifth-century inscriptions found near each other at the south end of the plain allow us to place the sanctuary just north of the Brexisa Marsh. About 1.5 kilometers to the north, corresponding to Herodotos' account of an Athenian charge at a run over 8 stades, is the most prominent feature in the plain, the *soros,* or burial mound of the Athenians (see figs. 48–51). It rises 9 meters and is about 50 meters across. Beneath it were buried the cremated remains of the 192 Athenians said to have died in the battle. A little over 5.5 kilometers to the northeast of the soros is the southern limit of the great marsh, where the majority of the 6,400 Persians were slain. Just south of the marsh is a medieval tower, in which were found several marble column drums and an Ionic capital dateable to the early fifth century, with cuttings to carry sculpture on top. This is almost certainly the trophy, set up at the turning pont (*trope*) of the battle, where the enemy suffered the greatest number of casualties.

Marathon was the home deme of the Athenian philanthropist Herodes Atticus (see fig. 208), and the plain was therefore a center of activity in the second century A.D. He had a large villa with baths and a shrine to the Egyptian gods near the Brexisa Marsh at the south end of the plain (see figs. 214, 215), and his wife, Regilla, apparently had a separate estate somewhat inland, reached through the arched Gate of Immortal Harmony (see fig. 216). There was also a Roman nymphaion built at Oinoe, perhaps by Herodes. A cave above the nymphaion (partially excavated in the 1950s) was worth a visit in Pausanias' time (1.32.6):

> A little way from the plain is a mountain of Pan and a grotto that is worth seeing;
> its entrance is narrow, but within are chambers and baths and what is called
> Pan's herd of goats, being rocks which mostly resemble goats.

The Plain of Marathon thus provides evidence of continuous human occupation and intensive use for more than seven thousand years, from Middle Neolithic times through the Roman era and beyond; in the Middle Ages one of the large Byzantine-Frankish towers was built at Oinoe and survives in good repair. The plain is under heavy cultivation today.

EXCAVATIONS

The soros was excavated first by H. Schliemann in the 1880s and by B. Staies in 1890–1891. Other excavations in the plain, including that of the Mycenaean tomb, were carried out by G. Soteriades in the 1930s; S. Marinatos excavated much prehistoric material and the "tomb of the Plataians" in the 1960s and 1970s. The most important topographical work on the battle of 490 was done over many years by E. Vanderpool. An excellent small museum at Vrana has material from all periods on display.

BIBLIOGRAPHY

Petrakos, B. Ὁ Μαραθὼν. Athens, 1995.

Travlos, J. *Bildlexikon zur Topographie des antiken Attika.* Tübingen, 1988. Pp. 216–257.

Vanderpool, E., and J. Camp. In Πρακτικά τῆς Δ' Ἐπιστημονικῆς Συνάντησης στην ΝΑ Ἀττικῆς. Kalyvia, Attica, 1993. Pp. 35–65.

PEIRAIEUS

DESCRIPTION, HISTORY, AND SIGNIFICANCE

Peiraieus was the port of Athens, a hilly peninsula with three natural harbors, Kantharos, Zea, and Mounychia, lying some 6 kilometers to the southwest of the city. Because of Athenian naval power and economic dependence on the sea, Peiraieus was perhaps the most important of all the demes of Attica, though not the largest (see figs. 5, 63). In many ways, it was almost an independent city, and on several occasions during times of trouble (404/3 and the third century B.C.), Peiraieus and Athens were actually held by different, warring factions. The dependence of the city on the port may be seen in the distribution of many offices; of ten *agoranomoi* (market police), ten *metronomoi* (officials in charge of weights and measures), or ten *sitophylakes* (grain commissioners), five would be assigned to Athens and five to Peiraieus.

The earliest Athenian harbor was at Phaleron, the broad open bay to the southeast of Peiraieus. It was Themistokles who first persuaded the Athenians to fortify the peninsula and to use its harbors as the port. The Themistoklean circuit wall, described by Thucydides, was largely destroyed at the end of the Peloponnesian War. The circuit which survives today, and which can be traced for long stretches, was the work of Konon in 394–391. It was maintained and repaired throughout the Hellenistic period and finally went out of use after Sulla's capture of the port in 86 B.C.

The largest harbor, Kantharos, lay to the northwest; its inner area served as the main commercial center. Five stoas, known from inscriptions as the *emporion*, lined its eastern side. Among them was the *deigma,* an area where merchants displayed their wares and where bankers' tables were set up. Boundary stones found in the harbor indicate that ferries left from these docks as well, just as they do today. In the fourth century B.C. the fare to Aigina was 2 obols (⅓ drachma; Plato, *Gorgias* 511D); by the second century A.D. it had doubled (Lucian, *Navig.* 15). A port tax of 1 drachma was payable to the principal sanctuary of Peiraieus, the temple of Zeus Soter and Athena Soteira (Savior). Several fifth-century Doric capitals found around the nearby church of Aghia Triada may indicate the location of the sanctuary.

The outer section of the harbor was used for the fleet; ship sheds there housed ninety-four triremes. At the entrance to the harbor was an unfluted marble Ionic column said to mark the tomb of Themistokles (see fig. 58). On the other side of the entrance was a huge marble lion, some 3 meters tall. It is not clear whether it stood there in antiquity, though lions were used to mark the entrance to the harbor of Miletos. It was certainly there in the eleventh century A.D., for it carries runic inscriptions carved at the order of the mercenary leader Harald of Norway after an attack on Athens in 1040:

260. Peiraieus, plan of the peninsula and harbors.

Asmond together with Asgeir, Thorlief, Thord, and Ivar carved these runes under the instruction of Harald the Long, despite the fact that the angry Greeks
wanted to prevent this action.

The lion was removed by Francesco Morosini following his assault on Athens in 1687–
1688 and stands today in front of the arsenal at Venice.

To the south of Kantharos lay Zea, the principal war harbor. Here ship sheds housed
196 triremes. Many of these were still visible in the nineteenth century, and parts of a handful are maintained in the basements of modern buildings (see fig. 144). The total number
of ship sheds in all three harbors in the second half of the fourth century was 372, the figure given in an inscription of 325/4 (*IG* II² 1629). These sheds were a source of particular
pride to the Athenians, especially in the fourth century, when they were rebuilt by Euboulos
and Lykourgos after the Thirty Tyrants pulled them down in 403. Most of the sheds were finally destroyed by Sulla in 86 B.C.

Behind the ship sheds lay the great *skeuotheke,* or arsenal, of Philon, where the hanging tackle of the fleet was stored (see fig. 145). Known from a detailed inscription listing its
building specifications, the structure has recently been located and partially excavated. Adjacent to the arsenal was the Agora, laid out in the fifth century by the Milesian urban plan-
ner Hippodamos, who also designed the rest of Peiraieus as well as the cities of Thurii and
Rhodes. A feature of his cities, though not his invention, was their regular orthogonal layout or grid plan.

The third harbor, Mounychia, was the smallest, but it still accommodated eighty-two
ship sheds. On a low hill to the southwest was an important sanctuary of Artemis Mounychia, and on a high, steep hill behind the harbor was the fort garrisoned by the Macedonians in the third century B.C.

Two theaters are known for Peiraieus, one dating to the fifth century at Mounychia
and another not far from Zea, dating to the second century. An unusual law court lay south
of Zea, called the Court in Phreatto; it was reserved for cases involving those who had already been exiled from Attica, who were therefore required to plead their case from a boat
offshore.

It is in Peiraieus especially that one can recover a sense of the cosmopolitan quality
of Athenian life. Athens was home to thousands of *metics,* resident aliens from other
Greek cities. These were free men who paid taxes but did not own land and were not citizens of Athens. They contributed much to Athenian success, however, and many were
prominent figures: Anaxagoras, the philosopher from Miletos; Polygnotos, the painter
from Thasos; and Aristotle, the philosopher from Stageira. An astounding 40 percent of

the thousands of gravestones known from Attica are for foreigners. Some from Peiraieus are even written in Phoenician script. Many of these foreigners, of course, lived and worked in the port, making Peiraieus a huge city, in which the foreigners perhaps almost overwhelmed the native Athenian population. This foreign presence can be appreciated if we consider the religious cults they brought with them; cults attested to for the Peiraieus include Bendis from Thrace, Aphrodite from Cyprus, Isis from Egypt, Baal from Phoenicia, Men from Lydia-Phrygia, and Zeus Labraundos from Caria. A decree proposed by Lykourgos in 333 (*IG* II² 337) preserves a record of the introduction of two such foreign cults:

> About those things which the merchants from Kition [in Cyprus] requested from the people, the right to legally own a property in which to found a sanctuary of Aphrodite. Resolved by the people, to give the merchants of Kition the right to own a plot of land in which to found the sanctuary of Aphrodite just as the Egyptians founded the sanctuary of Isis.

Many of these metics were very successful in business, and in 404/3 the Thirty Tyrants prosecuted them simply to get their hands on the money. Just north of Peiraieus, in the modern suburb of Kallithea, the huge tomb of a family from Istros was found. Raised on a high podium, decorated with sculpted friezes of battle scenes and animals, it was a small templelike building displaying life-sized statues of three members of the family. Reminiscent of the great Maussolleion at Halikarnassos, this tomb of a metic is among the most lavish of all the fourth-century graves of Attica. It is on display in the Peiraieus Museum.

EXCAVATIONS

There has been little systematic excavation of Peiraieus, though the rapid development of the modern city has produced considerable material from rescue excavations, as have repeated dredgings of the harbor. One rescue dig in 1959 uncovered a cache of four large bronze statues: an archaic Apollo in a kouros pose, a fourth-century armed Athena, an Artemis, and either a nymph or another Artemis. They were all buried together, presumably in a storeroom awaiting shipment, when the Mithradatic wars and Sulla's siege of Peiraieus caught up with them early in the first century B.C. They are now on display, together with other items of considerable interest, in the Peiraieus archaeological mu-

261

261. Bronze statue of Athena, found in Peiraieus, 4th century B.C.

262

seum near Zea. Here, too, are displayed a collection of marble reliefs dredged out of the large harbor. Dated to the second century A.D., they are copies or adaptations of Classical sculptures made for export to Rome. Among the scenes are several pairs of dueling figures taken from the Amazonomachy which adorned the shield of Pheidias' chryselephantine statue of Athena Parthenos in the Parthenon.

BIBLIOGRAPHY

General

Frazer, G. *Pausanias' Description of Greece.* London, 1898. Vol. 2, pp. 6–32.

*Garland, R. *The Piraeus.* Ithaca, 1987.

Judeich, W. *Topographie von Athen.* Munich, 1931. Pp. 430–456.

Panagos, C. *Le Pirée.* Athens, 1968.

Steinhauer, G. *Τά Μνημεῖα καί τό Ἀρχαιολογικό Μουσεῖο τοῦ Πειραιᾶ.* Athens 1998.

*Von Eickstedt, K. *Beiträge zur Topographie des antiken Piräus.* Athens, 1991.

Bronze Statues

Daux, G. "Chronique de fouilles, 1959." *BCH* 84 (1960), pp. 647–653.

Vanderpool, E. "News Letter from Greece." *AJA* 64 (1960), pp. 265–266.

Kallithea Tomb

Daux, G. "Archaeological Reports for 1967–68." *JHS* (1968), p. 6.

Daux, G. "Chronique de fouilles, 1967." *BCH* (1968), pp. 749 ff.

Tsirivakos, N. *AAA* (1968), pp. 35–36 and 108–109, and (1971), pp. 108–110.

262. Amazonomachy, marble relief copied from the shield of the Athena Parthenos in the 2nd century A.D.; found with several other similar reliefs in Peiraieus harbor.

Neo-Attic Reliefs

Harrison, E. B. "Motifs of the City-Siege on the Shield of Athena Parthenos." *AJA* (1981), pp. 281–317.
Stephanidou-Tiberiou, Th. *NEOATTIKA*. Athens, 1979.

Skeuotheke

Arch. Delt. 44 (1989, 1995), B, p. 50.
Jeppesen, K. *Paradeigmata*. Arhus, Denmark, 1958.

PHYLE

DESCRIPTION, HISTORY, AND SIGNIFICANCE

Phyle was the site of a deme and border fort on Mount Parnes, about 20 kilometers north of Athens (see figs. 128, 146). It was special to the Athenians as the place the exiled democrats first seized on their way to overthrow the Thirty Tyrants in 403 B.C. Xenophon (*Hell.* 2.4.2–7) and Diodorus Siculus (14.32–33) describe the campaign in detail; inscriptions record various rewards for those who fought; and orators refer to these events as well. The present, well-preserved fort is thought by most to date to a little later than the events of 403. It encircles the eastern half of a steep rocky crag overlooking the most direct north-south route from Attica to Boiotia. The walls still stand several meters high in places, broken at intervals by four towers and two gates. In later times Phyle was a regular Athenian garrison fort and appears in numerous military inscriptions. Repairs were carried out on it in the 330s (*IG* II² 244), and at the end of the fourth century it was garrisoned by Kassander before being seized by Demetrios Poliorketes (Plutarch, *Demetrios* 23.2).

The unexcavated deme site lies several hundred meters to the east, around an abundant spring. Farther east still, in a deep ravine, is a cave sacred to Pan; here were found fragments of reliefs and hundreds of late Roman lamps. The spot is usually identified as the shrine of Pan referred to by the god himself in the opening lines of Menander's *Dyskolos:*

> Imagine the scene is in Attica—it's Phyle—and the nymphaion from which I come belongs to the people of Phyle and those who can farm the rocks there, a very famous sanctuary.

EXCAVATIONS

Excavations at the fortress were carried out by the German Archaeological Institute in the 1920s. The cave of Pan was excavated by A. Skias for the Archaeological Society in 1900–1901.

BIBLIOGRAPHY

Cave of Pan

Rhomaios, K. *Arch. Eph.* (1905), pp. 99–158, and (1906), pp. 89–116.
Skias, A. *Arch. Eph.* (1918), pp. 1–28.

Fort

Wrede, W. "Phyle." *Ath. Mitt.* 49 (1924), pp. 153–224.

Notes

For honors paid to the heroes of Phyle, both citizens and foreigners, see Aeschines, *Against Ktesiphon* 187 and *IG* II² 10. For Demetrios' retaking of the fort, see Plutarch, *Demetrios* 23; and for assorted epigraphical references to the garrisons stationed there, see *IG* II² 244, 614b, 867 (= 998), 1299, 1304–1307, and 2971.

RHAMNOUS

DESCRIPTION, HISTORY, AND SIGNIFICANCE

Rhamnous was the northeasternmost deme of Attica, situated on the coast north of Marathon. It was famous in antiquity for its cult of Nemesis. Votive material at the sanctuary suggests that the cult goes back to the sixth century B.C. Before the Persian Wars there was a modest Doric temple and a simple fountain house on the site, but the main period of the sanctuary is in the fifth century. A small temple built in the polygonal style was erected first. It has a front porch, within which were found two marble thrones, one dedicated to Nemesis, the other to Themis. Inside the temple proper were several pieces of statuary, including a statue of Themis made in the third century, still standing on her inscribed base.

263, 264

265

Just north of this small temple was a larger Doric temple dedicated to Nemesis which is described by Pausanias (1.33; see figs. 106–108). It is a peripteral temple of six columns by twelve, with a *pronaos* (front porch), cella, and *opisthodomos* (back porch). Within the cella stood the statue of Nemesis, sculpted probably by Agorakritos, standing on a sculpted base. Fragments of both statue and base have been recovered, along with the cult or offering table which stood in front of the statue. The temple is built of local marble, and the final carving of the architecture was never completed.

The actual deme of Rhamnous and the garrison fort which protected it are located on a hill next to the sea, about 500 meters north of the sanctuary. A strong circuit wall with square towers was built around the lower part of the hill. Within, excavations have revealed traces of streets and houses and the remains of a small theater. Front-row seats of honor, in the form of marble thrones dedicated to Dionysos, indicate that the orchestra was rectilinear in plan. Also recovered have been numerous inscriptions carrying decrees in honor of many officers of the garrisons stationed on this stretch of the Attic frontier, particularly in the third century B.C.

On the slope opposite the town there was a small sanctuary of Amphiaraos. Early on,

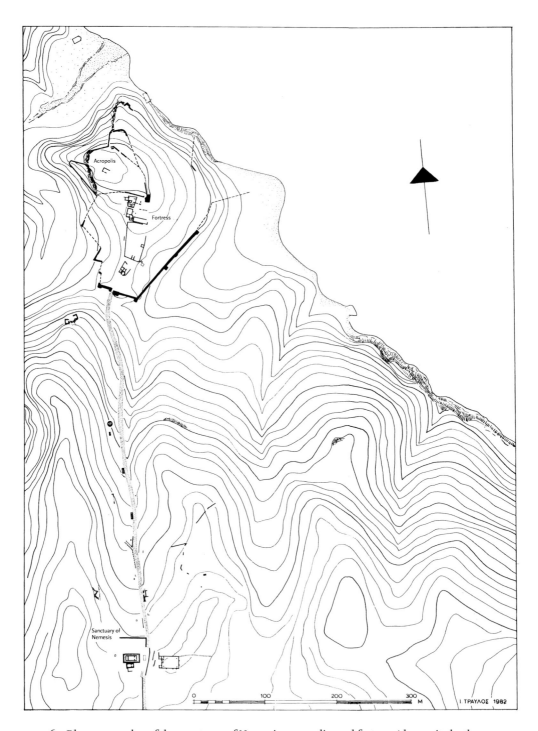

Labels within the map:

Acropolis

Fortress

Sanctuary of
Nemesis

0   100   200   300
                        M

I. ΤΡΑΥΛΟΣ 1982

263. Rhamnous, plan of the sanctuary of Nemesis, acropolis, and fortress/deme-site by the sea.

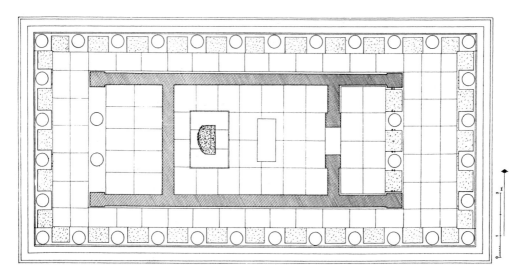

264. Ground plan of the Doric Temple of Nemesis at Rhamnous.

in the fourth century, there are dedications to a local healing deity, Aristomachos. In the third century Amphiaraos became increasingly prominent in the dedications. It may be that the emphasis on Amphiaraos at certain periods reflects the degree of Athenian control over his more famous sanctuary at Oropos, immediately to the north.

Connecting the town with the sanctuary and then continuing southward into the plain was a road, lined on either side with tombs. Many handsome sculpted grave stelai and inscriptions have been recovered, along with the terrace walls built to define individual family plots.

EXCAVATIONS

Rhamnous was first investigated by J. P. Gandy for the Society of the Dilettanti in 1813. D. Philios undertook work for the Archaeological Society in 1880, and B. Staies continued in 1891–1892. Since 1975 the work of the society has been carried out under the direction of B. Petrakos.

BIBLIOGRAPHY

Miles, M. M. "A Reconstruction of the Temple of Nemesis at Rhamnous." *Hesperia* 58 (1989), pp. 133–249.

265. Statue of Themis, dedicated in the small temple at Rhamnous, 3rd century B.C.

Petrakos, B. Annual reports in the *Praktika* and *Ergon* (Athens) throughout the 1990s.

*Petrakos, B. *Arch. Eph.* (1987), pp. 267–298.

Petrakos, B. *Ο ΔΗΜΟΣ ΤΟΥ ΡΑΜΝΟΥΝΤΟΣ.* 2 vols. Athens, 1999.

Petrakos, B. *Φιλία Έπη* (Mylonas festschrift). Athens, 1987. Vol. 2, pp. 295–326.

*Petrakos, B. *Rhamnous.* Athens, 1991.

Pouilloux, J. *La Forteresse de Rhamnonte.* Paris, 1954.

Society of the Dilettanti. *The Unedited Antiquities of Attica.* London, 1817.

SOUNION

DESCRIPTION, HISTORY, AND SIGNIFICANCE

Cape Sounion lies at the southernmost tip of Attica. On the cape itself were a sanctuary of Poseidon and a fortified settlement. A sanctuary of Athena lay on a lower hill to the northeast; here are found the earliest remains on the site. Sounion is not mentioned in the literary tradition as one of the early settlements of Attica, and only limited Bronze Age material has been found. The site was known in Homeric times, however, and the earliest material may be associated with that reference. According to the myth, when Menelaus was on his way back from the Trojan War he stopped and buried his helmsman, Phrontis, on the cape (*Odyssey,* 3.278–283):

Now we were sailing together on our way from Troy, the son of Atreus

266

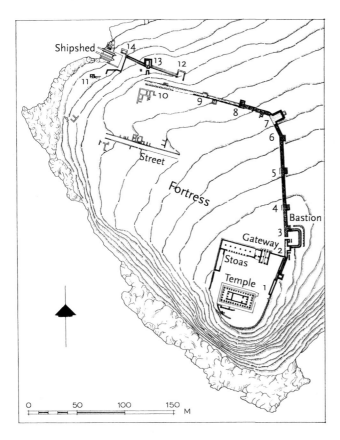

266. Sounion, plan of the fort and the sanctuary of Poseidon.

267. Terra-cotta plaque from Sounion, showing ship with helmsman (Phrontis?), 8th century B.C.

and I, in all friendship; but when we came to holy Sounion, the cape of Athens, there Phoibos Apollo assailed with his gentle shafts and slew the helmsman of Menelaus, as he held in his hands the steering oar of the speeding ship, Phrontis the son of Onetor, who excelled the tribes of men in piloting a ship when the storm winds blow strong. So Menelaus tarried there, though eager for his journey, that he might bury his comrade and over him pay funeral rites.

A rectangular pit more than 15 meters deep was found on the lower hill, full of early Archaic votive offerings which have been associated with a cult of Phrontis. The material includes Corinthian *aryballoi* (small oil jars), small terra-cotta figurines and heads, scarabs and carved seals, and black-figured plaques. One eighth-century plaque shows a warship under
267   way with the helmsman carefully depicted.

Next on the hill was the small temple with two prostyle columns, thought to have been built at the end of the sixth century B.C. Within is a statue base, presumably recovered and reused after the Persian destruction of 480/79. It is not clear who was worshiped in this little temple.

The principal temple on the lower hill was built in honor of Athena, probably in the

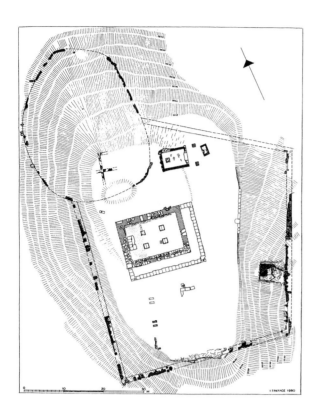

268. Sounion, plan of the sanctuary
of Athena, mid-5th century B.C.

decade 460–450 B.C. (see figs.
104, 105). It was of the Ionic order,   268
perhaps the earliest example on the
mainland, made of local marble
from nearby Agrileza to the north.
It has an unusual plan, with ten
columns across the eastern facade,
twelve down the southern flank,
and no columns on the west or
north.   269

The high headland itself was
appropriately dedicated to Poseidon, god of the sea. The earliest evidence of cult activity is a group of
more than a dozen sixth-century

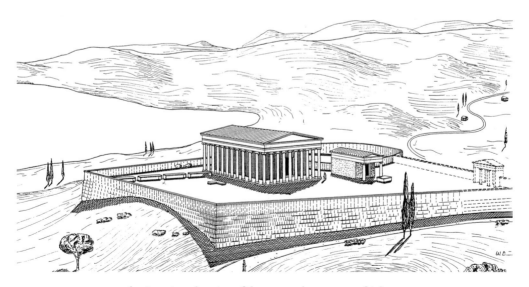

269. Sounion, drawing of the restored sanctuary of Athena.

kouroi, which were found buried in a pit east of the temple (see fig. 23). The earliest temple for which we have evidence dates somewhat later, around 490–480. Numerous fragments of its limestone Doric capitals, wall blocks, column drums, and architraves were built into the foundations of the later temple of Poseidon or reused in the sanctuary of Athena on the lower hill. The plan is similar to that of the later temple but slightly smaller; it was presumably destroyed by the Persians in 480/79.

The marble temple still crowning the cape today should probably be dated to the 440s as part of the Periklean building program (see figs. 100–103). It has the standard Doric plan, with six columns by thirteen, so close in design to the Hephaisteion above the Agora that it has been suggested that both were built by the same architect. The Sounion temple has three anomalies, however. All but one of the columns have drums of equal height (0.6 meters), and the walls of the cella had regular courses of alternating heights of 0.3 and 0.6 meters. Also, the columns have sixteen flutes, an archaizing feature; most Classical columns have twenty. There are several battered and worn sculpted frieze blocks which went in the pronaos (front porch) and, probably, the opisthodomos (back porch). One series depicts a boar hunt and the other a centauromachy. These are now stored in the closed museum at Laureion. Fragments of pedimental sculpture and an acroterion were also recovered and are on display in the National Museum. The temple stood within its own walled precinct, which was approached through a marble and limestone propylon, distyle-in-antis (two columns between the antae) in plan. To the west of the propylon, facing south, was a stoa, used presumably to display votives and perhaps for dining.

Soon after the construction of the sanctuary, the entire hill was fortified, in 413/2, according to Thucydides (see figs. 100, 163). The fort thereafter became an important garrison for the Athenians and was repaired and renewed in the troubled times of the third century. Two distinct building styles can be made out in the circuit, the later making liberal use of blocks taken from dismantled grave monuments. Two ship sheds were constructed at the northwest edge of the promontory. During a slave revolt in 104–100 B.C., Sounion was seized and used as a base for plundering Attica (Athenaios, *Deipnosophistai* 272E). In later times the cape and its sheltered beaches continued to attract travelers, many of whom inscribed their names on the Poseidon temple or carried off bits of the building to their homes.

The deme site of Sounion may be the collection of houses and streets that appear partially excavated within the fort, as at Rhamnous. An inscription (*IG* II² 1140) calling for the construction of a new agora for the deme was found several kilometers to the north, however, so the precise location of the deme center remains uncertain.

EXCAVATIONS

W. Dörpfeld of the German Archaeological Institute excavated the temple of Poseidon in 1884. B. Staies then excavated both sites for the Greek Archaeological Society between 1899 and 1915.

BIBLIOGRAPHY

Dinsmoor, W. B., Jr. *Sounion*. Athens, 1971.

Dinsmoor, W. B., Jr., and Thompson, H. A. *The Sanctuary of Athena Sounias*. Forthcoming.

Goette, H. *Ὁ Ἀξιόλογος δῆμος Σούνιον*. Athens, 1999.

Lauter, H. "Das Teichos von Sounion," Marburger-Winkelmann Program (1988), pp. 11–33.

Staies, B. *Τὸ Σούνιον καὶ οἱ ναοὶ Ποσειδῶνος καὶ Ἀθηνᾶς*. Athens, 1920, and *Arch. Eph.* (1911), pp. 168–213.

Travlos, J. *Bildlexikon zur Topographie des antiken Attika*. Tübingen, 1988. Pp. 404–429.

Frieze

Felton, F., and K. Hoffelener. "Die Relieffriese des Poseidontempels in Sunion." *Ath. Mitt.* 102 (1987), pp. 169–184.

Kouroi

Papathanasopoulos, G. *Σούνιον ἱερόν*. Athens, 1983.

Sanctuary

Sinn, U. "Sunion." *Ant. Welt.* 23 (1992), pp. 175–190.

Notes

For the quarries in Agrileza which provided marble for the temple of Poseidon, see H. Goette, "Die Steinbruche von Sounion." *Ath. Mitt.* 106 (1991), pp. 201 ff.

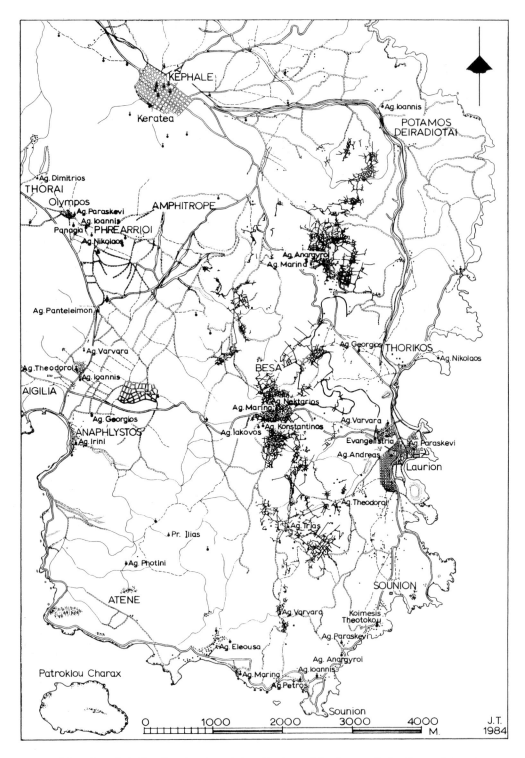

Map labels:

KEPHALE

Keratea

Ag. Ioannis

POTAMOS
DEIRADIOTAI

Ag. Dimitrios

THORAI

Olympos

AMPHITROPE

Ag. Paraskevi
Ag. Ioannis
Panagia   PHREARRIOI
Ag. Nikolaos

Ag. Anargyroi
Ag. Marina

Ag. Panteleimon

Ag. Georgios   THORIKOS

Ag. Nikolaos

Ag. Varvara

Ag. Theodoroi
Ag. Ioannis

BESA

AIGILIA

Ag. Marina   Ag. Nektarios

Ag. Georgios

ANAPHLYSTOS
Ag. Irini

Ag. Iakovos   Ag. Konstantinos

Ag. Varvara

Evangelistria   Ag. Paraskevi
Ag. Andreas   Laurion

Ag. Theodoroi

Pr. Ilias

Ag. Trias

Ag. Photini

SOUNION

ATENE

Ag. Varvara

Koimesis
Theotokou
Ag. Paraskevi

Ag. Eleousa

Ag. Anargyroi
Ag. Ioannis

Patroklou Charax

Ag. Marina
Ag. Petros

Sounion

| 0 | 1000 | 2000 | 3000 | 4000 |
M.

J.T.
1984

270. Map of south Attika, showing the mining district and the demes of Thorikos and Sounion.

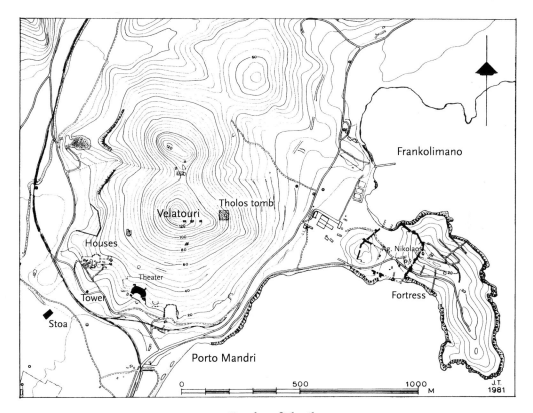

271. Site plan of Thorikos.

THORIKOS

DESCRIPTION, HISTORY, AND SIGNIFICANCE

The deme of Thorikos lies on the east coast of Attica, north of Cape Sounion. It be- 270
longed to the tribe of Akamantis and sent five representatives to the *boule* (senate). By tradition, it was one of the twelve cities founded by Kekrops before the synoicism of Theseus,
and this is confirmed archaeologically by a full range of Bronze Age material. The site oc-
cupies a steep hill with two peaks, the higher of which rises 145 meters above sea level. The 271

272. Thorikos, aerial view of the theater and adjacent areas excavated by the Belgian Mission. Note the reconstructed ore washery at left.

excavated prehistoric remains are largely near the top of the hill, while the Classical are on the lower southern slopes. The Aghios Nikolaos peninsula lies less than a kilometer to the east, providing safe anchorage for ships. Two rubble walls which run across the peninsula are thought to be the fortifications built during the Peloponnesian War referred to by Xenophon.

There are four Mycenaean tombs, two tholoi and two built chamber tombs. The earlier tholos, dating to the sixteenth century B.C., has an unusual form: the actual burial chamber is a long rectangle with rounded corners. The other tholos, from the fifteenth century, made deliberate use of colored stones for decorative effect and had a paved walkway running around the base of the mound. The Geometric period is represented by traces of houses and an extensive necropolis on the west slopes of the hill.

Excavations have uncovered a large part of the Archaic and Classical town, revealing public buildings, mines, private houses, industrial establishments, graves, and sanctuaries crowded together, with no obvious attempt to separate the various activities. Most impressive is the theater, which dates back to the late sixth century B.C., when a retaining wall was built to support an orchestra. A second phase dates to the mid-fifth century. At this time the orchestra was enlarged, and an auditorium consisting of twenty-one rows of stone seats was built. The form of the orchestra is noteworthy: most of the seating is set in straight rows, with only the ends curved. The terrain did not require this arrangement, and as this is our earliest dated stone theater in Attica—and far better preserved than the fifth-century theater of Dionysos in Athens—it offers important evidence for the original form of the orchestra in early Greek theaters. On present evidence, early orchestras appear to have been rectilinear rather than round. The theater was expanded one more time, in the mid-fourth century. A handsome new retaining wall was built at the back of the auditorium, approached from behind by two ramps, and twelve additional rows of seating were installed. This brought the capacity up to six thousand, an extraordinary number for a mid-sized deme; far less, to be sure, than the capacity of the theater of Dionysos at Athens, but comparable to the seating space available at the Pnyx. This great increase must be due in part to the extensive exploitation of the mines throughout southern Attica in the middle years of the fourth century.

Thorikos was one of the mining demes, and an adit and an ore-washing establishment are located just west of the theater. The ore washery has been partially reconstructed and gives a good idea of how such installations used running water to separate and clean the ore before smelting. Traces of mining activity going back to early and middle Helladic times have been found.

The religious life of the deme is reflected in a small, two-roomed building with an adjacent hall equipped with benches; a dedicatory inscription found nearby suggests that the shrine was sacred to Hygieia. From Thorikos also comes a sacred calendar inscribed on stone listing the sacrifices to be carried out for the well-being of the deme. Listed month by month and day by day are the deities to be honored, along with the sacrificial animal they should receive, sometimes even specifying its color and age. The calendar shows a mix of Olympian deities (who were worshiped also in Athens) with local heroes and heroines. Other such calendars are known from Attica (at Marathon and Erchia), and they too emphasize the local nature of much of Greek cult activity.

On the plain the remains of a fifth-century Doric building of marble with an unusual plan have been uncovered (see figs. 109, 110). The building was unfinished, though the remains of a peristyle survive: column drums on a stylobate with inexplicable gaps left in the two long sides. Because of alluviation the building has had to be excavated no fewer than five times since the 1750s. In the early Roman period several of the columns were taken down and reused in a temple in the Agora at Athens. Later still, they were built into the post-Herulian wall (276–282 A.D.), where the drums can still be seen today (see fig. 218).

Beyond the plundered and reused columns, Thorikos provides additional evidence for the abandonment of Attica, starting as early as the third century B.C. A hoard of 293 gold and silver coins was hidden when the Macedonians arrived in Athens in 295/4; it was never recovered, and the site as a whole seems to have been abandoned. The desolation continued into the Roman period, and Pomponius Mela, writing in the first century B.C., refers to "Thorikos and Brauron, once cities, now only names."

EXCAVATIONS

The theater at Thorikos was first excavated by the American School of Classical Studies in 1885–1886. The tholoi were explored in the 1890s by the Greek Archaeological Society. Additional work has been done throughout the site, particularly in the settlement and

273. Theater at Euonymon, 4th century B.C. Note the rectilinear orchestra and seats of honor (*proedria*).

cemeteries, by the Belgian Archaeological Mission under H. Mussche from the 1960s to the present time.

BIBLIOGRAPHY

Belgian Archaeological Mission. *Thorikos* 1–9. Brussels, 1963–1977 (1982).
Labarbe, J. *Thorikos, Les Testimonia.* Ghent, 1977.
Mussche, H. *Thorikos. A Guide to the Excavations.* Brussels, 1994.

Doric Building

Petrakos, B. *Ergon* (1996 [1997]), pp. 19–23.

Mining

Kakavoyianni, E. *Arch. Delt.* (1996), A, pp. 1–20, and *AAA* 22 (1989 [1995]), pp. 71–88.
Kalcyk, H. *Untersuchungen zum Attischen Silberbergbau.* Frankfurt, 1982.
Konophagos, K. *Le Laureion antique.* Athens, 1980.

WEST COAST: EUONYMON, AIXONE, CAPE ZOSTER, CAVE OF PAN (TRACHONES, GLYPHADA, VOULIAGMENI, VARI)

DESCRIPTION, HISTORY, AND SIGNIFICANCE

Several sites lie scattered along the west coast of Attica between Peiraieus and Cape Sounion (see fig. 248). The northernmost lies just north of the old Hellenikon Airport at modern Trachones. A fairly extensive Geometric cemetery has been excavated at a site identified as the deme of Euonymon. From the Classical period, rescue excavations have uncovered a well-preserved small theater. The scene-building stands 2 meters high, and the whole orchestra has been preserved, together with two types of front-row seats of honor (*proedria*): a set of marble thrones and a long bench with a dedicatory inscription. The sloping seating area behind can be made out, though the seat blocks have been removed. As with the other deme theaters (at Ikaria, Rhamnous, and Thorikos), the orchestra is rectilinear, not round. The theater seems to have been in use for a short time; built in the third quarter of the fourth century B.C., it was abandoned, like Thorikos and other Attic demes, early in the third.

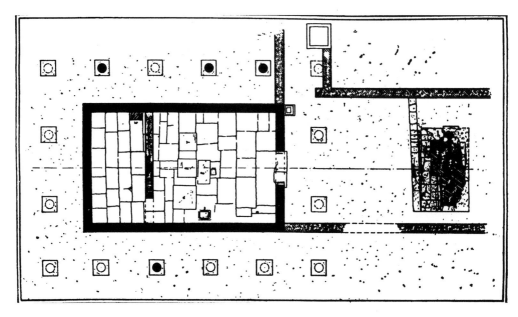

274. Plan of the temple of Apollo Zoster at Cape Zoster (Vouliagmeni), 6th century B.C., with later additions.

Just opposite the old airport at Hellenikon, a short cape known as Aghios Kosmas juts out into the Saronic Gulf (see fig. 7). Excavations here have uncovered a small settlement and cemetery of the Early Bronze Age.

South of the airport, in the modern suburb of Glyphada, an extensive area of houses, streets, and small shrines belonging to the deme of Aixone has been excavated and left uncovered. In many ways the buildings resemble the crowded neighborhoods excavated at Thorikos and southwest of the Athenian Agora. Numerous inscriptions have been uncovered at Glyphada which give a vivid picture of life in an ancient deme; many of the inscriptions concern the theater, which has not yet been excavated.

On the narrow neck of land connecting the Vouliagmeni Peninsula (ancient Cape Zoster) to the mainland lie the remains of an important shrine of the deme of Aixone: the sanctuary of Apollo Zoster. Here Apollo and Artemis were worshiped, together with their mother, Leto, who is said to have loosed her girdle here before giving birth to them on Delos. The sanctuary goes back at least to the sixth century B.C., and the temple contains bases for statues of the three deities, an offering table, and a throne for the priest. The temple is a simple chamber with a back room, or *adyton*. Columns are built around it, standing on individual bases rather than on a continuous stylobate; these were perhaps added later.

274

Nearby was a private house in use in the fifth and fourth centuries. Part of an inscription and an incised pot indicate that the house may have belonged to the priest of the cult; lead net weights suggest that he supplemented his priestly income with fishing.

Just outside the town of Vari, in the ancient deme of Anagyrous, a large early cemetery has been excavated, producing some of the best seventh-century B.C. pottery found anywhere in Attica. Among the latest pieces (around 610) is a large amphora decorated on the neck with a scene of Herakles killing the centaur Nessos; Perseus and the gorgons are depicted on the body (see fig. 22).

In the hills above Vari, about 290 meters above sea level at the end of Mount Hymettos, there is a cave dedicated to Pan and the Nymphs. It is the most ornately worked of all the caves in Attica, though it has suffered a great deal since it was first described by travelers early in the nineteenth century. Rock-cut statues and reliefs are reported, and several inscriptions were cut on the walls as well. Much of the work was apparently done by one Archedemos, from the island of Thera (Santorini), who describes himself as a *nympholept* (one siezed by the Nymphs):

Archedemos the Theran, the *nympholept,* worked out the cave at the orders of the Nymphs (*IG* I³ 980).

A second inscription tells us that Archedemos planted a garden for the Nymphs and built them a dancing ground (*IG* I³ 977), while another enjoins visitors to wash any innards outside the cave (*IG* I² 789).

BIBLIOGRAPHY

Aghios Kosmas

Mylonas, G. *Aghios Kosmas.* Princeton, N.J., 1959.

Aixone

Giannopoulou-Konsolaki, E. *ΓΛΥΦΑΔΑ.* Athens, 1990.

Cape Zoster

Kourouniotis, K. *Arch. Delt.* 11 (1927–1928), pp. 8–53.
Stavropoullos, Ph. *Arch. Eph.* (1938), pp. 1–31.

Cave of Pan

Weller, C., et al. "The Cave at Vari." *AJA* 7 (1903), pp. 263–349.

Wickens, J. "The Archaeology and History of Cave Use in Attica." Ph.D. diss., Indiana University, 1986. Pp. 90–121.

Cemetery at Vari

Kallipolitis, B. *Arch. Delt.* 18 (1963), A', pp. 115–132.

Papaspyridi-Karouzou, S. *Ἀγγεῖα τοῦ Ἀναγυροῦντος.* Athens, 1963.

Theater at Euonymon

Alexandri-Tsakou, O. *Praktika* (1980), pp. 65–67.

Border Areas

ELEUTHERAI

DESCRIPTION, HISTORY, AND SIGNIFICANCE

The town of Eleutherai lay on the northwest frontier of Athens (see fig. 146). At times it belonged to Boiotia and at times to Athens, according to both Strabo and Pausanias:

> Eleutherai is nearby, which some say belongs to Attica, others to Boiotia. (Strabo 9.2.31)

> Beyond Eleusis, in the direction of Boiotia, the Athenian territory marches with the Plataian. Formerly Eleutherai was the limit of Boiotia on the side of Attica, but when the Eleutherians cast in their lot with Athens, Kithairon became the boundary of Boiotia. The accession of Eleutherai to Athens was the result not of conquest but partly of a desire to share the Athenian citizenship and partly of a hatred of Thebes. In this plain there is a temple of Dionysos; it was from here that the old wooden image was brought to Athens. The image now in Eleutherai is a copy of it. (Pausanias 1.38.8–9)

The status of Eleutherai at any one period is by no means clear. It seems likely that the Athenians had control late in the sixth century B.C., after they defeated the Boiotians in 506. It would be about this time also that the worship of Dionysos Eleuthereus was imported to Athens. There was no known attempt to include Eleutherai in the political structure of

Athens, however, and it never became a deme. In the fifth century, a man from Eleutherai appears on an Athenian casualty list (*IG* I³ 1162), but otherwise the little evidence we have suggests that it was under the control of Boiotia. Myron, the sculptor of the famous fifth-century statue of the discus-thrower, was from Eleutherai and is referred to by Polemon, writing in the second century B.C., as a Boiotian. In addition, a great deal of fifth-century Boiotian pottery has been found on the site, including an incised dedication to Herakles in Boiotian dialect. The town may well have passed back and forth more than once, as is the case with Oropos on the northeast frontier.

The site is strategically located, on the principal pass leading north–south between Mount Parnes and Mount Kithairon. Anyone passing from northern Greece to the Peloponnese had to come through this pass, and the town was on the main route from Athens to Plataia. By the early fourth century the steep hill had been provided with a five-room blockhouse with thick walls built in a polygonal style of masonry. Somewhat later, a proper circuit wall was built, enclosing an area measuring roughly 100 meters north–south by 275 meters east–west. Well-built gates opened toward both the northwest and southeast. The northwest gate bears a battered inscription indicating that it led out toward Plataia, which indeed it does. A good long stretch of the northern wall stands well preserved, with square towers every 30 meters or so.

The fort features in discussions of the defenses of Attica, though a case can be made that it is actually Boiotian, built when Epaminondas led the Thebans to the hegemony of Greece between 371 and 362 B.C. The trapezoidal masonry in hard gray limestone and the consoles used in the gates find their best parallels in Boiotia rather than Attica. A later period of construction can also be made out, in which squared blocks of reddish conglomerate were used. In the plain below, the scant remains of a small Doric temple of the fourth century B.C. have been excavated and tentatively identified as the temple of Dionysos noted by Pausanias, though there is no trace of an earlier temple on the site.

Across the plain to the southeast, at Mazi, stand the remains of a large tower, reaching five stories high in places; and 2 kilometers farther east lies the fortified Attic deme of Oinoe, which had been walled by the start of the Peloponnesian War at the latest. Part of its north wall, with four towers, stands fairly well-preserved (see fig. 123). To the east-northeast, some 400 meters higher on Mount Parnes and overlooking the Skourta Plain, is the Athenian border fort of Panakton, which was taken by the Boiotians during the Peloponnesian War and demolished before it was returned to the Athenians as part of the settlement of the Peace of Nikias in 421. Inscriptions from the Athenian garrison which manned the fort in the fourth century have been found on the site.

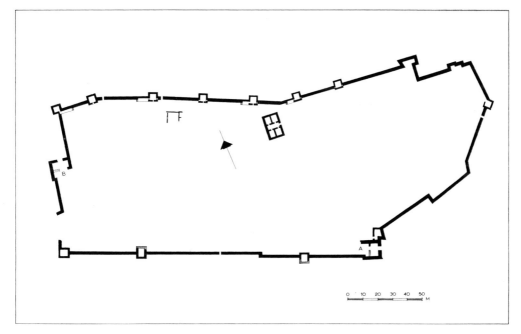

275. Plan of the fort at Eleutherai, 5th to 4th century B.C.

EXCAVATION

Eleutherai was excavated briefly by E. Stikas in the late 1930s. Panakton has been the subject of recent survey and excavation in a collaboration between the Thebes Ephoreia of the Archaeological Service and the American School of Classical Studies at Athens. Most of the work on the northwest frontier has not involved excavation.

BIBLIOGRAPHY

Camp, J. "Notes on the Towers and Borders of Classical Boiotia." *AJA* 95 (1991), pp. 193–202.

Munn, M. *The Defense of Attica.* Berkeley, 1993.

Ober, J. *Fortress Attika. Mnemosyne Suppl. 84.* Leiden, 1985.

Stikas, E. *Praktika* (1938), pp. 41–49, and (1939), pp. 44–52.

Vanderpool, E. "Roads and Forts in Northwestern Attica." *California Studies in Classical Antiquity* 11 (1978), pp. 227–245.

OROPOS (AMPHIAREION)

DESCRIPTION, HISTORY, AND SIGNIFICANCE

The town of Oropos lay on the east coast, north of Rhamnous (see fig. 248). Squeezed in between Athens and Thebes and across the straits from Eretria, the small city-state was often under the control of one of these three larger states. Between 490 and the first century b.c., the city is known to have changed hands twelve times, with short periods of independence. Athenian influence was particularly strong in the fifth century until 411 and on several occasions in the fourth century: 378/7–367/6, 338–322, and 304 until the 280s.

The principal sanctuary of Oropos was situated inland, well outside the city. It was
276   dedicated to Amphiaraos (see fig. 120), a healing deity similar to Asklepios who started life

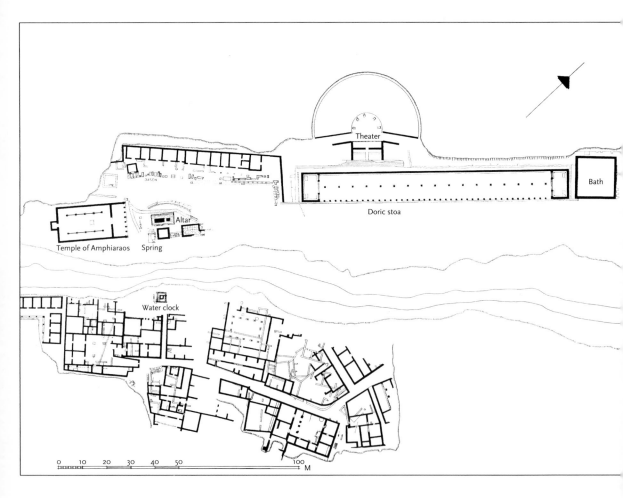

as a hero, one of the Seven against Thebes. He came to be regarded as a full-fledged god, a status which had to be confirmed by the Senate at Rome, according to an inscription found at the sanctuary (*IG* VII 413). In the 80s B.C., Sulla granted the area around the sanctuary the usual tax-free status awarded a god, but soon thereafter the *publicani,* or tax-farmers, tried to exact taxes from Oropos, on the grounds that Amphiaraos was only a hero and therefore not entitled to special privileges. In 73 a delegation, which included Cicero, was sent from Rome to look into the matter and determined that Amphiaraos was in fact a god and therefore the town was tax-exempt.

The sanctuary lies in a wooded ravine, along the banks of a small stream near a sacred spring. The earliest antiquities are two altars and a theatral seating area focused on the altars, all dating to the second half of the fifth century B.C. Around the end of the century the two altars were incorporated into a single large one, which was described by Pausanias (1.34.2–3). Various sections were dedicated to different deities:

> The altar is divided into parts. One part is sacred to Herakles, Zeus, and Paian Apollo, another to heroes and wives of heroes; a third to Hermes, Hestia, Amphiaraos, and the children of Amphilochos. . . . A fourth part of the altar is sacred to Aphrodite and Panacea, and also to Jason, Hygieia, and Healing Athena. A fifth part belongs to the Nymphs and Pan and the rivers Acheloos and Kephisos.

A stone plaque found at the altar inscribed with the names of Amphiaraos and Amphilochos is taken as one of several labels used to designate which part of the altar was appropriate for sacrifices to which deity.

Contemporary with this altar was a very small temple and a dormitory (*koimeterion*), where suppliants would stay. A contemporary sacred law (*IG* VII 235) lists various rules and regulations: The priest is required to be at the sanctuary for at least ten days a month during the summer, and he cannot be absent more than three days in a row. The names of those who are to sleep in the dormitory are to be posted on a board by the *neokoros* (custodian of the temple). Women and men must sleep separately, the men in the part of the building east of the altar (the larger part), the women to the west. There are fines for misbehavior. All meat from the sacrifices is to be consumed in the sanctuary.

To the middle years of the fourth century can be dated the large Doric prostyle temple, a long stoa provided with benches, and men's and women's baths. A little later the Athe-

Opposite 276. Oropos, plan of the Amphiareion, with temple, altars, stoa, and theater.

nians built a fountain house (*IG* II² 338) and, across the ravine, a monumental water clock, virtually identical to the one erected in the Agora in Athens (see fig. 156) and presumably designed by the same individual. In the Hellenistic period, when Oropos was largely independent, numerous statues were erected in the area of the old dormitory to honor various benefactors. In the second century B.C. the little theater with its well-preserved scene-building was erected.

The cult was a popular one, and the festival included musical and athletic contests. The stadium seems to have run in front of the stoa, and there was a hippodrome in the valley above. The Romans also maintained a considerable interest in the cult, and to honor prominent benefactors the Oropians simply reinscribed many of the old statue bases with new names; presumably the statues' heads were also changed. Many of the surviving bases therefore have a Roman name, such as that of Julius Caesar's assassin Brutus, with the signature of an earlier, Hellenistic sculptor. The site was abandoned in the late Roman period.

EXCAVATIONS

The site was excavated between 1884 and 1929 by B. Leonardos for the Archaeological Society. Work on inscriptions and the site was carried out by B. Petrakos in the 1960s.

BIBLIOGRAPHY

Petrakos, B. *The Amphiareion of Oropos.* Athens, ca. 1974.

Petrakos, B. *Οἱ Ἐπιγραφές τοῦ Ὠρωποῦ.* Athens, 1997.

*Petrakos, B. *Ὁ Ὠρωπός καί τὸ ἱερόν τοῦ Ἀμφιάραου.* Athens, 1968.

Roesch, P. "L'Amphiaraion d'Oropos." In *Temples et Sanctuaires,* ed. G. Roux. Paris, 1984.

Schachter, A. *The Cults of Boiotia.* London, 1981. Pp. 19–27.

SALAMIS

DESCRIPTION, HISTORY, AND SIGNIFICANCE

Salamis is an island lying just off the west coast of Attica, right outside the mouth of the harbor of Peiraieus (see fig. 7). At its western end it is equally close to the territory of Megara, and early in the sixth century Athens and Megara went to war over possession of it. The island was sacred to Ajax. A passage in the catalogue of ships in the *Iliad*—perhaps

277

277. View of northwest Attika from the east, showing the island of Salamis lying just offshore.
(Watercolor by Peter Connolly)

added by the Athenians to strengthen their claim to Salamis—describes Ajax drawing up his ships next to the Athenians at Troy.

According to Strabo, the early city faced southwest, toward Aigina, and Bronze Age remains are reported along the southern coast of the island. A sub-Mycenaean cemetery was excavated in the narrow waist of the island, not far from the Classical city, which lay on the east coast, around the modern village and peninsula of Ambelakia. Though supposedly acquired by the Athenians under the leadership of Solon—who was born on the island—early in the sixth century B.C., Salamis was not fully incorporated into the Athenian state during the Kleisthenic reforms at the end of the century. The island was never a deme and seems rather to have been regarded as a possession. Athenian klerouchs, those who held a share (*kleros*) of land, colonized the island, but they retained citizenship of some sort in Athens. There was an archon, appointed and paid for by Athens, and Athenian military commanders were in charge of some aspects of life on the island as well. Klerouchies became a common feature of Athenian foreign policy following military conquest, perhaps first used for Salamis. Despite the island's proximity, the status of Salamis vis-à-vis Athens was appreciably different from that of the rest of Attica.

Salamis is best known for the great sea battle which took place in the straits in late September 480 B.C., when a vastly outnumbered Greek fleet based on the island destroyed a Persian armada. The story is told by Herodotos (Book 8), Aischylos (*Persai*), and Plutarch (*Themistokles, Aristides*). After the victory, the Greeks dedicated a captured trireme to Poseidon at Cape Sounion (Herodotos 8.121), and others at the Isthmos and on Salamis. A trophy to celebrate the victory was set up at the end of the long, thin Kynosoura peninsula which extends eastward from the island toward Peiraieus; one or two worked blocks of the base have been reported from the site, but otherwise nothing remains.

During the Peloponnesian War, the Athenians built a fort at Boudoron on the west end of the island to blockade the harbor of Megara (Thucydides 2.93). Traces of its rubble wall, extending for several hundred meters, can still be made out, although the remains are suffering the effects of recent development of the area. In the Hellenistic period the island was a pawn in the wars of succession among the Macedonian successors to Alexander.

A cave on the south coast near Peristeria has recently been excavated and can perhaps be identified with the cave on Salamis where the playwright Euripides is said to have composed his plays. Few other significant antiquities have been found on the island. Little remains of what is known to be the principal sanctuary, dedicated to Athena Skiras. An interesting metrical relief has been found built into one of the churches on the north side of the island.

EXCAVATIONS

Except for the sub-Mycenaean cemetery, few systematic excavations or even surveys have been carried out on Salamis. Rescue work around Ambelakia has recovered some traces of the ancient town, and early travelers report having seen its circuit wall.

BIBLIOGRAPHY

Dekoulakou-Sideris, I. "A Metrological Relief from Salamis." *AJA* 94 (1990), pp. 445–451.

McLeod, W. E. "Budoron." *Hesperia* 29 (1960), pp. 316–323.

Muller, D. *Topographischer Bildkommentar zu den Historien Herodots.* Tübingen, 1987. Pp. 692–713.

Pallas, D. *Praktika* (1987), pp. 15–43, and *Arch. Delt.* 42 (1987), A', pp. 169–230.

Taylor, M. *Salamis and the Salaminioi.* Amsterdam, 1997.

Wallace, P. "Psyttaleia and the Trophies of the Battle of Salamis." *AJA* 73 (1969), pp. 293–303.

Wide, S. "Gräberfunde aus Salamis." *Ath. Mitt.* (1910), pp. 17–36.

Winters, T. "Literary and Epigraphical Testimonia of Salamis." M.A. thesis, Ohio State University, 1983.

ABBREVIATIONS

AA   *Archäologischer Anzeiger*

AAA   *Ἀρχαιολογικὰ ἀνάλεκτα ἐξ Ἀθηῶν*, Athens Annals of Archaeology (mostly modern Greek)

AJA   *American Journal of Archaeology*

ANRW   *Aufstieg und Niedergang der römischen Welt*

Ant. Welt.   *Antike Welt*

Arch. Delt.   *Archaiologikon Deltion*, Bulletin of the Archaeological Service, Ministry of Culture, Athens (mostly in modern Greek)

Arch. Eph.   *Ἀρχαιολογικὴ Ἐφημερίς*, Journal of the Archaeological Society, Athens (mostly in modern Greek)

Ath. Mitt.   *Mitteilungen des Deutschen Archäologischen Instituts. Athenische Abteilung*

BCH   *Bulletin de correspondence hellénique*, Ecole française, Athens

BSA   *Annual of the British School in Athens*

CJ   *Classical Journal*

CRAI   *Comptes rendus des séances de l'Académie des inscriptions et belles-lettres*

Ergon   *Ἔργον τῆς ἐν Ἀθήναις Ἀρχαιολογικῆς Ἑταιρείας*, Proceedings of the Athens Archaeological Society (modern Greek)

IG   *Inscriptiones Graecae*, Berlin, 1873 and following

JDAI   *Jahrbuch des Deutschen Archäologischen Instituts*

JHS   *Journal of the Hellenic Society*, London

JÖAI   *Jahreshefte des Österreichischen Archäologischen Institutes in Wien*

Praktika   *Πρακτικα τῆς ἐν Ἀθήναις Ἀρχαιολογικῆς Ἑταιρείας*, Proceedings of the Archaeological Society, Athens (modern Greek)

RE   Pauly-Wissowa, *Real-Encyclopädie der klassischen Altertumswissenschaft*

Illustration Credits

Numbers refer to figures.

American School of Classical Studies—Agora Excavations: 4, 12, 16, 17, 18, 30, 31, 32, 44, 45, 46, 55, 60, 61, 65 (B 262), 66, 67, 75, 80, 83, 84, 93, 94, 95, 96, 97, 104, 110, 112, 121, 122, 131, 134, 135, 147, 150, 151, 152, 153, 154, 155, 156, 164, 166, 167, 168, 169, 170, 175, 176, 177, 178, 182, 183, 184, 185, 186, 190, 191, 192, 193, 194, 196, 198, 199, 210, 212, 218, 220, 221, 222, 223, 224, 225, 226, 229, 231, 233, 234, 235, 237, 238, 239, 240, 241, 242, 243, 244, 245

American School of Classical Studies—Alison Frantz Collection: 2, 13, 21, 22, 23, 25, 26, 28, 36, 40, 43, 56 (National Museum, Athens, No. 2687), 69, 71, 72, 73, 78, 79, 86, 88, 90, 91, 92, 101, 102, 107, 127, 133, 138, 148, 159 (Athens, National Museum, No. 3624), 173, 174, 188

Archaeological Society (including John Travlos Archive), Athens: 8, 9, 11, 14, 15, 24, 37, 47, 48, 50, 51, 52, 57, 63, 68, 70, 77, 89, 98, 105, 106, 108, 114, 119, 124, 125, 126 (National Museum, Athens, Nos. 1592 and 1593), 128, 145, 149, 162, 165, 172, 187, 189, 197, 200, 203, 204, 206, 207, 214, 215, 217, 228, 230, 232, 246, 249, 250, 251, 252, 254, 255, 256, 258, 259, 260, 263, 264, 265, 266, 268, 269, 270, 271, 274, 275, 276

British Museum: 10 (BM E 84), 35 (BM 605), 38

John Camp: 27, 33, 34, 53, 81, 111, 129, 132, 146, 157, 158, 160, 161, 208, 273

Peter Connolly (watercolors): 3, 5, 54, 59, 64, 76, 87, 99, 137, 139, 144, 257, 277

Deutsches Archäologisches Institut, Athens: 19 (National Museum, Athens, No. 804), 20, 29, 42 (No. 679), 49, 58, 82, 103, 109, 115 (National Museum, Athens, No. 400), 116, 117, 120, 123, 130, 136, 140, 141, 142, 143, 163, 171, 179, 180, 181, 195, 201, 202, 205, 209, 211, 213, 216, 219, 227, 236, 247, 253, 261, 262, 267

Epigraphical Museum, Athens: 6 (EM 12553), 113 (*IG* II², 2893)

Michael Djordjevitch: 1, 7, 248

Hans Goette, DAI, Athens: 100, 118, 272

Louvre Museum, Paris: 62

Craig and Marie Mauzy: 74

John Traill: 39

R. A. Tomlinson: 41 (No. 675), 85

Index